D0649464

THE COMMONWEALTH AND I[

Joint Chairmen of the Honorary -
SIR ROBERT ROBINSON, O[
DEAN ATHELSTAN SPIL[

Publisher: ROBERT MAX[

MATHEMATICS
General Editors: W. J. LANGFO[

FUNDAMENTA[

ALGEBRA FO[

FUNDAMENTAL MODERN ALGEBRA FOR A-LEVEL

by

K. H. OKE, B.Sc.

*Assistant Lecturer in Mathematics, Kingston College of
Further Education, Kingston upon Thames*

PERGAMON PRESS

OXFORD · LONDON · EDINBURGH · NEW YORK
TORONTO · SYDNEY · PARIS · BRAUNSCHWEIG

Pergamon Press Ltd., Headington Hill Hall, Oxford
4 & 5 Fitzroy Square, London W.1

Pergamon Press (Scotland) Ltd., 2 & 3 Teviot Place, Edinburgh 1

Pergamon Press Inc., 44–01 21st Street, Long Island City, New York 11101

Pergamon of Canada Ltd., 6 Adelaide Street East, Toronto, Ontario

Pergamon Press (Aust) Pty. Ltd., 20–22 Margaret Street,
Sydney, New South Wales

Pergamon Press S.A.R.L., 24 rue des Écoles, Paris 5e

Vieweg & Sohn GmbH, Burgplatz 1, Braunschweig

Copyright © 1967 Pergamon Press Ltd.
First edition 1967
Library of Congress Catalog Card No. 66-29596

Printed in Great Britain by The Camelot Press Ltd.
London and Southampton

Library
I.U.P.
Indiana, Pa.

512.8 Ok2f
c. 1

This book is sold subject to the condition
that it shall not, by way of trade, be lent,
resold, hired out, or otherwise disposed
of without the publisher's consent,
in any form of binding or cover
other than that in which
it is published.

(3113/67)

Contents

Preface

THIS book is aimed at the A-level student who is studying the new "modern mathematics" syllabus, the student specializing in mathematics in a College of Education (Teacher Training College), and the student who will very soon have to study some modern algebra in O.N.D. and H.N.D. courses. It is also hoped that this book will serve as a useful introduction to some of the aspects of modern algebra included in the various mathematics degree courses. The presentation is straightforward without being unduly rigorous and it is therefore hoped that any cultured adult should follow the book easily.

The first chapter on simple propositional logic has been written in order to encourage the reader in precise expression in the language of mathematics generally. Chapter 1 also serves as an introduction to set theory and Boolean algebra developed in Chapter 2. It was decided in Chapter 2 to include a short section on transfinite cardinals as a natural and very interesting extension to the concept of number of elements in a set. In Chapter 3, after a brief look at the principle of mathematical induction, permutations and combinations, and the binomial theorem, the concepts of Boolean algebra are used to develop probability theory. Relations, equivalence classes, functions, mappings and transformations are briefly dealt with in the language of sets in Chapter 4. In Chapter 5 on matrices, a large number of worked examples and exercises have been included so that, with the text, the reader should not only gain a firm grasp of the fundamentals involved but become proficient in manipulating elementary matrix forms. Second and third order determinants are dealt with quite comprehensively. Chapter 6 serves to illustrate some of the most important aspects of algebraic structure and often refers to earlier chapters as background, as well as introducing the concepts of the group, ring and field.

It is hoped that this book will stimulate the reader into investigating this subject in greater detail. A bibliography for further reading has been included.

I wish to thank my colleagues and Dr. J. N. A. Ridyard for their helpful comments. I should also like to thank for his valuable comments Mr. W. J. Langford, General Editor of the Mathematics Division of the Commonwealth Library.

Kingston upon Thames   K. H. OKE
March, 1966

List of Symbols

$\bar{p}$	negation: **not** p
$\underline{\vee}$	exclusive disjunction: **or**
$\vee$	inclusive disjunction: **and/or**
$\wedge$	conjunction: **and**
$\rightarrow$	conditional: **if . . . then;** also a mapping
$\leftrightarrow$	biconditional: **if and only if;** also one–one correspondence
$\Rightarrow$	implication: **if . . . then** logically true
$\Leftrightarrow$	equivalence: **if and only if** logically true
$\in$	membership
:	such that
$\varnothing$	the null set
J	the set of all integers
J^+	all positive integers
J_0^+	all non-negative integers
R	all rational numbers; also a ring
R^+	all positive rational numbers
R^*	all real numbers
R^{*+}	all positive real numbers, etc.
$\subseteq$	subset
$\subset$	proper subset
U	universal set
$\cup$	union
$\cap$	intersection
A'	complement of the set A; also the transpose of the matrix A
c	contradiction ⎫
t	tautology ⎬ in Boolean algebra
$n(A)$	number of elements in set A

$\aleph_0$	smallest transfinite cardinal (where $\aleph$ is the Hebrew letter aleph)
$\aleph_1$	the next transfinite cardinal to $\aleph_0$, etc.
μ_r	weight assigned to each element r of a set
$\mu(A)$	measure of a set
$P(a)$	probability of a proposition a being true
$P(a_1 \mid a_2)$	conditional probability of a_1 given a_2
$A \times B$	the cartesian product of the sets A and B
$a \equiv b \pmod{m}$	a is congruent to b (mod m), i.e. $\dfrac{a-b}{m}$ has zero remainder
f or $f(x)$	a function
$X \underset{f}{\rightarrow} Y$	a mapping from a set X to a set Y by a function f
f^{-1} or $f^{-1}(x)$	an inverse function
$X \underset{T}{\rightarrow} Y$	a transformation T from a set X to a set Y
$T(x_1, y_1) \rightarrow (x_2, y_2)$	(x_1, y_1) transformed to (x_2, y_2)
T^{-1}	inverse transformation
A or (a_{ij})	a matrix A
$\bar{A}$	conjugate matrix
Δ	determinant
$\mid A \mid$	determinant of the matrix A
adj A	adjoint of a matrix
A^{-1}	inverse matrix
$\exists$	there exists
$*$	any binary operation

CHAPTER 1

Simple Propositional Logic

1.1. The purpose of this first chapter is to look closely at the statements or propositions commonly used in mathematics: more exactly to investigate how propositions are combined rather than study the nature of the propositions themselves—this latter study being very difficult and belonging more to linguistics than mathematics. For example, consider the proposition: "This is a triangle *and* two of its angles are equal." This **proposition** is made up of two simpler propositions or **subpropositions:** "This is a triangle." "Two of its angles are equal." The two subpropositions are joined together by the word "and" which we call a **connective.** Any subproposition may itself be made up of subpropositions. For example, "This is white and this is black, whereas these two are both green" where "whereas" is meant in the sense "and", and the subproposition "This is white and this is black" is made up from the two subpropositions: "This is white." "This is black."

Consider the following simple propositions: "England is in the southern hemisphere." "All even numbers are divisible by 2." Clearly the first proposition is false, whereas the second proposition is true. Suppose we have the following compound propositions: "$a(b + c) = ab + ac$, and $a \times (b \times c) = (a \times b) \times c$", "England is in the southern hemisphere and all even numbers are divisible by 2". The first compound proposition is true (in ordinary algebra) and so are both of its subpropositions, but how can we decide on the **truth value** (i.e. truth or falsity) of the second compound proposition where its subpropositions are respectively false and true?

We now concern ourselves with the problem of compounding propositions and determining their truth values.

1.2. Connectives

(i) *Negation* (*not*)

p	$\bar{p}$
1	0
0	1

Negation of a proposition p (written $\bar{p}$) is defined by the above **truth table** where 1 and 0 denote truth and falsity respectively. Thus $\bar{p}$ is true when p is false, and $\bar{p}$ is false when p is true.

(ii) *Disjunction* (*or*)

It is helpful here if we first of all look at some examples:

(a) Either two straight lines intersect *or* they are parallel (in plane Euclidean geometry).
(b) Some aspects of number may be studied either by geometric methods *or* by algebraic methods.
(c) Tomorrow's weather may be sunny *or* windy.
(d) Any real number is either rational *or* irrational.

In (a) and (d), *or* is meant in the sense p or q but not both, where p and q are the subpropositions; whereas in (b) and (c), *or* is meant in the sense p or q with the possibility of both p and q, i.e. p and/or q. In mathematics we must be quite clear in what we mean by "or". In the first sense we call the connective "or" the **exclusive disjunction**, and in the second sense we call it the **inclusive disjunction**.

EXCLUSIVE DISJUNCTION (WRITTEN $(p \underline{\vee} q)$ (OR)

p	q	$p \underline{\vee} q$
1	1	0
1	0	**1**
0	1	1
0	0	0

INCLUSIVE DISJUNCTION (WRITTEN $p \vee q$) (AND/OR)

p	q	$p \vee q$
1	1	1
1	0	1
0	1	1
0	0	0

The truth table definitions of the two types of disjunction are given above. Thus the exclusive disjunction of two propositions which are both true or both false is not true; the inclusive disjunction of two propositions which are both false is not true, although it is true in the remaining **logical possibilities.**

The inclusive disjunction is the more common of the two forms, and unless otherwise specified, the word disjunction in the rest of the book will mean inclusive disjunction.

(iii) *Conjunction* (*written* $p \wedge q$) (*and*)

p	q	$p \wedge q$
1	1	1
1	0	0
0	1	0
0	0	0

The truth table definition of conjunction is shown above; thus the conjunction of two propositions which are both true is true, although it is false in the remaining logical possibilities.

Referring to an earlier example in §1.1, if we let p be "England is in the southern hemisphere" and q be "All even numbers are divisible by 2", we see that the truth value of $p \wedge q$ is 0 (false) *by definition*.

Suppose, in the above example, we negate p (say) so that $p = 1$ and $q = 1$, then according to the truth table for a conjunction, $p \wedge q = 1$. However, it is most important to note that we are in no position to deduce the following: the falsity of "England is in the southern hemisphere and all even numbers are divisible by 2" *implies* the truth of "England is not in the southern hemisphere and all even numbers are divisible by 2". For, although it is most tempting to find such a relation, there is nothing stated in the definitions of connectives which permits us to relate propositions in this way. We will be dealing with the problem of defining a **relation** between propositions in §1.5.

EXAMPLES

1. If p be "Jack likes Jill" and q be "Jill likes Jack", then
    (a) Jack likes Jill or Jill likes Jack is $p \vee q$.
    (b) Jack likes Jill and Jill likes Jack is $p \wedge q$.
    (c) Neither Jack likes Jill nor Jill likes Jack is $\bar{p} \wedge \bar{q}$.
    (d) It is not true that Jack likes Jill or Jill likes Jack is $\overline{(p \vee q)}$.
Note that (c) and (d) are identical.

2. If we had to construct the truth table for the proposition $p \vee (q \wedge r)$ (say), we would determine firstly the number of logical possibilities (i.e. the total number of propositions that can be formed by giving the truth values 1 and 0 to p, q and r, is 8), secondly the truth values of $q \wedge r$, and finally the truth values of $p \vee (q \wedge r)$. The number of rows in the truth table is therefore 8 as follows:

p	q	r	$q \wedge r$	$p \vee (q \wedge r)$
1	1	1	1	1
1	1	0	0	1
1	0	0	0	1
0	0	0	0	0
0	1	0	0	0
0	1	1	1	1
0	0	1	0	0
1	0	1	0	1

                     ↑   ↑
Using the definition   Using the definition
of conjunction   of disjunction

3. Construct truth tables for each of the following:

   (a) $\bar{\bar{p}}$ (b) $\overline{(p \wedge q)}$ (c) $\overline{(p \vee q)} \vee \overline{(q \vee p)}$.

(a)

p	$\bar{p}$	$\bar{\bar{p}}$
1	0	1
0	1	0

i.e. $\bar{\bar{p}}$ is identical with p.

(b)

p	q	$p \wedge q$	$\overline{(p \wedge q)}$
1	1	1	0
1	0	0	1
0	1	0	1
0	0	0	1

(c)

p	q	$p \vee q$	$\overline{(p \vee q)}$	$q \vee p$	$\overline{(q \vee p)}$	$\overline{(p \vee q)} \vee \overline{(q \vee p)}$
1	1	1	0	1	0	0
1	0	1	0	1	0	0
0	1	1	0	1	0	0
0	0	0	1	0	1	1
		(i)	(ii)	(iii)	(iv)	(v)

Note that (i) and (iii) are identical, and (ii), (iv) and (v) are identical. We will be looking closely at identities in §1.5.

EXERCISES 1a

1. Let p be "I will read a book" and q be "It is summer". Interpret in good English, each of the following:

(a) $p \wedge q$ (b) $p \vee q$ (c) $\bar{p} \vee q$ (d) $p \wedge \bar{q}$ (e) $\overline{(p \wedge q)}$ (f) $(p \wedge \bar{q}) \vee (\bar{p} \wedge q)$
(g) $(p \vee q) \wedge \overline{(p \wedge q)}$.

Questions 2–4 should be done using truth tables.

2. Prove the following rules of identity:

(a) $p \equiv p$ (b) $p \vee p \equiv p$ (c) $p \wedge p \equiv p$.

3. Prove the following rules:

(a) Associativity. $p \vee (q \vee r) = (p \vee q) \vee r$.
$\qquad\qquad\qquad p \wedge (q \wedge r) = (p \wedge q) \wedge r$.

(b) Commutativity. $p \vee q = q \vee p$
$\qquad\qquad\qquad p \wedge q = q \wedge p$.

(c) Distribution of disjunction over conjunction.

$$p \vee (q \wedge r) = (p \vee q) \wedge (p \vee r).$$

(d) Distribution of conjunction over disjunction.

$$p \wedge (q \vee r) = (p \wedge q) \vee (p \wedge r).$$

4. Prove the following (De Morgan's laws):

(a) $\overline{(p \vee q)} = \bar{p} \wedge \bar{q}$ (b) $\overline{(p \wedge q)} = \bar{p} \vee \bar{q}$.

1.3. Conditionals

In addition to the above connectives there are two more very important ones: the **conditional** and the **biconditional.**

As examples, take the following propositions:

"*If* the equation of a curve in the plane (referred to rectangular coordinates) is $x^2 + y^2 + 2gx + 2fy + c = 0$, *then* the curve is a circle whose centre lies at $(-g, -f)$ and whose radius is the positive square root of $(g^2 + f^2 - c)$."

"*If* a system of forces acting in the plane is in equilibrium, *then* the algebraic sum of the moments of the forces about any point in the plane is zero."

"A number is rational *if and only if* it can be put in the form a/b, where a and b are integers, $b \neq 0$."

"The weather is fair *if and only if* the barometer is high."

The first two are examples of the conditional and the last two are examples of the biconditional. Complete definitions of these connectives are given in the following truth tables.

CONDITIONAL (WRITTEN $p \rightarrow q$) (IF . . . THEN)

p	q	$p \rightarrow q$
1	1	1
1	0	0
0	1	1
0	0	1

Thus the proposition $p \rightarrow q$ is false when p is true and q is false, although it is true in the remaining logical possibilities.

BICONDITIONAL (WRITTEN $p \leftrightarrow q$) (IF AND ONLY IF)

p	q	$p \leftrightarrow q$
1	1	1
1	0	0
0	1	0
0	0	1

The proposition $p \leftrightarrow q$ is true whenever both p and q are true or both p and q are false, otherwise it is false.

A word of warning. Sometimes paradoxical situations will occur if the reader applies the definition of the conditional to everyday usage of language. For example, according to the truth table for a conditional, the proposition "If black is white, then red is blue" is true, whereas "If $2 \times 2 = 4$, then I am a monkey's uncle" is false. In everyday language we use the conditional in a *causal sense* (e.g. $2 \times 2 = 4$ causes me to be a monkey's uncle), whereas in the above definitions of connectives there is no such limitation due to a causal relationship. Normally, in everyday language, we would say that both propositions are nonsensical, and not entertain the notion of the truth or falsity of each.

1.4. Tautology. Contradiction

If we construct truth tables for propositions such as $(p \to q) \leftrightarrow (\bar{q} \to \bar{p})$ or $p \lor \bar{p}$ for example, we see that the propositions are always true, i.e. *logically true for all logical possibilities*, i.e. for all possible truth values of their subpropositions.

p	q	$p \to q$	$\bar{q}$	$\bar{p}$	$\bar{q} \to \bar{p}$	$(p \to q) \leftrightarrow (\bar{q} \to \bar{p})$
1	1	1	0	0	1	1
1	0	0	1	0	0	1
0	1	1	0	1	1	1
0	0	1	1	1	1	1

p	$\bar{p}$	$p \vee \bar{p}$
1	0	1
0	1	1

Such propositions we call **tautologies**. On the other hand, propositions which are *logically false*, i.e. false for *all logical possibilities* are called **contradictions**. Examples of contradictions are $p \wedge \bar{p}$ and $\overline{p \rightarrow (p \vee q)}$.

p	$\bar{p}$	$p \wedge \bar{p}$
1	0	0
0	1	0

p	q	$p \vee q$	$p \rightarrow (p \vee q)$	$\overline{p \rightarrow (p \vee q)}$
1	1	1	1	0
1	0	1	1	0
0	1	1	1	0
0	0	0	1	0

We will now prove that the negation of a tautology is a contradiction, and the negation of a contradiction is a tautology:

(i) Consider the last column of a tautology truth table; it consists entirely of 1's. Hence, negating a tautology requires adding a further column to the truth table corresponding to the logically possible truth values of the negated tautology. By definition of the negation, this column will consist entirely of 0's. Thus by definition of the contradiction, it follows that a negated tautology is a contradiction.

(ii) Negating a contradiction is similar in proof.

1.5. Logical relations

Until now we have considered statements in isolation, although we discussed the possibility of relating propositions (or statements) in §1.2. Two of the most important relations are those of **implication** and **equivalence**.

Implication (*written* $p \Rightarrow q$)

We say that $p \Rightarrow q$ (p implies q) if the conditional $p \rightarrow q$ is a tautology, i.e. logically true. For example, $p \wedge q \Rightarrow p \vee q$.

p	q	$p \wedge q$	$p \vee q$	$p \wedge q \Rightarrow p \vee q$
1	1	1	1	1
1	0	0	1	1
0	1	0	1	1
0	0	0	0	1

It should be noted in the above example that $p \vee q \not\Rightarrow p \wedge q$ (where $\not\Rightarrow$ signifies "does not imply").

Equivalence (*written* $p \Leftrightarrow q$)

If $p \leftrightarrow q$ is a tautology, then we say that p and q are equivalent or identical. For example, $\overline{p \vee q} \Leftrightarrow \bar{p} \wedge \bar{q}$.

p	q	$p \vee q$	$\overline{p \vee q}$	$\bar{p}$	$\bar{q}$	$\bar{p} \wedge \bar{q}$	$\overline{p \vee q} \Leftrightarrow \bar{p} \wedge \bar{q}$
1	1	1	0	0	0	0	1
1	0	1	0	0	1	0	1
0	1	1	0	1	0	0	1
0	0	0	1	1	1	1	1

So, in §1.4, $(p \rightarrow q) \leftrightarrow (\bar{q} \rightarrow \bar{p})$ may be written $(p \rightarrow q) \Leftrightarrow (\bar{q} \rightarrow \bar{p})$. We now see exactly what is meant by "identity" in §1.2.

EXERCISES 1b

1. Show that $(p \leftrightarrow q) \to (p \to q)$ is a tautology and may therefore be written: $(p \leftrightarrow q) \Rightarrow (p \to q)$. Also show that $(p \leftrightarrow q) \to (p \lor q)$ is not a tautology.

2. Prove that the following are tautologies:

    (a) $[p \land (p \to q)] \to q$

    (b) $\bar{q} \to \overline{q \land r}$

    (c) $(p \to q) \leftrightarrow (\bar{p} \lor q)$

    (d) $\overline{(p \to q)} \leftrightarrow p \land \bar{q}$

    (e) $(p \to q) \land (r \to s) \to [(p \lor r) \to (q \lor s)]$.

3. If p is logically true, prove that:

    (a) $p \lor q$ is a tautology

    (b) $\bar{p} \land q$ is a contradiction

    (c) $p \land q \leftrightarrow q$ is a tautology

    (d) $\bar{p} \lor q \leftrightarrow q$ is a tautology.

[*Hint*: each truth table starts off with the columns

p	q
1	1
1	0

i.e. there are only *two* logical possibilities, since p is logically true (i.e. always true).]

4. Construct truth tables for $p \Rightarrow q$ and $p \Leftrightarrow q$.

(*Hint:* in the case $p \Rightarrow q$, it is impossible for $p = 1$ and $q = 0$ at the same time. Also, in the case $p \Leftrightarrow q$, it is impossible for $p = 1$ and $q = 0$ at the same time or $p = 0$ and $q = 1$ at the same time.)

5. Which of the following conditions are implications?

    (a) If $a^2 = b^2$, then $a = b$ (a and b real).

    (b) If $a = b$, then $a^2 = b^2$ (a and b real).

    (c) If n is even, then it is divisible by 2.

    (d) If $x \not< y$, then $x > y$.

    (e) If n is prime, then it is odd.

    (f) If it is sunny, then the weather is fine.

6. Which of the following biconditionals are equivalences?

    (a) The weather will be fine if and only if the barometer is high.

    (b) $a = b$ if and only if $a^2 = b^2$ (a and b real).

    (c) $a\alpha^2 + b\alpha + c = 0$ if and only if $x = \alpha$ is a root of $ax^2 + bx + c$ (a, b, c real and non-zero).

    (d) Two sides of a triangle are equal if and only if the triangle has its base angles equal.

(e) Three forces acting in the plane are concurrent if and only if they are in equilibrium.

(f) $a(b + c) = ab + ac$ if and only if the distributive law of multiplication over addition holds (a, b, c real or complex).

1.6. Relatives of a conditional

There are three common conditionals often associated with a conditional $p \rightarrow q$. They are:

(i) $q \rightarrow p$ the **converse** of $p \rightarrow q$;
(ii) $\bar{p} \rightarrow \bar{q}$ the **inverse** of $p \rightarrow q$;
(iii) $\bar{q} \rightarrow \bar{p}$ the **contrapositive** of $p \rightarrow q$.

To see how these conditionals are related to the conditional $p \rightarrow q$, let us look at the following combined truth table:

p	q	$p \rightarrow q$	$q \rightarrow p$	$\bar{p} \rightarrow \bar{q}$	$\bar{q} \rightarrow \bar{p}$
1	1	1	1	1	1
1	0	0	1	1	0
0	1	1	0	0	1
0	0	1	1	1	1

We note that $\bar{q} \rightarrow \bar{p} \Leftrightarrow p \rightarrow q$, i.e. *the conditional is equivalent to its contrapositive*. Also, $q \rightarrow p \Leftrightarrow \bar{p} \rightarrow \bar{q}$, i.e. *the inverse of a conditional is equivalent to the converse*. However, the conditional is not equivalent to its inverse or its converse.

These three conditionals often arise in mathematics and are very useful in classifying certain fallacies. For example, consider the conditional "If two triangles each have their base angles equal to 60°, then both triangles are isosceles":

Conditional. If two triangles each have their base angles equal to 60°, then both triangles are isosceles. (Given, true.)

Converse. If two triangles are isosceles, then each have their base angles equal to 60°. (False.)

Inverse. If two triangles do not each have their base angles equal to 60°, then neither triangle is isosceles. (False.)

Contrapositive. If two triangles are not isosceles, then each of their base angles are not equal to 60°. (True.)

The converse is considered false in the above example, since the base angles may each be equal to 47° (say). Similarly, the inverse is considered false. Too often the converse of a conditional is assumed to be true in mathematics, when in fact it is not. Of course, the converse may be true in certain cases, for example: "If n is an even number, then it is divisible by 2" is true and so is its converse, "If n is a number that is divisible by 2, then it is an even number". By definition of the conditional and the converse, it is clear that the converse of $p \rightarrow q$ will be true if $p \leftrightarrow q$. (An instance of this is the example above.)

A further important point to note is that since $p \rightarrow q \Leftrightarrow \bar{q} \rightarrow \bar{p}$, then if $p \rightarrow q$ is logically true, i.e. $p \Rightarrow q$, then $\bar{q} \rightarrow \bar{p}$ is an implication and can be written $\bar{q} \Rightarrow \bar{p}$.

1.7. Some important methods of proof

Before we discuss methods of proof, we must clarify the various modes of expression used in this connection. That some confusion might arise is immediately obvious when one considers that "if $\bar{q}$ then $\bar{p}$" is equivalent to saying "if p then q". An alternative way of stating "if p then q" is "q if p"; the latter expression suggests that p is required for q, although other possibilities are left (e.g. "q if r"). So p is not *necessary* for q but is *sufficient* for q. On the other hand consider "p only if q" (not to be confused with "$p \leftrightarrow q$"); since we have p *only if* we have q, it follows that we do not have p if we do not have q, i.e. "p only if q" is an alternative way of stating "$\bar{q} \rightarrow \bar{p}$" or its equivalent "$p \rightarrow q$". So q is *necessary* for p.

Turn now to the biconditional "$p \leftrightarrow q$". We know that "$p \leftrightarrow q$" is equivalent to "$p \rightarrow q$ and $q \rightarrow p$", and from above "$p \rightarrow q$" may be stated as "p is sufficient for q and q is necessary for p" and "$q \rightarrow p$" may be stated as "q is sufficient for p and p is necessary for q". Thus "$p \leftrightarrow q$" may be interpreted as "p is *necessary and sufficient* for q, and q is *necessary and sufficient* for p." Also, "$p \leftrightarrow q$" can be written "p only if q and q only if p", that is, "p *if and only if* q" (this form being very familiar now).

The following table summarizes what has so far been discussed in this section:

$p \rightarrow q$	If p then q	q if p	p only if q	p is sufficient for q	q is necessary for p
$p \leftrightarrow q$	If p then q and if q then p	p if q and q if p	p if and only if q	p is necessary and sufficient for q	

A **proof** is essentially an argument which shows that a conditional of the form $p \rightarrow q$ is logically true, i.e. $p \Rightarrow q$; p is the conjunction of the **premises** and q is the **conclusion**. We now exemplify this:

(i) *Given* (i.e. the premises). In the right-angled triangle shown,

$$\sin\theta = \frac{a}{c}, \qquad \cos\theta = \frac{b}{c}, \qquad \tan\theta = \frac{a}{b}.$$

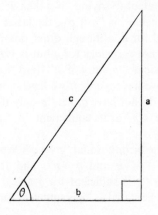

Prove. $\dfrac{\sin \theta}{\cos \theta} = \tan\theta$ (i.e. the conclusion).

Proof. $\sin\theta = \dfrac{a}{c}$ and $\cos\theta = \dfrac{b}{c}$ and $\tan\theta = \dfrac{a}{b}$

$$\Rightarrow \frac{\sin\theta}{\cos\theta} = \frac{a}{c} \times \frac{c}{b} = \frac{a}{b} = \tan\theta.$$

(ii) *Given.* All men are mortal. All Greeks are men.

Prove. All Greeks are mortal.

Proof. All Greeks are men and all men are mortal.

$\Rightarrow$ All Greeks are mortal.

(iii) *Given.* The quadratic equation $ax^2 + bx + c = 0$.

Prove. $x = \dfrac{-b \pm \sqrt{(b^2 - 4ac)}}{2a}$ gives the roots of the equation.

Proof. $ax^2 + bx + c = 0$

$$\Rightarrow x^2 + \frac{bx}{a} + \frac{c}{a} = 0$$

$$\Rightarrow \left(x + \frac{b}{2a}\right)^2 - \frac{b^2}{4a^2} + \frac{c}{a} = 0$$

$$\Rightarrow \left(x + \frac{b}{2a}\right) = \pm \sqrt{\left(\frac{b^2 - 4ac}{4a^2}\right)} = \frac{\pm \sqrt{(b^2 - 4ac)}}{2a}$$

$$\Rightarrow x = \frac{-b \pm \sqrt{(b^2 - 4ac)}}{2a}$$

where $\sqrt{(b^2 - 4ac)}$ is known as the discriminant.

(iv) *Given.* If $(b^2 - 4ac) \geqslant 0$, then $ax^2 + bx + c = 0$ has real roots. Consider $x^2 - 7x + 12 = 0$.

Prove. $x^2 - 7x + 12 = 0$ has real roots.

Proof. In the equation $x^2 - 7x + 12 = 0$, the discriminant $=$

$$(49 - 48) > 0$$

$\Rightarrow x^2 - 7x + 12 = 0$ has real roots.

(v) *Given.* If $a = b$, then $a^2 = b^2$, where a and b are real. Consider $a = b = 2$.

Prove. $2^2 = 2^2$.

Proof. Since 2 is real, $2^2 = 2^2$.

(vi) *Given.* xy is odd where x and y are integers.

Prove. Both x and y are odd.

Proof. Suppose x and y are not both odd, say x is even and y odd. Then $x = 2n$, where n is any integer, and $xy = 2(ny)$ which is even. But xy is odd (given), and we have arrived at a contradiction. Similar arguments dispose of the possibilities of x odd and y even, and x and y both even. Thus both x and y must be odd (the only possibility left).

(vii) *Prove.* $\sqrt{2}$ is irrational.

Proof. Assume on the contrary that $\sqrt{2}$ is rational and let $\sqrt{2} = a/b$, where a and b are relatively prime integers (i.e. highest common factor of a and b is 1 which means that a/b is in its simplest form). So squaring, we obtain

$$a^2 = 2b^2 \Rightarrow a^2 \text{ is even} \Rightarrow a \text{ is even.}$$

Let $a = 2n$, where n is any integer, then $a^2 = 4n^2 = 2b^2$, i.e.

$$2n^2 = b^2 \Rightarrow b^2 \text{ is even} \Rightarrow b \text{ is even.}$$

Since both a and b are even, a/b can be simplified by cancellation; this is contrary to the assumption that a/b is in its simplest form. Thus $\sqrt{2}$ cannot be rational and must therefore be irrational (only possibility left).

(viii) *Given.* $a/b = c \Rightarrow a = bc$, where a, b and c are any real numbers.

Prove. Division by zero is meaningless.

Proof. Assume on the contrary that $a/0$ is meaningful, and let $a \neq 0$, then $a/0 = c \Rightarrow a = 0 \times c = 0$ (whether or not $c = 0$). Thus $a \neq 0$ and $a = 0$. We have arrived at a contradiction, and so $a/0$ must be meaningless (only possibility left).

As one goes down the list of examples from (i) to (viii) one realizes that the proofs appear to be more and more removed from the simple definition of a proof given earlier. However, this is an illusion as we shall now see:

In (i) no explanation required; it is a straightforward example of $p \Rightarrow q$.

In (ii) and (iii) the reasoning is of the form

$$(p \Rightarrow q) \wedge (q \Rightarrow r) \Rightarrow (p \Rightarrow r);$$

here $(p \Rightarrow q)$ and $(q \Rightarrow r)$ are the premises and $(p \Rightarrow r)$ is the conclusion. In (ii) p is Greeks, q is men, and r is mortal. In (iii),

$$p \text{ is } ax^2 + bx + c = 0,$$

$$q \text{ is } x^2 + \frac{bx}{a} + \frac{c}{a} = 0,$$

$$r \text{ is } \left(x + \frac{b}{2a}\right)^2 - \frac{b^2}{4a^2} + \frac{c}{a} = 0,$$

$$s \text{ is } \left(x + \frac{b}{2a}\right) = \pm \sqrt{\left(\frac{b^2 - 4ac}{4a^2}\right)},$$

i.e.
$$s \text{ is } \left(x + \frac{b}{2a}\right) = \frac{\pm \sqrt{(b^2 - 4ac)}}{2a},$$

and
$$t \text{ is } x = \frac{-b \pm \sqrt{(b^2 - 4ac)}}{2a};$$

so, $\quad (p \Rightarrow q) \wedge (q \Rightarrow r) \wedge (r \Rightarrow s) \wedge (s \Rightarrow t) \Rightarrow (p \Rightarrow t).$

In (iv) and (v) the argument is of the form $(p \Rightarrow q) \wedge (p \text{ is true})$ $\Rightarrow (q \text{ is true})$. In the case of (iv), $p \Rightarrow q$ is "If $(b^2 - 4ac) \geqslant 0$, then $ax^2 + bx + c = 0$ has real roots" and that p is true is evident in the case $x^2 - 7x + 12 = 0$. In the case of (v), $p \Rightarrow q$ is "If $a = b$, then $a^2 = b^2$" and p is clearly true as $2 = 2$.

Example (vi) is an argument of the form $(\bar{q} \Rightarrow \bar{p})$ which we know is equivalent to $(p \Rightarrow q)$. Here p is "xy is odd where x and y are integers" and q is "Both x and y are odd".

In (vii) and (viii) the proof is of the form $(p \wedge \bar{q}) \Rightarrow (r \wedge \bar{r})$. In the case of example (vii), p is "$\sqrt{2}$ is a number and 2 is not a perfect square" and q is "$\sqrt{2}$ is irrational" and r is "$\sqrt{2} = a/b$ where a and b are relatively prime integers". In (viii), p is "$a/b = c \Rightarrow a = bc$, where a, b, and c are any real numbers" and q is "division by zero is meaningless" and r is "$a \neq 0$".

The different forms of proof, then, are all basically the same as $p \Rightarrow q$; truth tables below show this:

RULE OF SYLLOGISM $[(p \Rightarrow q) \land (q \Rightarrow r) \Rightarrow (p \Rightarrow r)]$

p	q	r	$p \Rightarrow q$	$q \Rightarrow r$	$(p \Rightarrow q)$ $\land (q \Rightarrow r)$	$p \Rightarrow r$	$(p \Rightarrow q) \land (q \Rightarrow r)$ $\Rightarrow (p \Rightarrow r)$
1	1	1	1	1	1	1	1
1	1	0	1	0	0	0	1
1	0	0	0	1	0	0	1
0	0	0	1	1	1	1	1
0	1	1	1	1	1	1	1
0	0	1	1	1	1	1	1
0	1	0	1	0	0	1	1
1	0	1	0	1	0	1	1

therefore $[(p \Rightarrow q) \land (q \Rightarrow r) \Rightarrow (p \Rightarrow r)] \Leftrightarrow (p \Rightarrow q)$

The second, third, seventh and eighth rows have been deleted from the truth table since in one or more of these rows either $p \not\Rightarrow q$ or $q \not\Rightarrow r$ (i.e. the simultaneous truth values of p, q and r are not logically possible in these rows).

Modus Ponens $[(p \Rightarrow q) \land (p \text{ is true}) \Rightarrow (q \text{ is true})]$

p	q	$p \Rightarrow q$
1	1	1
0	1	1
0	0	1

From the first row of the truth table for an implication, it is seen that q is true if p is true.

Reductio ad Absurdum $[(p \wedge \bar{q}) \Rightarrow (r \wedge \bar{r})]$

p	q	r	$p \wedge \bar{q}$	$r \wedge \bar{r}$	$(p \wedge \bar{q}) \Rightarrow (r \wedge \bar{r})$	$p \Rightarrow q$
1	1	1	0	0	1	1
1	1	0	0	0	1	1
-1-	-0-	-0-	-1-	-0-	-0-	-0-
0	0	0	0	0	1	1
0	1	1	0	0	1	1
0	0	1	0	0	1	1
0	1	0	0	0	1	1
-1-	-0-	-1-	-1-	-0-	-0-	-0-

therefore $[(p \wedge \bar{q}) \Rightarrow (r \wedge \bar{r})] \Leftrightarrow (p \Rightarrow q)$

The third and eighth rows have been deleted from the truth table since in both these rows $(p \wedge \bar{q}) \not\Rightarrow (r \wedge \bar{r})$.

We summarize in the following table:

Direct proofs			Indirect proofs	
Direct application of implication	Rule of syllogism	*Modus ponens*	Contra-positive	*Reductio ad absurdum*
$p \Rightarrow q$	$(p \Rightarrow q) \wedge (q \Rightarrow r)$ $\Rightarrow (p \Rightarrow r)$	$(p \Rightarrow q) \wedge$ (p is true) $\Rightarrow q$ is true	$(\bar{q} \Rightarrow \bar{p})$ $\Leftrightarrow (p \Rightarrow q)$	$(p \wedge \bar{q}) \Rightarrow$ $(r \wedge \bar{r})$
Ex. (i)	Ex. (ii) and (iii)	Ex. (iv) and (v)	Ex. (vi)	Ex. (vii) and (viii)

This table shows some of the most common forms of proof by **deduction** in mathematics. A different approach to proving theorems, that by **induction,** is given in Chapter 3.

EXERCISES 1c

1. "For a system of coplanar forces to be in equilibrium it is necessary that the algebraic sum of the moments of the forces about any point in their plane be zero." (Given.)

Which of the following are true?

(a) If a system of coplanar forces is in equilibrium, then the algebraic sum of the moments of the forces about any point in their plane is zero.

(b) A sufficient condition for a system of coplanar forces to be in equilibrium is that the algebraic sum of the moments of the forces about any point in their plane be zero.

(c) A system of coplanar forces is in equilibrium only if the algebraic sum of the moments of the forces about any point in their plane is zero.

(d) If the algebraic sum of the moments of the forces, in a coplanar system, about a point in their plane is not zero, then the forces are not in equilibrium.

2. "A necessary and sufficient condition that two triangles be similar is that they be equiangular." (Given.)

"A necessary and sufficient condition that two triangles be similar is that an angle of one should equal an angle of the other and that the ratios of the corresponding sides containing these angles should be equal." (Given.)

It should be noted that we have here an example of the rule that "necessary and sufficient conditions" are not necessarily **unique.**

Which of the following are true?

(a) Two triangles are similar only if they are equiangular.

(b) If in the case of two triangles an angle of one equals an angle of the other and the ratios of the corresponding sides containing these angles are equal then the triangles are similar.

(c) Two triangles are equiangular if and only if they are similar.

3. Test the validity of the following argument:

"For me to go for a walk it is sufficient that the weather be hot and sunny. The weather is hot and sunny only if it is summer. It is not summer, and therefore I will not go for a walk."

4. Test the validity of the following argument:

"If he studies hard then he will get well qualified and get a good job. Therefore, if he does not get well qualified or does not get a good job then he has not studied hard."

5. Give a direct proof then an indirect proof of:

"If a positive integer a divides bc and is relatively prime to one factor b, it must divide the other factor c."

6. Using *reductio ad absurdum* as method of proof, prove that the number of primes is infinite. [*Hint*: assume on the contrary and let n be the greatest prime number, then consider the product $2.3.5.7.11 \ldots n$ in which each factor is a prime number. What sort of number is formed by adding 1 to this product? (two possibilities).]

7. Examine the statement "All prime numbers are odd". (*Hint*: a single counterexample will disprove a theorem.)

CHAPTER 2

Elementary Set Theory and Boolean Algebras

2.1. Notation and idea of a set

A **set** is a well-defined collection of objects. This concept is of fundamental importance since the whole of mathematics can be developed from it.

People sitting in a bus form a set. Other examples of sets are: all the integers between 3 and 500; all the people living in a town; all the quadrupeds in the world; all the real numbers between 0 and 1; all prime numbers; the roots of $2x^3 + 9x^2 + 4x - 15 = 0$. In other words, there is an infinite variety of objects that may at one time or another be considered; in mathematics we prefer to use the abstract term **element** for object. The qualification "well-defined" is important in the concept of set; it means that we must be able to distinguish between the elements in a particular set and yet at the same time all the elements must have something in common in order that the totality of them may be grouped together as a unique set. Put another way, a set is uniquely determined by its elements—the latter being distinct.

A set with a finite number of elements in it ("all the quadrupeds in the world" for example) is called a **finite set,** whereas a set with an infinite number of elements in it ("all the real numbers between 0 and 1" for example) is called an **infinite set.** There are essentially two ways of specifying a set: (i) by listing, and (ii) by description. In case (i) a complete list, usually enclosed by braces { }, of all the elements in the set is given: $\{-2\frac{1}{2}, -3, +1\}$ for example is the solution set of the equation given above. In case (ii) a rule is given by which it can be determined whether or not a given element is a member of the set: the set comprising "all prime numbers" for example tells us that 7 is a member of this set. Clearly, listing cannot be done for infinite sets.

The membership of an element of a set is denoted by $\in$. Thus if P denotes the set of all prime numbers, we write for example $7 \in P$. Frequently, in specifying sets a combination of "description", "listing", and "membership ($\in$)" is used: $J = \{x: x \text{ is an integer}\}$, $S = \{x \in J^+: x^2 - 7x + 12 = 0\}$ are examples, where the colon ":" inside the braces denotes "such that". $J = \{x: x \text{ is an integer}\}$ is then read as "J is the set comprising of x's such that each x is an integer"—in other words J is the set of integers. $S = \{x \in J^+: x^2 - 7x + 12 = 0\}$ is read as "S is the set comprising of x's which are members of the set of positive integers such that $x^2 - 7x + 12 = 0$", i.e. $S = \{3, 4\}$.

Usually, capital letters are used for sets and small letters for elements.

If each element of a set A is also a member of a set B, then we say that A is a **subset** of B. Written $A \subseteq B$. For example, the set R of all rational numbers is a subset of the set R^* of all real numbers, i.e. $R \subseteq R^*$. A set that contains no elements at all is called the **null set** and is denoted by $\varnothing$. For example, $\{n \in R^+: n \leqslant 0\} = \varnothing$, where R^+ is the set containing positive rational numbers; $\{x: x \neq x\} = \varnothing$, where the x's signify anything under the sun! The null set is considered to be a subset of every set. Consider now a totality of elements, and form all possible sets $A, B, C, \ldots,$ from them; clearly one of the sets will be the null set $\varnothing$, and there will be one set containing all the elements—this latter set is called the **universal set** and is usually denoted by U. The universal set is considered to be a subset of itself. Thus we have $\varnothing \subseteq A \subseteq U$ for *any* set A. A **proper subset** A of the set B is such that A is a subset of B and B contains at least one element not in A; written $A \subset B$. For example, the proper subsets of $\{a, b, c\}$ are $\{a, b\}$, $\{a, c\}$, $\{b, c\}$, $\{a\}$, $\{b\}$, $\{c\}$ and $\varnothing$. $\varnothing$ is considered a proper subset of every set except itself.

Two sets are said to be *equal* if they have the same elements. From this definition of equality and the definition of a subset it follows that for any two sets A and B if $A \subseteq B$ **and** $B \subseteq A$ **then** $A = B$; this important result is often used in proving set relationships (e.g. example 6 in §2.3).

The total possible number of subsets that can be formed from a set containing n elements is 2^n; by the definition of subset, this includes the set itself. We prove this as follows (see Chapter 3 for permutations, combinations and the binomial theorem): we form $\emptyset$ by choosing no element from the n elements—there are $^nC_0 = 1$ ways of doing this; we then form all the subsets having one element in each—there are $^nC_1 = n$ ways of doing this; next, we form all the subsets having two elements in each—there are $^nC_2 = \dfrac{n(n-1)}{2!}$ ways of doing this; continuing in this fashion we exhaust all the possibilities. The total possible number of subsets that may be formed is then equal to the sum

$$^nC_0 + {}^nC_1 + {}^nC_2 + \ldots + {}^nC_{n-1} + {}^nC_n,$$

and if we put $x = 1$ in the expansion of $(1 + x)^n$ we obtain

$$(1 + 1)^n = 2^n = {}^nC_0 + {}^nC_1 + {}^nC_2 + \ldots + {}^nC_{n-1} + {}^nC_n.$$

2.2. Operations on sets

Definition. An **operation** is an instruction for obtaining sets from given sets.

We concern ourselves with three different operations in set algebra: (i) The **complement** of a set A, written A'. (ii) The **union** of two sets A and B, written $A \cup B$. (iii) The **intersection** of two sets A and B, written $A \cap B$. The operation in (i) is an example of a **unary operation,** whereas in (ii) and (iii) we have examples of a **binary operation.**

Definitions. (i) The **complement** A' of a set A is the set of those and only those elements which are *not* in A.

(ii) The **union** $A \cup B$ of two sets A and B is the set which contains either the elements of A *or* the elements of B or the elements in both A *and* B.

(iii) The **intersection** $A \cap B$ of two sets A and B is the set which contains those and only those elements which are in A *and* B.

For example, if $A = \{a, b, c, d\}$ and $B = \{b, c, f, g, h, j\}$,

then $\qquad A \cup B = \{a, b, c, d, f, g, h, j\}$

and $\qquad A \cap B = \{b, c\}$.

If in this case we take the universal set to be

$$U = \{a, b, c, d, f, g, h, j, p, q, r, v, w\},$$

then $\qquad A' = \{f, g, h, j, p, q, r, v, w\},$

$$B' = \{a, d, p, q, r, v, w\},$$

$$(A \cup B)' = \{p, q, r, v, w\}, \text{ and}$$

$$(A \cap B)' = \{a, d, f, g, h, j, p, q, r, v, w\}.$$

If $A \cap B = \varnothing$, that is if two sets have no elements in common, then the sets are called **disjoint**.

Operations on sets can be illustrated by means of **Venn diagrams.** The universal set U is represented by the space inside the rectangle, and the sets A and B are represented by spaces inside circles as shown in Fig. 2.1. Note also that by universal set we mean *universal in a relative sense*, that is to say in a particular context the universal set contains *at least* all the elements in the sets under consideration: put another way, if we consider the sets $A = \{\alpha, \beta, \gamma\}$, $B = \{\delta, \varepsilon, \zeta, \eta\}$, and $C = \{\beta, \gamma, \omega\}$, for example, then

$$(A \cup B) \cup C = A \cup (B \cup C) = A \cup B \cup C$$
$$= \{\alpha, \beta, \gamma, \delta, \varepsilon, \zeta, \eta, \omega\} \subseteq U.$$

That $A \cup B \cup C = (A \cup B) \cup C = A \cup (B \cup C)$ can easily be *verified* by a Venn diagram, but we will *prove* this *associative law* in the next section.

Library
I.U.P.
Indiana, Pa.

512.8 Ok2f
c.1

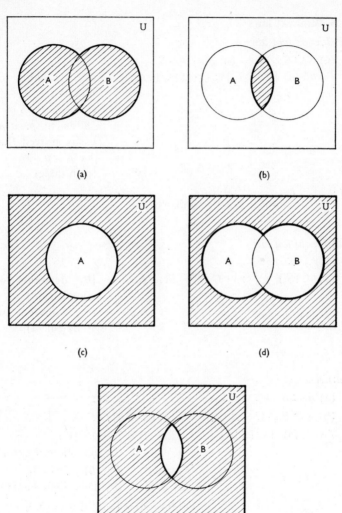

FIG. 2.1.
(a) $A \cup B$.　(b) $A \cap B$.　(c) A'.　(d) $(A \cup B)'$.　(e) $(A \cap B)'$.

2.3. Basic set laws

(i) *Idempotent law*

  (a) $S \cup S = S$　　(b) $S \cap S = S$

Proof. (a) $S \cup S = \{x: (x \in S) \vee (x \in S)\}$　　(by definition of union)

$$= \{x: x \in S\}$$

(putting $x \in S =$ statement p, it is easily proved that $p \vee p = p$ by a truth table)

$$= S.$$

(b) The proof is exactly similar to (a).

(ii) *Involution law*

  $(S')' = S$

Proof. $(S')' = \{x: x \in (S')'\} = \{x: x \notin S'\}$　　(by definition of complement)

$$= \{x: x \in S\}$$

(by definition of complement)

$$= S.$$

(iii) *Associative law*

  (a) $A \cup B \cup C = A \cup (B \cup C) = (A \cup B) \cup C$

  (b) $A \cap B \cap C = A \cap (B \cap C) = (A \cap B) \cap C$

Proof. (a) $A \cup (B \cup C) = \{x: (x \in A) \vee [x \in (B \cup C)]\}$

(by definition of union)

$$= \{x: (x \in A) \vee [(x \in B) \vee (x \in C)]\}$$

(by definition of union)

$$= \{x: [(x \in A) \vee (x \in B)] \vee (x \in C)\}$$

(associative law for disjunction; see exercises 1a)

$$= (A \cup B) \cup C.$$

(b) Proof exactly similar to (a).

We now see that $A \cup B \cup C$ and $A \cap B \cap C$ may be written without ambiguity.

(iv) *Commutative law*

   (a) $A \cup B = B \cup A$ (b) $A \cap B = B \cap A$

   Proof. (b) $A \cap B = \{x : (x \in A) \wedge (x \in B)\}$

$$\text{(by definition of intersection)}$$

$$= \{x : (x \in B) \wedge (x \in A)\}$$

$$\text{(commutative law for conjunction;}$$
$$\text{see exercises 1a)}$$

$$= B \cap A.$$

(a) Proof exactly similar to (b).

(v) *Distributive law*

   (a) $A \cup (B \cap C) = (A \cup B) \cap (A \cup C)$, distribution of union over intersection.

   (b) $A \cap (B \cup C) = (A \cap B) \cup (A \cap C)$, distribution of intersection over union.

   Proof. (b) $A \cap (B \cup C) = \{x : (x \in A) \wedge [x \in (B \cup C)]\}$

$$\text{(by definition of intersection)}$$

$$= \{x : (x \in A) \wedge [(x \in B) \vee (x \in C)]\}$$

$$\text{(by definition of union)}$$

$$= \{x : [(x \in A) \wedge (x \in B)] \vee [(x \in A) \wedge (x \in C)]\}$$

$$\text{(distributive law of conjunction over dis-}$$
$$\text{junction; see exercises 1a)}$$

$$= (A \cap B) \cup (A \cap C).$$

(a) Proof exactly similar to (b).

(vi) *De Morgan's laws* [after Augustus de Morgan (1806–71)]

   (a) $(A \cup B)' = A' \cap B'$ (b) $(A \cap B)' = A' \cup B'$.

   Proof. (a) $(A \cup B)' = \{x : [(x \in A) \vee (x \in B)]'\}$

$$\text{(definition of union)}$$

$$= \{x: (x \in A)' \land (x \in B)'\}$$

(De Morgan's law for conjunction; see exercises 1a)

$$= \{x: (x \notin A) \land (x \notin B)$$

(definition of complement)

$$= A' \cap B'.$$

(b) Proof exactly similar to (a).

A few of the set laws are illustrated in Venn diagrams in Fig. 2.2.

It should be noted that given either form of any one of the laws (iii)–(vi), we may obtain its counterpart simply by interchanging the operation symbols $\cup$ and $\cap$. Thus, in law (iii) given $A \cup (B \cup C)$ (or $A \cap (B \cap C)$) we obtain $A \cap (B \cap C)$ (or $A \cup (B \cup C)$) writing $\cap$ for $\cup$ (or $\cup$ for $\cap$); likewise for laws (iv), (v) and (vi). When one law or statement may be deduced from another law or statement by interchanging in this way, the first law (or second) is said to be the **dual** of the second law (or first). A familiar example of duality in plane geometry is: "Any two distinct points determine a unique line" and "Any two distinct lines determine a unique point"; here, the terms "point" and "line" are interchangeable. The dual of a statement or proposition should not be confused with its converse (see § 1.6).

In addition to the laws (i)–(vi) there are some important theorems:

(vii) (a) $S \cup S' = U$ (b) $S \cap S' = \emptyset$

(viii) (a) $U' = \emptyset$ (b) $\emptyset' = U$

(ix) (a) $S \cup U = U$ (b) $S \cap U = S$

(x) (a) $S \cup \emptyset = S$ (b) $S \cap \emptyset = \emptyset$

The proofs of theorems (vii)–(x) are left to the reader.

The algebra of sets which is based on the above laws and theorems is called a **Boolean algebra** after George Boole (1815–64). As the reader has probably noticed, the algebra of sets is of the same form as the two-valued (i.e. 0 and 1) algebra of propositions developed in Chapter 1; this algebra of propositions is also Boolean and in § 2.5 we will meet yet another Boolean algebra.

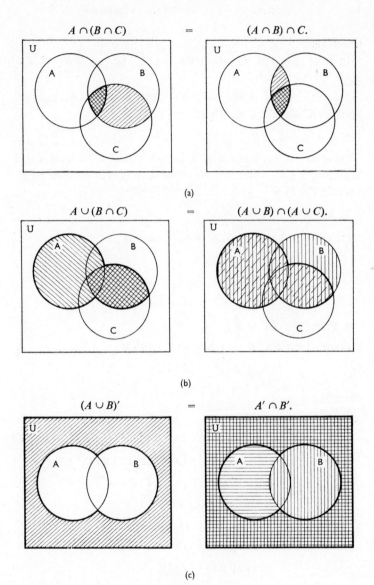

FIG. 2.2.

EXAMPLES

1. If $A \subseteq B$ and $B \subseteq C$, then $A \subseteq C$, i.e. $(A \subseteq B \wedge B \subseteq C) \Rightarrow (A \subseteq C)$.

Proof. If x is any element of A, i.e. $x \in A$, then $x \in B$ since $A \subseteq B$. Thus $x \in C$ since $B \subseteq C$. Therefore $A \subseteq C$.

2. $A \subseteq B \Leftrightarrow A \cap B' = \varnothing$.

Proof. If x is any element of A, i.e. $x \in A$, then $x \in B$ since $A \subseteq B$. Therefore $x \notin B'$. Therefore no element in A is a member of B'. Therefore $A \cap B' = \varnothing$.

3. $A \subseteq B \Leftrightarrow B' \subseteq A'$.

Proof. $A \subseteq B \Leftrightarrow A \cap B' = \varnothing$ (see example 2)

$$\Leftrightarrow B' \cap A = \varnothing$$
$$\Leftrightarrow B' \cap (A')' = \varnothing$$
$$\Leftrightarrow B' \subseteq A' \text{ (see example 2)}.$$

4. Prove $A \cap (A' \cup B') = A \cap B'$.

Proof. $A \cap (A' \cup B') = (A \cap A') \cup (A \cap B')$

$$= \varnothing \cup (A \cap B')$$
$$= A \cap B'.$$

5. Prove

$$(A \cap B \cap C) \cup (A \cap B' \cap C) \cup (A \cap B \cap C') = A \cap (B \cup C)$$

Proof. L.H.S. $= (A \cap C) \cap (B \cup B') \cup (A \cap B \cap C')$

$$= [(A \cap C) \cap \mathrm{U}] \cup (A \cap B \cap C')$$
$$= (A \cap C) \cup (A \cap B \cap C')$$
$$= A \cap [(B \cap C') \cup C]$$
$$= A \cap [(B \cup C) \cap (C' \cup C)]$$
$$= A \cap [(B \cup C) \cap \mathrm{U}]$$
$$= A \cap (B \cup C).$$

6. Prove $[(A \cap B') \cup B']' = B$

Proof.
$$
\begin{aligned}
[(A \cap B') \cup B']' &= (A \cap B')' \cap B'' \\
&= (A \cap B')' \cap B \\
&= (A' \cup B'') \cap B \\
&= (A' \cup B) \cap B \qquad\qquad\text{(a)} \\
&= (A' \cap B) \cup (B \cap B) \\
&= (A' \cap B) \cup B \\
&= (A' \cup B) \cap (B \cup B) \\
&= (A' \cup B) \cap B. \qquad\qquad\text{(b)}
\end{aligned}
$$

In going from (a) to (b) we have arrived back at (a); the proof between (a) and (b) is therefore "circular". To overcome this difficulty let us try an alternative proof from (a):

Let x be any element which is a member of $[(A' \cup B) \cap B]$,
i.e. $x \in [(A' \cup B) \cap B]$
$\Rightarrow [x \in (A' \cup B)]$ and $[x \in B]$
$\Rightarrow [x \in A'$ and/or $x \in B]$ and $[x \in B]$
$\Rightarrow$ *if* $x \in A'$ (in the first bracket), we have $[x \in A']$ and $[x \in B]$, i.e. $x \in B$;
and, *if* $x \in B$ (in the first bracket), we have
$[x \in B]$ and $[x \in B]$, i.e. $x \in B$;
and, *if* $x \in A'$ and $x \in B$ (in the first bracket), we have
$[x \in A'$ and $x \in B]$ and $[x \in B]$,
i.e. $x \in A'$ and $x \in B$, i.e. $x \in B$.
In any case, $x \in B$. Thus $[(A' \cup B) \cap B] \subseteq B$.

All that remains to complete the proof is to prove that
$$B \subseteq [(A' \cup B) \cap B]:$$

Let y be any element which is a member of B,
i.e. $y \in B$,
then $y \in (A' \cup B)$,
$\Rightarrow y \in [(A' \cup B) \cap B]$
$\Rightarrow B \subseteq [A' \cup B) \cap B]$.

Thus, since $[(A' \cup B) \cap B] \subseteq B$ and $B \subseteq [(A' \cup B) \cap B]$, we have (from the definition of equal sets in §2.1) $[(A' \cup B) \cap B] = B$, and therefore $[(A \cap B') \cup B']' = (A' \cup B) \cap B = B$.

A much more elegant proof may be obtained by making the substitution $B' = B' \cap U$:

$$[(A \cap B') \cup B']' = [(A \cap B') \cup (B' \cap U)]'$$

$$= [B' \cap (A \cup U)]'$$

$$= [B' \cap U]'$$

$$= [B']'$$

$$= B.$$

Sometimes, the complement of a set S is written as $(U-S)$, i.e. $S' = (U-S) = (U \cap S')$ (see theorem (ix)). If in the case of two sets A and B we take A as the universal set, then we define $(A-B) = (A \cap B')$ as a natural extension to the above definition of S'. Thus, for example, De Morgan's laws would become: $A-(B \cup C) = (A-B) \cap (A-C)$ and $A-(B \cap C) = (A-B) \cup (A-C)$; both forms being deducible from the definition of $(A-B)$.

Two more examples, and their proofs, follow:

7. Prove $B \cap (A-B) = \emptyset$.

Proof. L.H.S. $= B \cap (A \cap B')$

$$= (B \cap B') \cap A$$

$$= \emptyset \cap A$$

$$= \emptyset$$

8. Prove $B \cup (A-B) = A \cup B$.

Proof. L.H.S. $= B \cup (A \cap B')$

$$= (B \cup A) \cap (B \cup B')$$

$$= (B \cup A) \cap U$$

$$= B \cup A$$

$$= A \cup B.$$

EXERCISES 2a

Prove the following equalities, illustrating each with a Venn diagram.

1. $A \cap (A' \cup B) = (A \cap B)$.

2. $A \cup (A' \cap B) = A \cup B$.

3. $(A \cap B') \cup (A \cap B) = A$.

4. $(A \cup B) \cap (A \cup B') = A$.

5. $A \cup (A \cap B) = A$. (*Hint*: use $A \cap U = A$.) Also write an alternative proof.

6. $A \cap (A \cup B) = A$. (*Hint*: use $A \cup \emptyset = A$.) Also write an alternative proof.

7. $[(A \cap B) \cup B]' = B'$.

8. $[A \cup (B \cap C)]' = (A' \cap B') \cup (A' \cap C')$.

9. $(A \cap B) \cup (A' \cap B) \cup (A \cap B') = A \cup B$.

10. $(A \cup B) \cap (A' \cup B) \cap (A \cup B') = A \cap B$.

11. $A \cap [B \cup (B' \cap C)] = (A \cap B) \cup (A \cap C)$.

12. $(A \cap B) \cup (B' \cap C') \cup (A \cap C') = (A \cap B) \cup (B' \cap C')$.

13. $(A \cap B') \cup (B \cap C') \cup (C \cap A') = (A' \cap B) \cup (B' \cap C) \cup (C' \cap A)$.

14. $A - B' = A \cap B$.

15. $A - (B \cup C) = (A - B) \cap (A - C)$.

16. $A - (B \cap C) = (A - B) \cup (A - C)$.

17. Prove that if $A \subset B$ and $B \subseteq C$, then $A \subset C$.

18. Prove that if $B \subseteq A$, then $(B - C) \subseteq (A - C)$.

19. Deduce the duals of the distributive law using the involution law and De Morgan's laws.

20. With reference to the diagram shown in Fig. 2.3, write down in terms of A, B, C, D, the disjoint subsets numbered 1 to 16, respectively. (*Hint*: subset 1 is $A \cap B \cap C \cap D$, subset 2 is $A' \cap B \cap C \cap D$, subset 3 is $A \cap B' \cap C \cap D$.)

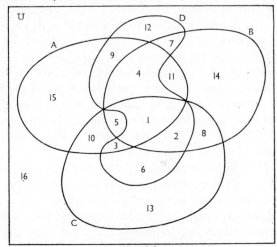

Fig. 2.3.

2.4. Comparing a Boolean algebra with ordinary elementary algebra

Ordinary elementary algebra may be viewed as a generalization of the arithmetic of real numbers (see number systems in Chapter 6). The tables opposite show the operational rules for both types of algebra (the algebra of sets is given in the Boolean case). A set is said to be closed under the operation of *, if for any two elements a and b belonging to this set we have $a * b = c$, where c also belongs to this set. Comparing the entries in both tables strongly suggests that the operation of union is similar to the operation of addition, and the operation of intersection is similar to the operation of multiplication. Further, the identities $\varnothing$ and U may be compared with 0 and 1. Writing $+$ for $\cup$ and $\times$ for $\cap$ in both forms of the distributive rule in a Boolean algebra, we have,

$$A + (B \times C) = (A + B) \times (A + C) \text{ and}$$
$$A \times (B + C) = (A \times B) + (A \times C).$$

The latter form is the same as in ordinary algebra, whereas the former certainly has no counterpart in ordinary algebra. The idempotent rule becomes $A + A = A$, or generalizing, $A + A + A + \ldots + A$ (to n terms) $= A$; likewise, the generalization of $A \times A = A$ is $A \times A \times A \times \ldots \times A$ (to n terms) $= A$. In ordinary algebra we have, $A + A + A + \ldots + A$ (to n terms) $= nA$, and $A \times A \times A \times \ldots \times A$ (to n terms) $= A^n$. Ordinary algebra, then, has the same symmetry or duality as a Boolean algebra for rules (i)–(iv), whereas this symmetry breaks down in the distributive rule for ordinary algebra; it must also be admitted that the idempotent rule in Boolean algebra is completely symmetrical (in that both its forms are duals) and therefore much simpler than its counterpart in ordinary algebra.

From §2.3, we have theorems (ix)(a) and (x)(b): $A \cup U = U$ and $A \cap \varnothing = \varnothing$ respectively; in order to compare these results with ordinary algebra we write $A + 1 = 1$ and $A \times 0 = 0$. The latter is familiar enough, but $A + 1 = 1$ certainly looks odd; here again there is duality, e.g. writing $+$ for $\times$ and at the same time

THE OPERATIONAL RULES FOR ORDINARY ALGEBRA

Rule	Addition ($+$)	Multiplication ($\times$)
(i) Closure	$(a+b) \in R^*$	$(a \times b) \in R^*$
(ii) Associative	$a+(b+c)=(a+b)+c$	$a \times (b \times c) = (a \times b) \times c$
(iii) Commutative	$a+b=b+a$	$a \times b = b \times a$
(iv) Identity	0 such that $a+0=0+a=a$	1 such that $a \times 1 = 1 \times a = a$
(v) Inverse	$(-a)$ such that $a+(-a)=(-a)+a=0$	a^{-1} such that $a \times a^{-1} = a^{-1} \times a = 1$
(vi) Distributive	$a \times (b+c) = (a \times b) + (a \times c)$	

THE OPERATIONAL RULES FOR A BOOLEAN ALGEBRA

Rule	Union ($\cup$)	Intersection ($\cap$)
(i) Closure	$A \cup B$ is a set	$A \cap B$ is a set
(ii) Associative	$A \cup (B \cup C) = (A \cup B) \cup C$	$A \cap (B \cap C) = (A \cap B) \cap C$
(iii) Commutative	$A \cup B = B \cup A$	$A \cap B = B \cap A$
(iv) Identity	$\varnothing$ such that $A \cup \varnothing = \varnothing \cup A = A$	U such that $A \cap U = U \cap A = A$
(v) Distributive	$A \cup (B \cap C) = (A \cup B) \cap (A \cup C)$ and $A \cap (B \cup C) = (A \cap B) \cup (A \cap C)$	
(vi) Idempotent	$A \cup A = A$	$A \cap A = A$
(vii) Complement	$A \cup A' = U$	$A \cap A' = \varnothing$
(viii) Involution	$(A')' = A$	

writing 1 for 0, we obtain $A+1 = 1$ from $A \times 0 = 0$—there being no such dual in ordinary algebra.

Clearly one wants an algebraic system to be as simple as possible—that way the manipulation involved in solving a problem is reduced to a minimum. The redeeming feature of a Boolean algebra is its symmetry—where one form of a rule may be deduced from the other by a simple interchange of operating symbols and identities (where the latter are present). Ordinary algebra lacks such symmetry, but is less limited than a Boolean algebra in that the operations of subtraction ($-$) and division ($\div$) are defined in addition to the operations of addition ($+$) and multiplication ($\times$). That we have subtraction in ordinary algebra is guaranteed by the definition of an inverse ($-a$) (called a negative); multiplication also being guaranteed by the definition of an inverse (a^{-1}) (called a reciprocal—see number systems in Chapter 6). We might try extending a Boolean algebra in order that it may include the operations of subtraction and division: we can define subtraction from the definition of complement, $A - B = A \cap B'$ (so long as $B \subseteq A$), and putting $A = B$, we have $A - A = A \cap A' = \varnothing$, i.e. the inverse ($-A$) of any set A with respect to union is defined by the following:

$$A \cup (-A) = (-A) \cup A = A - A = \varnothing,$$

or for comparison with ordinary algebra we may write,

$$A + (-A) = (-A + A) = A - A = 0.$$

Now, division; we know in general that given any set A it is impossible to find a set B such that $A \cap B = U$, or keeping up the analogy with ordinary algebra, $A \times B = 1$ (naturally if $A = 1$ then we should write $B = 1$ and then $1 \times 1 = 1$ so that 1 is the reciprocal of itself). Thus there are no reciprocals and therefore no division operation is possible in a Boolean algebra. Further, there is no cancellation law (since division cannot be defined). One last point: $A \cap B = \varnothing$, i.e. $A \times B = 0$ does *not* imply that $A = 0$ or $B = 0$, in fact $A \cap B = \varnothing \Rightarrow A$ and B disjoint.

2.5. General form of a Boolean algebra. Isomorphism. Switching circuits

We have discussed a Boolean algebra up till now only in terms of the algebra of sets, although it was briefly mentioned that the algebra of propositions as developed in Chapter 1 is also

Boolean. In this section we will show precisely how the algebra of sets, algebra of propositions, and an algebra of circuit designs (to be developed later) are of the *same form*. It is first of all convenient to write a Boolean algebra in a general form; let the set B of elements $x, y, z, \ldots$, be operated on by operators $'$ (e.g. b'), $+$ and $\times$ as follows:

B (i)	*Closure*	(a) $(x+y) \in B$	(b) $(x \times y) \in B$.
B (ii)	*Idempotent law*	(a) $x+x = x$	(b) $x \times x = x$.
B (iii)	*Involution law*	$(x')' = x$.	
B (iv)	*Associative law*	(a) $x+(y+z) = (x+y)+z$	
		(b) $x \times (y \times z) = (x \times y) \times z$.	
B (v)	*Commutative law*	(a) $x+y = y+x$	(b) $x \times y = y \times x$.
B (vi)	*Distributive law*	(a) $x+(y \times z) = (x+y) \times (x+z)$	
		(b) $x \times (y+z) = (x \times y)+(x \times z)$.	
B (vii)	*De Morgan's laws*	(a) $(x+y)' = x' \times y'$	
		(b) $(x \times y)' = x'+y'$.	
B (viii)	*Complement*	(a) $x+x' = 1$	(b) $x \times x' = 0$.
B (ix)	*Identities*	(a) $x+1 = 1$	(b) $x \times 1 = x$.
B (x)		(a) $x+0 = x$	(b) $x \times 0 = 0$.

0 and 1 are the **identity elements.**

We may then define a Boolean algebra as a set B where we operate on the elements according to the above ten axioms or rules. These ten axioms are by no means minimal, i.e. they do not form the least number of axioms that define a Boolean algebra, however, they do form a very valuable basis for such an algebra.†

Let us now list the most important properties of an algebra of propositions P (see Chapter 1, especially exercises 1a), where $p, q, r, \ldots \in P$:

P (i)	*Closure*	(a) $p \vee q$ is a proposition
		(b) $p \wedge q$ is a proposition.
P (ii)	*Idempotent law*	(a) $p \vee p = p$ (b) $p \wedge p = p$.
P (iii)	*Involution law*	$\bar{\bar{p}} = p$.

† It is possible to define a Boolean algebra in terms of six axioms concerning: (i) closure, (ii) commutativity, (iii) distributivity, (iv) complement, (v) identity, (vi) inclusion, i.e. $x \subset y$. The remaining properties may then be deduced from these axioms.

P (iv)   *Associative law*   (a) $p \vee (q \vee r) = (p \vee q) \vee r$

(b) $p \wedge (q \wedge r) = (p \wedge q) \wedge r$.

P (v)   *Commutative law*   (a) $p \vee q = q \vee p$

(b) $p \wedge q = q \wedge p$.

P (vi)   *Distributive law*   (a) $p \vee (q \wedge r) = (p \vee q) \wedge (p \vee r)$

(b) $p \wedge (q \vee r) = (p \wedge q) \vee (p \wedge r)$.

P (vii)   *De Morgan's laws*   (a) $\overline{(p \vee q)} = \bar{p} \wedge \bar{q}$

(b) $\overline{(p \wedge q)} = \bar{p} \vee \bar{q}$.

P (viii)   (a) $p \vee \bar{p} = t$ (b) $p \wedge \bar{p} = c$.

P (ix)   (a) $p \vee t = t$ (b) $p \wedge t = p$.

P (x)   (a) $p \vee c = p$ (b) $p \wedge c = c$.

Here t denotes tautology (and therefore truth value of t can only be 1), and c denotes contradiction (and therefore truth value of c can only be 0). The equals sign $=$ in P(i)–P(x) really denotes equivalence and may be replaced by $\Leftrightarrow$. Any of the properties in P(i)–P(x) not mentioned explicitly in Chapter 1 can easily be proved by truth tables, e.g. for P(x) (a):

p	c	$p \vee c$
1	0	1
0	0	0

i.e. $p \vee c \Leftrightarrow p$.

Comparing P(i)–P(x) with B(i)–B(x), we see that we have exactly similar lists of operational rules or axioms; p corresponds to x (say), q corresponds to y (say), $\bar{p}$ corresponds to x', t corresponds to 1 and c corresponds to 0, $p \vee q$ corresponds to $x + y$, and $p \wedge q$ corresponds to $x \times y$, etc. Formally stated: there exists an **isomorphism**† between the algebra of propositions P and the Boolean algebra B; and by isomorphism we mean that for each element in P (or B) there corresponds one and only one element in B (or P) and to each operation in P (or B) there corresponds one and only one operation in B (or P).

† From Greek: isos—equal, and morphe—form.

Likewise there exists an isomorphism between the algebra of sets and the Boolean algebra B; this is hardly surprising since we constructed our general form of a Boolean algebra B by setting up an isomorphism between it and the algebra of sets! All algebras which are isomorphic with B are called Boolean and are clearly isomorphic to each other.

Let us now consider some simple electrical circuits which comprise essentially simple on–off switches p, q, r, . . . , connected in series and parallel.

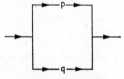

FIG. 2.4. Parallel.

The arrows in Fig. 2.4 indicate the direction of flow of the electric current; however, this direction is unimportant, for all we are interested in is whether current flows in the circuit or not for all possibilities of the switches p and q being on or off. (In all

FIG. 2.5. Series.

future circuit diagrams the arrows will be omitted.) The table below shows the analysis ("on" for the circuit means current flowing, "off" for the circuit means no current flowing).

p	q	parallel circuit
on	on	on
on	off	on
off	on	on
off	off	off

p	q	series circuit
on	on	on
on	off	off
off	on	off
off	off	off

Consider one switch p

p	$\bar{p}$	
on	off	Where $\bar{p}$ denotes switch p in the "off" position.
off	on	

Writing 1 for "on" and 0 for "off", it is clear that the parallel circuit corresponds to disjunction and so when two switches p and q are connected in parallel we write $p \vee q$ to represent the parallel circuit. It is also clear that the series circuit corresponds to conjunction ($p \wedge q$), and that $\bar{p}$ (p switched off) corresponds to the negation of a proposition p. We can therefore build up more complex circuits based on the simple parallel and series circuits shown in Figs. 2.4 and 2.5, that is we can build up more complex circuits and find corresponding expressions for them in the algebra of propositions. To make this quite clear consider, for example, the circuit shown in Fig. 2.6.

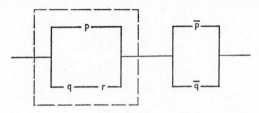

Fig. 2.6.

In Fig. 2.6, switches q and r are in series and such that part of the circuit is equivalent to $(q \wedge r)$; p is connected in parallel with $(q \wedge r)$ and so the whole of the circuit enclosed by the rectangle (drawn with broken lines) is equivalent to $p \vee (q \wedge r)$; $\bar{p}$ is connected in parallel with $\bar{q}$ and so this part of the circuit is equivalent to $(\bar{p} \vee \bar{q})$; since the circuit represented by $p \vee (q \wedge r)$ is in series with the circuit represented by $(\bar{p} \vee \bar{q})$, the whole circuit is equivalent to $[p \vee (q \wedge r)] \wedge (\bar{p} \vee \bar{q})$. Such complex circuits are easily realized in practice by using mechanically coupled switches, or relays, or better still by transistors (or some other electronically bistable devices).

Having set up a one–one correspondence between circuits and expressions in the algebra of propositions we see that the algebra of circuits is isomorphic to the algebra of propositions and is therefore a Boolean algebra. We can therefore operate on such circuits using Boolean methods; one such operation is the replacement of a complex circuit (Fig. 2.7) by an equivalent simpler circuit.

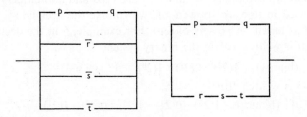

FIG. 2.7.

The circuit is equivalent to

$$[(p \wedge q) \vee (\bar{r} \vee \bar{s} \vee \bar{t})] \wedge [(p \wedge q) \vee (r \wedge s \wedge t)]$$
$$= (p \wedge q) \vee [(\bar{r} \vee \bar{s} \vee \bar{t}) \wedge (r \wedge s \wedge t)] \quad \text{(distributive rule)}$$

Now, $\qquad \bar{r} \vee \bar{s} \vee \bar{t} = \overline{(r \wedge s)} \vee \bar{t} \quad$ (De Morgan's law)

$$= \overline{(r \wedge s \wedge t)} \quad \text{(De Morgan's law)},$$

and so the circuit expression becomes:

$$(p \wedge q) \vee [\overline{(r \wedge s \wedge t)} \wedge (r \wedge s \wedge t)]$$
$$= (p \wedge q) \vee c \qquad \text{[P(viii) (b)]}$$
$$= p \wedge q \qquad\qquad \text{[P(x) (a)]},$$

and the simpler circuit is shown in Fig. 2.8.

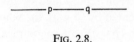

FIG. 2.8.

The circuit in Fig. 2.7 has eight switches (the two p's and the two q's are coupled) whilst the equivalent circuit in Fig. 2.8 has only two switches – a considerable saving!

Boolean algebra is a valuable tool in the design of computer circuits and other automatic control systems. In order to see basically how our switching circuits can be used in the design of computers we will now construct a circuit which will function as an adding machine (a **binary adder** in this case); in this connection we take a brief glimpse at the binary number system. In the binary system only two digits "0" and "1" are used and all numbers are expressed in terms of powers of two (unlike the decimal system which is based on powers of ten). For example, 5 in the decimal system is written 101 in the binary system

$$101 \text{ (binary)} = 1(2^2) + 0(2^1) + 1(2^0) = 5 \text{ (decimal)}$$

and 43 is written 101011

$$101011 \text{ (binary)} = 1(2^5) + 0(2^4) + 1(2^3) + 0(2^2) + 1(2^1) + 1(2^0)$$
$$= 43 \text{ (decimal)}.$$

More briefly, we could use the suffix notation when expressing a number in two different bases, e.g. $101011_2 \equiv 43_{10}$.

Binary addition, $(23 + 56)$ say, is as follows:

	10111	=	23
	111000	=	56
"Carries"	10000	=	0
	1001111	=	79

In general for the addition of two binary numbers a_i, b_i where the carries are c_i, we have the sum s_i; $i = 0, 1, 2, \ldots$:

$$
\begin{array}{rcccc}
& \ldots a_3 & a_2 & a_1 & a_0 \\
& \ldots b_3 & b_2 & b_1 & b_0 \\
\text{"Carries"} & \ldots c_3 & c_2 & c_1 & c_0 \\
\hline
& \ldots s_3 & s_2 & s_1 & s_0 \\
\end{array}
$$

where c_i denotes the carry from the ith column (reading from right to left). Considering any one column (the ith, say) in our "addition sum" and ignoring the carry from the right (c_{i-1}) for the moment, all possible values for a_i, b_i, s and c are given in the following table; s is the sum of a_i and b_i and c is the carry from this sum—of course, to obtain s_i we must add c_{i-1} to s and this will be done a little later. We also show later how to obtain c_i.

a_i	b_i	s	c
1	1	0	1
1	0	1	0
0	1	1	0
0	0	0	0

The last column shows us that we may write $c = a_i \wedge b_i$. To find a Boolean expression for s we note that s has the value 1 if and only if $a_i = 1$ and $b_i = 0$ or $a_i = 0$ and $b_i = 1$; this suggests that $s = a_i \wedge \bar{b}_i$ or $s = \bar{a}_i \wedge b_i$:

a_i	b_i	$\bar{a}_i$	$\bar{b}_i$	$a_i \wedge \bar{b}_i$	$\bar{a}_i \wedge b_i$	$(a_i \wedge \bar{b}_i) \vee (\bar{a}_i \wedge b_i)$
1	1	0	0	0	0	0
1	0	0	1	1	0	1
0	1	1	0	0	1	1
0	0	1	1	0	0	0

Clearly $s \neq a_i \wedge \bar{b}_i$, $s \neq \bar{a}_i \wedge b_i$ and so we try $s = (a_1 \wedge \bar{b}i) \vee (\bar{a}_i \wedge b_i)$ which is true. A circuit that represents s is shown in Figs. 2.9a and 2.9b (the circuit in Fig. 2.9b is identical to the circuit in Fig. 2.9a except that the switches have been drawn "facing" each other).

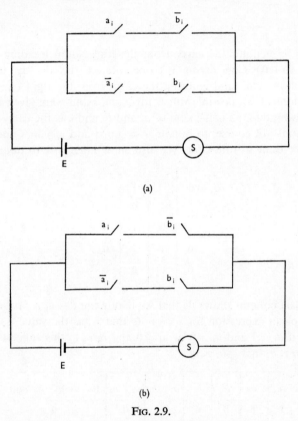

(a)

(b)

Fig. 2.9.

A battery E supplies the electric current, and the sum s is indicated by a small lamp—when the lamp is on, $s = 1$, and when the lamp is off, $s = 0$. A much neater equivalent circuit that represents s is obtained by using single-pole double-throw switches

(Fig. 2.10). The single pole or lever AT shown in Fig. 2.10 may be in either position AP or position AQ, but not both. The neater circuit for s is shown in Fig. 2.11. Since $c = a_i \wedge b_i$, the complete

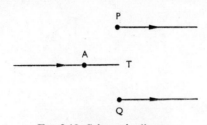

FIG. 2.10. Schematic diagram of a single-pole double-throw switch.

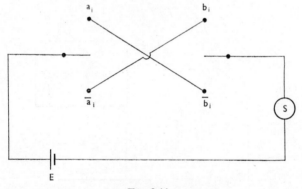

FIG. 2.11.

circuit for s and c is shown in Fig. 2.12; this circuit functions as a **half adder** as it does not add in the carry from the column on the right [$(i-1)$th]. The right-hand switch has an extra b_i contact for the carry c series circuit.

To find the complete sum s_i by adding the carry c_{i-1} from the $(i-1)$th column to s, we have only to use a second half adder; two half adders connected together to give the complete sum s_i form a unit called a **full adder** which is shown in Fig. 2.13. To understand how the carry c_i is obtained we note that the carry c from

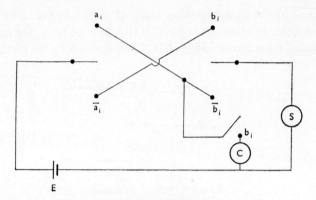

FIG. 2.12. Half adder.

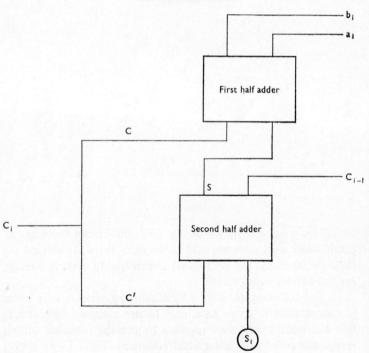

FIG. 2.13. Full adder.

the addition of a_i and b_i, and the carry c' (say) from the addition of s and c_{i-1}, cannot both be 1; and so the wire carrying the "signal c" may be joined with the wire carrying the "signal c'" to form a common wire carrying the "signal c_i"—this can easily be checked using a truth table.

The numbers a_i and b_i are "fed" into our full adder by manual switching, whereas, of course, it is much more convenient to have relays to operate the switches in the second half adder; so by merely setting two switches manually, we automatically obtain s_i and c_i. To complete the circuit for the binary adder we have only to connect together full adders as shown in Fig. 2.14.

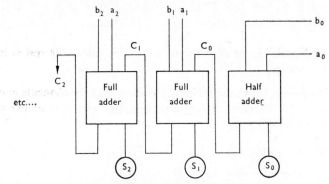

FIG. 2.14. Complete binary adder.

In the extreme right column (the *zero*th) of our addition sum there is no carry to be added and therefore a half adder suffices to add a_0 to b_0. We may build our binary adder as large as we please (within practical limits) depending on how many digits we wish to include in each of the numbers a and b; the last carry will clearly be the last digit (in the extreme left position) of the sum. Using additional relays which function as a **store** or **memory** it is easy to extend our binary adder† so that it may add together a large number of numbers (not just two), subtract one number from another, multiply a large number of numbers together, and divide one number into another.

† Such an extension was organized by the author at Kingston.

EXAMPLES

1. Show that the set of four elements, combined as shown in the tables below, is a Boolean algebra:

+	a	b	c	d
a	a	b	a	b
b	b	b	b	b
c	a	b	c	d
d	b	b	d	d

×	a	b	c	d
a	a	a	c	c
b	a	b	c	d
c	c	c	c	c
d	c	d	c	d

We will verify some of the most important rules—the rest is left to the reader.

(i) *Closure.* From the tables it is evident that the elements combine to give elements which are themselves members of the set of elements a, b, c, d.

(ii) *Associative law*

(a) $a + (b + d) = a + b = b$

$(a + b) + d = b + d = b.$

(b) $a \times (b \times d) = a \times d = c$

$(a \times b) \times d = a \times d = c.$

(iii) *Commutative law*

(a) $a + c = a$ (b) $a \times c = c$

$c + a = a.$ $c \times a = c.$

(iv) *Distributive law*

(a) $b + (c \times d) = b + c = b$

$(b + c) \times (b + d) = b \times b = b.$

(b) $b \times (c + d) = b \times d = d$

$\quad (b \times c) + (b \times d) = c + d = d.$

(v) *Identities*

(a) $c = 0$, e.g. $c + a = a$ and $c \times a = c$.

(b) $b = 1$, e.g. $b + a = b$ and $b \times a = a$.

2. Prove that in a Boolean algebra $x + (y - x) = x + y$. (The equivalent expression in sets is: $A + (B - A) = A + B$, where we defined $A - B = A \cap B'$; see §2.2, examples 7 and 8.)

Proof. Now $x - y = x \times y'$ by definition, since this is equivalent to $A - B = A \cap B'$, where A and B are sets.

Therefore $x + (y - x) = x + (y \times x')$

$$= (x + y) \times (x + x')$$
$$= (x + y) \times 1$$
$$= x + y.$$

3. The complement x' of any element $x \in B$ is unique.

Proof. Assume the contrary and let x_1' and x_2' both be complements of x.

Then $x + x_1' = 1; \qquad x + x_2' = 1$

$\quad x \times x_1' = 0; \qquad x \times x_2' = 0.$

Therefore $x_1' = x_1' \times 1 = x_1' \times (x + x_2') = (x_1' \times x) + (x_1' \times x_2')$

$$= 0 + (x_1' \times x_2')$$
$$= x_1' \times x_2'.$$

Similarly, $x_2' = x_1' \times x_2'$.

Therefore $x_1' = x_2'$, therefore the complement of $\dot{x}$ is unique.

4. Prove the tautology $p \wedge [q \vee (\bar{q} \wedge r)] \Leftrightarrow p \wedge (q \vee r)$, (i) by truth table method; (ii) using the general Boolean method; illustrate with a Venn diagram.

(i)

p	q	r	$\bar{q}$	$\bar{q} \wedge r$	$q \vee (\bar{q} \wedge r)$	$p \wedge [q \vee (\bar{q} \wedge r)]$	$q \vee r$	$p \wedge (q \vee r)$
1	1	1	0	0	1	1	1	1
1	1	0	0	0	1	1	1	1
1	0	0	1	0	0	0	0	0
0	0	0	1	0	0	0	0	0
0	1	1	0	0	1	0	1	0
0	0	1	1	1	1	0	1	0
0	1	0	0	0	1	0	1	0
1	0	1	1	1	1	1	1	1

$$\therefore p \wedge [q \vee (\bar{q} \wedge r)] \Leftrightarrow p \wedge (q \vee r).$$

(ii) The equivalent Boolean expression, where x, y, z, say, are the elements corresponding to p, q and r respectively, is:

$$x \times [y + (y' \times z)] = x \times (y + z).$$

Now, $\text{L.H.S.} = x \times [(y + y') \times (y + z)]$

$$= x \times [1 \times (y + z)]$$

$$= x \times (y + z) = \text{R.H.S.}$$

If the sets A, B, C correspond to p, q, r respectively (and therefore x, y, z respectively), the corresponding set expression is

$$A \cap [B \cup (B' \cap C)] = A \cap (B \cup C).$$

Venn diagrams in Fig. 2.15 illustrate the expression.

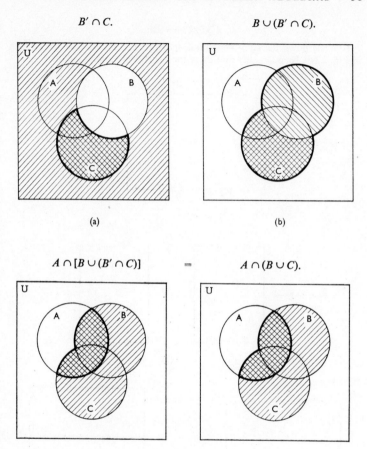

$B' \cap C.$

$B \cup (B' \cap C).$

(a)

(b)

$A \cap [B \cup (B' \cap C)]$ $=$ $A \cap (B \cup C).$

(c)

FIG. 2.15.

EXERCISES 2b

1. Write down the equivalent Boolean expression for each of the circuits in Fig. 2.16. Then simplify and draw the equivalent simpler circuit.

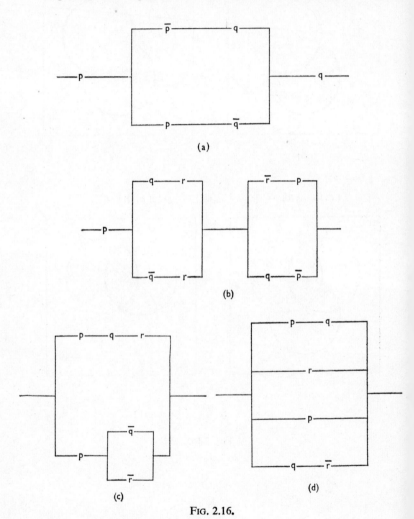

Fig. 2.16.

2. Show that the two circuits in Fig. 2.17 are equivalent.

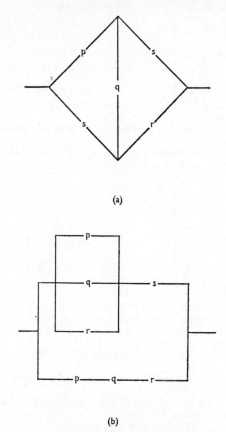

(a)

(b)

FIG. 2.17. Bridge circuit.

3. Prove that the sum s in the binary half adder can also be expressed as $s = (a_i \vee b_i) \wedge (\bar{a}_i \vee \bar{b}_i)$. Accordingly draw another circuit which will function as a half adder.

4. Instead of designing a full adder by combining two half adders, do it directly.

5. Design a circuit which will enable a house owner to switch on (or off) a stair light at one end of the stairs (either end) and switch off (or on) the light at the other end of the stairs, i.e. design a "two-way circuit".

6. Show that the set $\{0, 1\}$ of two elements under the operations of $+$ and $\times$ as defined in the tables below, is a Boolean algebra.

+	0	1
0	0	1
1	1	1

×	0	1
0	0	0
1	0	1

Which are the identities?

7. Show that there exists a Boolean algebra with only one element. (*Hint:* consider $0 = 1$.)

8. Is the set of four elements under the operations of $+$ and $\times$ as defined in the tables below a Boolean algebra?

+	a	b	c
a	a	a	c
b	a	b	c
c	c	c	c

×	a	b	c
a	a	b	a
b	b	b	b
c	a	b	c

Which element is 0? 1? a'? b'? c'? (See §2.6.)

9. Show that in any Boolean algebra $0' = 1$ and $1' = 0$.

10. Let B be a subset of the positive integers and for any a and b in B let $a + b$ be the least common multiple of a and b and let $a \times b$ be the highest common factor of a and b. Then,

(a) show that B is a Boolean algebra when B is the set of integers $1, 2, 5, 7, 10, 14, 35$, and 70,

(b) show that $1, 2, 4, 6, 9, 18, 24$ is not a Boolean algebra under these operations.

11. Prove that the identities 0 and 1 in a Boolean algebra are unique.

12. Using the definition that for any two elements a and b of a Boolean algebra B, $a \leqslant b$ if and only if $a + b = b$, prove that:

(a) $b \leqslant b$

(b) if $a \leqslant b$ and $b \leqslant a$, then $a = b$.

(c) if $a \leqslant b$ and $b \leqslant c$, then $a \leqslant c$ $(c \in \mathrm{B})$

(d) $0 \leqslant a \leqslant 1$

(e) $a \leqslant b$ if and only if $b' \leqslant a'$.

13. Write down the equivalent expressions for (a)–(e) in No. 12, in the algebra of sets and the algebra of propositions.

14. Construct a Boolean algebra of four elements and show that it is isomorphic with the algebra of propositions which has four elements in it.

15. Compare and contrast Boolean algebra with ordinary algebra; how many instances of duality are there in ordinary algebra?

2.6. Number of elements in sets and the unions and intersections of sets. Transfinite cardinals

In considering the number of elements in a given set, the union of two sets, or the intersection of two sets, the reader may think that our attention will be confined to finite sets only. That the union of two infinite sets is an infinite set strongly suggests that there is nothing more to be said about infinite sets. Consider for example the two sets J^+ (set of all positive integers—sometimes called the **natural numbers**) and $E = \{x : (x = 2n) \wedge n \in J^+\}$ (set of all even natural numbers); then, $J^+ \cup E = J^+$, and $J^+ \cap E = E$ (since $E \subset J^+$). In any case, J^+, E, and therefore $J^+ \cup E$ ($= J^+$) and $J^+ \cap E$ ($= E$) are all infinite sets. Now, $E \subset J^+$, so surely the number of elements in E [written $n(E)$] is less than the number of elements in J^+, i.e. $n(E) < n(J^+)$? On the other hand if we set up a one–one correspondence between E and J^+, it seems that $n(E) = n(J^+)$:

$$
\begin{array}{cccccc}
1 & 2 & 3 & 4 & 5 & \ldots \\
\updownarrow & \updownarrow & \updownarrow & \updownarrow & \updownarrow & \\
2 & 4 & 6 & 8 & 10 & \ldots
\end{array}
$$

It has therefore become necessary to make clear what we mean by the number of elements in a set.

Definition. Two sets A and B have the same number of elements (written $A \sim B$) if there exists a one–one correspondence between the elements in A and the elements in B. So, referring to the sets J^+ and E above, we have by definition $J^+ \sim E$, i.e. $n(J^+) = n(E)$; the two sets are said to have the same **cardinal number,** which in this case may be denoted by either $n(J^+)$ or $n(E)$. We will look more closely at infinite sets later in this section.

When the elements of a set S can be placed in one–one correspondence with the subset of natural numbers $(1, 2, 3, \ldots, n)$, S is called a **finite set** and has the cardinal number n. For example, the cardinal number of the set $\{a, v, w, \alpha, \beta\}$ is 5 and the cardinal number of $\{x, x, y, z, b\}$ is 4 as this set should be written $\{x, y, z, b\}$ (since the elements in a set must be distinct).

We can now find the number of elements in the union of two finite sets A and B. Referring to the Venn diagram in Fig. 2.18, it is clear that $n(A \cup B) = n(A) + n(B) - n(A \cap B)$; this also follows from the definitions of union, intersection and cardinal number.

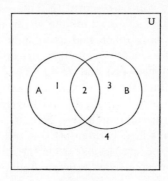

FIG. 2.18.

The expression for the number of elements in the union of two sets may also be obtained as follows:

Referring to Fig. 2.18, we have the four exhaustive disjoint sets $A \cap B'$ (1), $A \cap B$ (2), $A' \cap B$ (3), and $(A \cup B)' = A' \cap B'$ (4),

therefore, $\quad n(A \cup B) = n(A \cap B') + n(A \cap B) + n(A' \cap B)$

$$n(A) = n(A \cap B') + n(A \cap B)$$

$$n(B) = n(A \cap B) + n(A' \cap B).$$

Thus, $\quad n(A \cup B) = n(A) + n(B) - n(A \cap B).$

An expression for $n(A \cup B \cup C)$ may be derived from the above expression for $n(A \cup B)$ as follows:

$$n[A \cup (B \cup C)] = n(A) + n(B \cup C) - n[A \cap (B \cup C)],$$

i.e. $\quad n[A \cup B \cup C] = n(A) + n(B) + n(C) - n(B \cap C)$
$$- n[(A \cap B) \cup (A \cap C)] \qquad \text{(i)}$$

Now, $\quad n[(A \cap B) \cup (A \cap C)] = n(A \cap B) + n(A \cap C)$
$$- n(A \cap B \cap A \cap C),$$

i.e. $\quad n[(A \cap B) \cup (A \cap C)] = n(A \cap B) + n(A \cap C)$
$$- n(A \cap B \cap C), \qquad \text{(ii)}$$

therefore from (i) and (ii),

$$n(A \cup B \cup C) = n(A) + n(B) + n(C) - n(A \cap B)$$
$$- n(B \cap C) - n(A \cap C) + n(A \cap B \cap C).$$

Forming the eight disjoint sets as shown in Fig. 2.19, one has the basis for an alternative derivation for $n(A \cup B \cup C)$; the derivation is left to the reader.

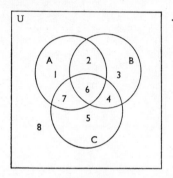

FIG. 2.19.

Clearly, if A, B and C are disjoint sets,

$$n(A \cup B) = n(A) + n(B),$$

and $\qquad n(A \cup B \cup C) = n(A) + n(B) + n(C).$

There are some interesting applications of the foregoing theory of which one is as follows:

In a certain college students pass an examination only if they are successful in three papers A, B and C. For a particular year the results were: 3% failed all three papers, 9% failed in papers B and C, 10% failed in papers A and C, 12% failed in papers A and B, 32% failed in paper A, 30% failed in paper B, and 46% failed in paper C. What percentage of students qualified? What percentage of students failed in exactly one paper?

Solving the problem amounts to sorting out overlapping sets of students; for example, when we are told that 10% failed in papers A and C this figure will include the 3% who failed in all three papers. The Venn diagram in Fig. 2.20 shows the percentage of students in each disjoint subset; we start off by writing 3 in the space representing $A \cap B \cap C$, and since $n(B \cap C) = 9$ we write 6 in the space representing $A' \cap B \cap C$, and so on.

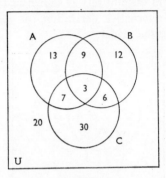

FIG. 2.20.

$$n(A \cup B \cup C)' = 100 - (3 + 6 + 7 + 9 + 12 + 30 + 13) = 20.$$

Therefore, the percentage of students that qualified is 20. The percentage of students that failed in one paper $= 13 + 12 + 30 = 55$. These results could have been obtained by using formulae for the numbers of elements in unions and intersections of sets, but using a Venn diagram is much simpler. It is important to note that for any subset, the number of elements in it must be positive; bearing this in mind one can easily detect an inconsistency in any given information; e.g. suppose that the information given is exactly the same as in the above example except that the percentage of students who failed in paper A is 15% (instead of 32%), then $n(A \cap B' \cap C') = -4$ (instead of $+13$).

We noted earlier that in the case of the two **infinite sets** E and J^+ that although $E \subset J^+$ we have $n(E) = n(J^+)$; whereas for *any two finite sets*, A and B, where $B \subset A$, we have, by definition of a finite set, $n(B) < n(A)$. It is not always the case that for any two infinite sets S and T (say) where $T \subset S$ that $n(T) = n(S)$, that is, it is possible for $n(T) < n(S)$. Consider the set of all real numbers

R^* for example; unlike the set E we cannot set up a one–one correspondence between the elements of R^* and the elements of J^+, and we prove this as follows: We assume that we can set up a one–one correspondence for all the real numbers between 0 and 1 and the elements in the set J^+. We then produce a single counter-example which contradicts the assumption thereby proving the original statement (namely that such a correspondence is impossible). Now any real number between 0 and 1 can be written as an infinite decimal (merely by writing an infinite number of 0's if necessary, e.g. $\frac{1}{2}$ may be written $0 \cdot 5000 \ldots$). The correspondence is shown below:

$$1 \leftrightarrow 0 \cdot x_{11} x_{12} x_{13} \ldots$$
$$2 \leftrightarrow 0 \cdot x_{21} x_{22} x_{23} \ldots$$
$$3 \leftrightarrow 0 \cdot x_{31} x_{32} x_{33} \ldots$$
$$\cdot \quad \cdot \qquad \cdot$$
$$\cdot \quad \cdot \qquad \cdot$$
$$\cdot \quad \cdot \qquad \cdot$$

where x_{ij} is the jth figure after the decimal place of the real number corresponding to the natural number i. We now construct the real number (between 0 and 1): $0 \cdot r_1 r_2 r_3 \ldots$, where $r_1 \neq x_{11}$, $r_2 \neq x_{22}$, $r_3 \neq x_{33}$, and so on. Clearly this number does not belong to the list enumerated above, since it differs in at least the first figure after the decimal place of the first real number, it differs in at least the second figure after the decimal place of the second real number, and so on. Thus it is impossible to set up a one–one correspondence between the numbers in R^* (between 0 and 1) and the natural numbers J^+. Obviously, if we cannot set up a one–one correspondence between the real numbers (between 0 and 1) and the set J^+ then we cannot set up a one–one correspondence between the set R^* (*all* real numbers) and the set J^+. Sets, like E for example, are called **denumerable,** that is, they can be placed in one–one correspondence with the set J^+. We have just proved, then, that the set R^* of real numbers is non-denumerable. Since R^* is non-denumerable it seems natural to have the following definition:

Definition. The cardinal number of R^* is greater than the cardinal number of J^+, i.e. $n(R^*) > n(J^+)$.

Two questions probably enter the mind of the reader now:

(i) Are there any more non-denumerable sets and if so do they have a cardinal number which is less than, equal to, or greater than $n(R^*)$? (ii) Are there any more denumerable sets? The answer to question (i) is that there are infinitely many non-denumerable sets whose cardinal numbers are greater than or equal to $n(R^*)$ (*not less than* $n(R^*)$); some of the most important sets whose cardinal numbers are *equal to* $n(R^*)$ are the set P of points on a line segment (finite or infinite in length), the set T of transcendental numbers, the set R_i of irrational numbers (which includes the set T). We will consider briefly the non-denumerably infinite sets whose cardinal numbers are *greater than* $n(R^*)$ in a moment. The answer to question (ii) is that there are infinitely many denumerable sets and examples are: any finite set A, the set R of all rational numbers (surprisingly enough), the set F of all algebraic numbers (again surprisingly). That the set P of points on any straight line has a cardinal number equal to $n(R^*)$ is clear enough (and it may also be shown that the cardinal numbers of each of the following sets are equal to $n(R^*)$: the set of points in the plane, the set of points in three-dimensional space and, in general, in n-dimensional space). We will prove that $n(T) = n(R_i) = n(R^*)$, and $n(R) = n(F) = n(J^+)$ in the list of examples at the end of this section.

Earlier in this section we said that two sets had the same cardinal number, by definition, if there existed a one–one correspondence between the elements in one set and the elements in the other set. This definition is perfectly general; it applies to both finite and infinite sets. The study of the cardinal numbers of infinite sets was first made by the German mathematician, G. Cantor (1845–1918); the basis for this study was the above general definition. Cantor called the cardinal numbers of infinite sets **transfinite cardinals** and built up a whole new arithmetic called **transfinite arithmetic.** Although this transfinite arithmetic is very interesting in itself, it has few, if any, practical applications and so we will only take a glimpse at it in this book. Cantor showed that the smallest transfinite cardinal was $n(J^+)$ and he wrote this as $\aleph_0$ (where $\aleph$ is the Hebrew letter aleph). The next transfinite cardinal he wrote as $\aleph_1$, the next as $\aleph_2$, and so on. That we have an infinite number of larger and larger transfinite cardinals is guaranteed by a theorem due to Cantor: If we have an infinite set V and construct the infinite set S_v of all subsets of V, then $n(S_v) > n(V)$. We will not attempt a proof of this theorem as it is rather beyond the scope of this book; however, we can easily illustrate it in the case of the set J^+ and the set S_{J^+} of all the subsets of J^+:

Firstly, we show that it is possible to place the elements of S_{J^+} in one–one correspondence with the elements of R^* (between 0 and 1), and then show how to set up a one–one correspondence between the elements of R^* (between 0 and 1) and *all* the elements of R^*. To each subset of J^+, i.e. to each element of S_{J^+}, we can assign a unique number of the form $0 \cdot n_1 n_2 n_3 \ldots$; the number is written in the binary scale and therefore any one n will have the value 0 or 1. The elements of each subset J^+ are written down in order of magnitude, e.g. $\{1, 4, 8, 9\}$ and for any elements of J^+ not appearing in a particular subset we agree to write a dash $(-)$, e.g. $\{1, -, -, 4, -, -, -, 8, 9, -, -, -, \ldots\}$. Treating the dashes as elements also, we then represent the ith element in any one subset by n_i where $n_i = 0$ or 1 according to whether the ith element is a dash or not, e.g. the unique number assigned to $\{2, 4, 5, 6, 10\}$ is $0 \cdot 01011100010000 \ldots$, the number assigned to $\{1, 2, 3, 4, 8, 10\}$ is $0 \cdot 11110001010000 \ldots$, the number assigned to the set of all even numbers is $0 \cdot 0101010101 \ldots$, the number assigned to J^+ is $0 \cdot 11111111, \ldots$ and so on. Since the smallest subset of J^+ is the null set (which we represent by $0 \cdot 0000 \ldots$), and the largest subset of J^+ is J^+ itself (which we represent by $0 \cdot 1111 \ldots$), that is we assign to the smallest and largest subsets the unique numbers 0 and 1 (in the decimal scale) respectively, and also since we cover all real numbers between 0 and 1, then we clearly have a one–one correspondence between the real numbers R^* (between 0 and 1) and the subsets of J^+, i.e. S_{J^+}. Using the function $y^2 = 1 - x^2$, where $0 \leqslant x \leqslant 1$ and $-1 \leqslant y \leqslant 1$ we have a mapping between the real numbers between 0 and 1 and the real numbers between -1 and 1; using the function $y = \tan(\pi x/2)$, where

$$-1 \leqslant x \leqslant 1 \text{ and } -\infty \leqslant y \leqslant +\infty$$

we have a mapping between the real numbers between -1 and 1 and all real numbers R^* (see Chapter 4 on functions). Thus

$$n\{x \in R^* : 0 \leqslant x \leqslant 1\} = n\{x \in R^* : -1 \leqslant x \leqslant 1\} = n(R^*),$$

and so from above, $n(S_{J^+}) = n(R^*)$; now $n(R^*) > n(J^+)$ by definition, and therefore $n(S_{J^+}) > n(J^+)$, thus proving an interesting instance of the general theorem due to Cantor. Although our theorem guarantees larger and larger transfinite cardinals, it does not imply that for any infinite set V whose cardinal number is $\aleph_i$ that $n(S_v) = \aleph_{i+1}$; that is, it does not imply that the cardinal number of the set S_v of all the subsets of V is the next larger cardinal number to $\aleph_i$. However, Cantor was able to show that there was a next larger transfinite cardinal $\aleph_{i+1}$ to any transfinite cardinal $\aleph_i$ (this is by no means trivial, since for instance there is no "next larger number" in the set R of rational numbers).

Finally, since $n(R^*) > \aleph_0 [= n(J^+)]$, and since there is an infinite number of transfinite cardinals then $n(R^*)$ must occur somewhere amongst the transfinite cardinals, but where? Cantor assigned $\aleph_1$ to the transfinite cardinal of R^* but was unable to prove that $n(R^*) = \aleph_1$; to this day it has not been proved that $n(R^*) = \aleph_1$. That $\aleph_1 = n(R^*)$ is called the **continuum hypothesis** since the geometrical representation of R^* is a straight line called the **continuum**.

EXAMPLES

1. The set R of all rational numbers is denumerable, i.e. $n(R) = n(J^+) = \aleph_0$. To see this it is necessary only to arrange the positive rational numbers "diagonally" as shown below, and generalize to include the negative rational numbers:

The rational number p/q is situated in the pth row and qth column; the arrows in the above array show the correspondence, i.e.

$$
\begin{array}{ccccccc}
1 & 2 & 3 & 4 & 5 & 6 & 7 \quad \ldots \\
\updownarrow & \updownarrow & \updownarrow & \updownarrow & \updownarrow & \updownarrow & \updownarrow \\
{}^1/_1 & {}^1/_2 & {}^2/_1 & {}^3/_1 & {}^2/_2 & {}^1/_3 & {}^1/_4 \quad \ldots
\end{array}
$$

The enumeration of the positive rational numbers includes "overlap", e.g. ${}^1/_1, {}^2/_2, \ldots$, and ${}^1/_2, {}^2/_4, \ldots$; eliminating such overlapping clearly does not affect the correspondence. The general correspondence which includes the negative rationals is easily set up as shown below:

$$
\begin{array}{ccccccccc}
1 & 2 & 3 & 4 & 5 & 6 & 7 & 8 & 9 \quad \ldots \\
\updownarrow & \updownarrow & \updownarrow & \updownarrow & \updownarrow & \updownarrow & \updownarrow & \updownarrow & \updownarrow \\
+{}^1/_1 & -{}^1/_1 & +{}^1/_2 & -{}^1/_2 & +{}^2/_1 & -{}^2/_1 & +{}^3/_1 & -{}^3/_1 & +{}^2/_2 \, . \, .
\end{array}
$$

2. The set F of all algebraic numbers is denumerable, i.e. $n(F) = n(J^+) = \aleph_0$.

Now, an algebraic number is any number x, real or complex, that satisfies some algebraic equation of the form

$$a_0 x^n + a_1 x^{n-1} + a_2 x^{n-2} + \ldots + a_{n-1}x + a_n = 0$$

$(n \geqslant 1, a_0 \neq 0)$ where a_i $(i = 0, 1, \ldots, n)$ are integers. For example, $\sqrt[3]{3}$ is an algebraic number since it satisfies the equation $x^3 - 3 = 0$. An algebraic equation of degree n (the degree is defined to be the highest power to which x is raised) has n roots; the proof of this **fundamental theorem of algebra** lies outside the scope of this book, although the theorem can easily be illustrated: for example, the three roots of $x^3 - 3 = 0$ are $3^{\frac{1}{3}}$, $\dfrac{-3^{\frac{1}{3}}}{2}(1 - 3^{\frac{1}{2}}i)$, $\dfrac{-3^{\frac{1}{3}}}{2}(1 + 3^{\frac{1}{2}}i)$, where $i = \sqrt{-1}$, $3^{\frac{1}{3}} =$ the ordinary positive cube root of 3, and $3^{\frac{1}{2}} =$ the ordinary positive square root of 3; these cube roots are calculated using **De Moivre's theorem.**

We now define the *height* h of an algebraic equation:

$$h = |a_0| + |a_1| + \ldots + |a_{n-1}| + |a_n| + n,$$

i.e. the height is the sum of the absolute values of the coefficients to which the degree is added. Since $n \geqslant 1$, and $a_0 \neq 0$, i.e. $|a_0| \geqslant 1$ (since coefficients are integers), then $h \geqslant 2$. For any *finite h*, there are only a *finite* number of equations; each of these equations can have at most n roots. Therefore, there can be only a finite number of algebraic numbers whose equations are of height h. So we can arrange all the algebraic numbers in sequence by starting with those from equations of height 2, then taking those from equations of height 3, and so on. Thus, $n(F) = \aleph_0$.

3. The set T of transcendental numbers is non-denumerable and $n(T) = \aleph_1$.

That the set F of all algebraic numbers is denumerable and the set R^* of all real numbers is non-denumerable implies the existence of a subset of R^* that must be non-denumerable. Further, this subset of numbers can never be obtained as roots of algebraic equations since the latter numbers can be denumerated. This subset of R^* is the set T of transcendental numbers.† So $n(T) = \aleph_1$ by definition, and furthermore $F \cup T = R^*$ by definition.

4. The set R_i of irrational numbers is non-denumerable and $n(R_i) = \aleph_1$.

Since $R \cup R_i = R^*$ by definition, where R is the set of all rational numbers, which can be denumerated, it follows that R_i cannot be denumerated and therefore $n(R_i) = \aleph_1$.

5. The number of points on any line segment is equal to the number of points in the entire continuum, i.e. $\aleph_1$.

To prove this it is necessary to show the one–one correspondence between the line segment and an infinitely long straight line; Fig. 2.21 is self-evident, the line segment being bent at right angles at two points of trisection.

---

† Term used by the Swiss–German mathematician Euler (1707–83) who said of these numbers "they transcend the power of algebraic methods".

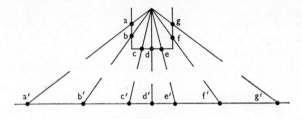

Fig. 2.21.

Exercises 2c

1. In a school the numbers of students taking various combinations of subjects are as follows:

60 students take Mathematics
55 students take English
44 students take French
21 students take Mathematics and English
23 students take English and French
25 students take Mathematics and French
9 students take all three subjects

Assuming that every student in the school takes one of the courses, find the total number of students in the school.

2. The results of a series of tests carried out on a number of applicants for a job are as follows:

50% applicants having good education
61% applicants having good personality
60% applicants having good health
24% applicants having good education and personality
35% applicants having good personality and health
27% applicants having good education and health
5% applicants *not* having any of the three assets.

Assuming that in order to get the job applicants must have a good education, good personality and good health, find the number of applicants that were successful out of a total number of 230 applying.

3. In a small international gathering there are 6 English males, 7 foreign boys, 7 foreign females, 14 English people, 9 boys, 9 men, and 5 English children. What is the number of people in the gathering?

4. Comment on question 3 if the number of foreign boys is 8 and the number of English boys is 1, the other numbers remaining unchanged.

5. For the three sets A, B, C, the following information is given:

$$n(A \cap B \cap C) = 5, \qquad n(A \cap B \cap C') = 7, \qquad n(B \cap C \cap A') = 3,$$
$$n(A \cap C \cap B') = 10, \qquad n(A \cap B' \cap C') = 6, \qquad n(B \cap A' \cap C') = 4,$$
$$n(A' \cap B' \cap C') = 20, \qquad n(U) = 70.$$

Find $n(C \cap A' \cap B')$.

6. Write down the formula for $n(A \cup B \cup C \cup D)$ in each of the following cases:

(a) A, B, C, D all mutually disjoint.

(b) $(A \cup B) \cap (C \cup D) = \varnothing$, $(A \cap B) \neq \varnothing$, $(C \cap D) \neq \varnothing$.

(c) $(A \cup B \cup C) \cap D = \varnothing$, $(A \cap B \cap C) \neq \varnothing$, $D \neq \varnothing$.

(d) $(A \cup B \cup C) \cap D = \varnothing$, $(A \cap B \cap C) = \varnothing$, $(A \cap B) \neq \varnothing$,
   $(B \cap C) \neq \varnothing$, $D \neq \varnothing$.

It will be helpful to draw a Venn diagram for each case.

7. Prove that there exists a one–one correspondence between the set of all natural numbers and the set of all lattice points (i.e. the points whose co-ordinates are integers) in the plane.

8. Show that the set of complex numbers with integral real and imaginary parts can be denumerated.

9. Prove that "if there are more people in this world than hairs on any human head, then there are at least two people in the world who have an equal number of hairs". (A well-known conundrum.)

10. Prove that if two infinite sets A and B are denumerable then so is their union $A \cup B$.

(*Hint:* consider separately the cases when (i) A and B are disjoint and (ii) A and B are not disjoint. Write $A = \{a_1, a_2, a_3, \ldots\}$ and $B = \{b_1, b_2, b_3, \ldots\}$.)

11. Prove that the union of a denumerable number of denumerable sets is also denumerable.

(*Hint:* consider separately the cases when (i) the sets are mutually disjoint and (ii) when some of the sets are not disjoint. Write the sets as $S_1, S_2, S_3, \ldots,$ $S_i, \ldots$, where $S_i = \{a_{i1}, a_{i2}, a_{i3}, \ldots\}$.)

12. Show that the intersection of two denumerable sets is denumerable. Discuss separately the cases when (i) the intersection is finite and (ii) the intersection is infinite.

13. $\aleph_i + \aleph_j$ is by definition the cardinal number of the union of any two sets A and B where $n(A) = \aleph_i$ and $n(B) = \aleph_j$. Prove, using the general theorem of Cantor developed in the last section, that (a) $\aleph_i + \aleph_i = \aleph_i$, (b) $\aleph_i + \aleph_j = \aleph_j$ if and only if $j > i$.

14. Prove the following:

(a) $F \cup T = R^*$ (e) $F \cup R_i = R^*$

(b) $F \cap T = \varnothing$ (f) $F \cap R_i = F \cap T'$

(c) $F \cup R = F$ (g) $J \cup R \cup (F \cap T') = F$

(d) $F \cap R = R$ (h) $R^* - (R \cup R_i) = J$.

CHAPTER 3

Mathematical Induction. Binomial Theorem. Elementary Probability Theory

MATHEMATICAL INDUCTION

3.1. Well-ordering principle

Given any two real numbers a and b we can tell which is greater; there are two possibilities, either a is greater than b, i.e. $a > b$, or a is less than b, i.e. $a < b$. Furthermore, if $a > b$ and $b > c$, then $a > c$. So we can conceive that *all* real numbers can be arranged in their order of magnitude (does this contradict the fact that R^* is non-denumerable?—see §2.6). This property of "greater than" or "less than" is called **well-ordering.** The set of all complex numbers is *not* well-ordered since for any two distinct complex numbers it is possible for them to have the same modulus but have different arguments (see Chapter 6 on number systems).

In any finite subset of the real numbers there exists a **least member** and a **greatest member**; for example, the least and greatest members in the finite subset $\{7, \sqrt{2}, 3, \pi\}$ are $\sqrt{2}$ and 7 respectively. On the other hand, for any infinite subset of the real numbers there need not be either a least member or a greatest member; for example, the least member of the infinite subset $\{x \in R^* : x \geqslant 0\}$ is 0 and there is no greatest member; in the case of the infinite subset $\{x \in R^* : x > 0\}$ there is no least member or greatest member.

In any subset (infinite or not) of non-negative integers there is a

least member. This property of the integers is called the **well-ordering principle.** We shall return to the concept of order when dealing with relations in Chapter 4.

3.2. Principle of mathematical induction

Consider the following tentative method of obtaining a formula. Suppose that we wish to find a formula for the sum of the first n of the cubes of the positive integers, $1^3, 2^3, 3^3, \ldots$. We examine the cases for $n = 1, 2, 3, 4$ (say) and try to pick out a pattern:

$$S_1 = 1^3 = 1$$

$$S_2 = 1^3 + 2^3 = 9$$

$$S_3 = 1^3 + 2^3 + 3^3 = 36$$

$S_4 = 1^3 + 2^3 + 3^3 + 4^3 = 100$, where S_r = the sum of the first r cubes.

Assuming that we know $\sum\limits_{r=1}^{n} r = \dfrac{n(n+1)}{2}$ (sum of A.P.), then we could reasonably get to $\sum\limits_{r=1}^{n} r^3$ by seeing that for $n = 1, 2, 3, 4$ (say), $(\Sigma r)^2 = \Sigma r^3$ and from *this* approach *guess* that

$$\sum\limits_{r=1}^{n} r^3 = \frac{n^2(n+1)^2}{4}.$$

$$S_1 = 1 = \tfrac{1}{4}(1 \times 2)^2$$

$$S_2 = \tfrac{1}{4}(2 \times 3)^2$$

$$S_3 = \tfrac{1}{4}(3 \times 4)^2$$

$$S_4 = \tfrac{1}{4}(4 \times 5)^2$$

$$\cdot \qquad \cdot \qquad \cdot$$

$$S_n = \tfrac{1}{4}[n(n+1)]^2$$

We can test the formula $S_n = \tfrac{1}{4}[n(n+1)]^2$ for as many values of n as we desire, but this amounts to *validating* the formula and not *proving* it. To prove the formula we must show that it is true for *all* n. We do this using the following theorem:

Given a set of theorems $\{T_n : n = 1, 2, 3, \ldots\}$ then, (i) if T_1 is true and (ii) for every positive integer k the truth of T_k implies the truth of T_{k+1}, then T_n is true for every positive integer n. This is the principle of mathematical induction.

Proof. We use the *reductio ad absurdum* method. Suppose that some of the T_n are false, then by the well-ordering principle there will be a least value m of n for which T_n is false. Thus T_{m-1} must be true, where $m - 1 \geqslant 1$, i.e. $m \geqslant 2$ from (i). From (ii), T_m must be true; but we earlier deduced that T_n for $n = m$ is false. We have therefore reached a contradiction, and so the theorem must be true.

Part (ii) of the theorem is often referred to as the **inductive hypothesis.**

We may now return to proving our formula $S_n = \frac{1}{4}[n(n+1)]^2$.

(i) If $n = 1$, then $S_1 = 1^3 = 1$, and $\frac{1}{4}[1(1+1)]^2 = 1$. So the formula is true for the case $n = 1$.

(ii) Assuming the formula to be true for any positive integer k, then $S_k = \frac{1}{4}[k(k+1)]^2$ and therefore

$$S_{k+1} = S_k + (k+1)^3 = \frac{1}{4}\{k^2(k+1)^2 + 4(k+1)^3\}$$
$$= \frac{(k+1)^2}{4}(k^2 + 4k + 4),$$

i.e. $S_{k+1} = \frac{1}{4}[(k+1)(k+2)]^2$, the formula that we would obtain by writing $(k+1)$ for k in S_k. Thus the truth of S_k implies the truth of S_{k+1}.

We have now proved that $S_n = \frac{1}{4}[n(n+1)]^2$.

EXERCISES 3a

Prove the following using the principle of mathematical induction.

1. $1 + 2 + 3 + \ldots + n = \dfrac{n}{2}(n+1)$.

2. $2 + 4 + 6 + \ldots + 2n = n(n+1)$.

3. $1^2 + 2^2 + 3^2 + \ldots + n^2 = \dfrac{n}{6}(n+1)(2n+1)$.

4. $a + (a+d) + (a+2d) + \ldots + [a + (n-1)d] = \dfrac{n}{2}[2a + (n-1)d]$.

5. $a + ar + ar^2 + ar^3 + \ldots + ar^{n-1} = \dfrac{a(1-r^n)}{1-r}$.

6. Each of the following represents a positive integer for every non-negative n (n can be 0, in which case statement (i) in the induction principle should be interpreted as "T_0 is true").

(a) $\dfrac{7^n - 2^n}{5}$ (b) $\dfrac{8^n - 3^n}{5}$ (c) $\dfrac{2^{2n+1} + 3^{2n+1}}{5}$ (d) $\dfrac{3^{2n+1} + 4^{2n+1}}{7}$

(e) $\dfrac{n^5 - n}{5}$.

BINOMIAL THEOREM

3.3. Permutations and combinations

In this section we will concern ourselves with "counting problems" of the type that are met in dealing with the binomial theorem and in probability theory. This type of problem may be formulated in the following way: we want to count the number of subsets each containing r elements that can be formed from the n elements of a given set; clearly, $r \leqslant n$. Any one subset is uniquely determined by the r elements contained in it *irrespective of the order in which the elements may have been written*. (This follows immediately from the concept of set.) The subsets formed in this way are called **combinations** and the number of combinations of r elements from n is written ^nC_r.

Suppose now that we want to know the number of subsets each containing r elements that can be formed from the n elements of a given set *where the order of the elements in each subset is important*. We should first of all find ^nC_r and then work out *how many "arrangements" could be made of each combination*. For example, the combinations of two elements from the set $\{a, b, c, d\}$ are: $\{a, b\}$, $\{a, c\}$, $\{a, d\}$, $\{b, c\}$, $\{b, d\}$, and $\{c, d\}$; thus $^4C_2 = 6$ and each combination has two arrangements: $\{a, b\}, \{b, a\}; \{a, c\}, \{c, a\}; \{a, d\}$, $\{d, a\}$; etc. Thus the total number of arrangements in this case = $6 \times 2 = 12$. We call these arrangements **permutations** and the number of permutations of r elements formed from n is written ^nP_r; so from the above example, $^4P_2 = 12$. It follows from the definitions of combinations and permutations that $^nP_r \geqslant {}^nC_r$ and it is left to the reader in the exercises below to investigate when $^nP_r = {}^nC_r$.

In such problems the following general principle is most useful: **If there are p ways of doing a thing and q ways of doing another**

thing and *r* ways of doing still another thing, etc., then the number
of ways of doing all the things in sequence is *pqr* . . . .

Proof. Consider *any one* of the *p* ways of doing the first thing,
then we have *q* ways of doing the second thing. If on the other
hand we consider any other one of the *p* ways of doing the first
thing, then we still have *q* ways of doing the second thing. So, in
short, for each of the *p* ways of doing the first thing we have *q* ways
of doing the second thing and therefore the total number of ways
of doing both things in sequence in *pq*. The **tree diagram** in Fig. 3.1
illustrates this; each *point* of the tree represents the number of
ways of doing a thing, and each *branch* represents a particular way
of doing it.

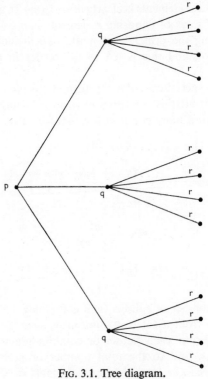

FIG. 3.1. Tree diagram.

Similarly, for each of the pq ways of doing the first two things there are r ways of doing the third, and therefore the number of ways of doing the three things in sequence is pqr. Thus the number of ways of doing n things in sequence is $pqr \ldots$ (to n terms).

We now derive formulae for ^nP_r and ^nC_r:

$$^nP_r = n(n-1)(n-2) \ldots (n-r+1).$$

Proof. Consider a set of n elements. The number of ways of choosing any one element is n and the number of ways of choosing any other element out of the remaining $(n-1)$ elements is $(n-1)$. Thus, according to our general principle, the number of ways of choosing any two elements is $n(n-1)$. The number of ways of choosing any three elements is clearly $n(n-1)(n-2)$, and therefore the number of ways of choosing r elements is $n(n-1)(n-2) \ldots (n-r+1)$. Using the principle of mathematical induction completes the proof, and this is left to the reader in the exercises below.

Consider the special case of $n = r$, then $^nP_n = n(n-1)(n-2) \ldots 3.2.1$, and for short this is written $n!$ (read **n factorial**). We may now write down a more compact formula for ^nP_r:

$$^nP_r = n(n-1)(n-2) \ldots (n-r+1)$$

$$= \frac{n(n-1)(n-2) \ldots (n-r+1)(n-r)(n-r-1) \ldots 3.2.1}{(n-r)(n-r-1) \ldots 3.2.1},$$

i.e.

$$^nP_r = \frac{n!}{(n-r)!}$$

$$^nC_r = \frac{n(n-1)(n-2) \ldots (n-r+1)}{r!}.$$

Proof. The number of subsets each containing r elements that can be formed from a set containing n elements $(n \geqslant r)$ is ^nC_r by definition. From each subset or combination we can form $r!$ permutations, and so the total number of permutations of r elements that can be formed from n elements is $^nC_r \cdot r! = {}^nP_r$.

Thus, $\quad {}^nC_r = \dfrac{{}^nP_r}{r!} = \dfrac{n(n-1)(n-2)\ldots(n-r+1)}{r!}.$

Using the compact form for ${}^nP_r$, we have,

$$ {}^nC_r = \frac{n!}{(n-r)!\,r!}. $$

It follows from the formula for ${}^nC_r$, that ${}^nC_r = {}^nC_{n-r}$, and ${}^nC_{r-1} + {}^nC_r = {}^{n+1}C_r$ $(n \geqslant r \geqslant 1)$; we prove these relations in the examples below.

The number of combinations each containing n elements that can be formed from a set of n elements is clearly one. However, if we write $n = r$ in the formula for ${}^nC_r$, we have,

$$ {}^nC_r = \frac{n!}{0!\,n!} = \frac{1}{0!}. $$

From the definition of factorial, it is immediately evident that 0! is meaningless, although it is natural to give 0! the value 1. We therefore have the following definition:

Definition. $0! = 1$.

Finally, we consider the problem of finding the number of permutations of n elements taken n at a time, where not all the elements are distinct. For example, if the elements are *abbc*, then we may list all the possible permutations or arrangements:

$$
\left.
\begin{array}{cccc}
a & b & b & c \\
a & b & c & b \\
b & a & b & c \\
b & a & c & b \\
c & b & b & a \\
b & c & b & a \\
c & b & a & b \\
\cdot & \cdot & \cdot & \cdot
\end{array}
\right\} 12 \text{ permutations}
$$

From any one permutation, *b a b c* say, we could make $2! = 2$ permutations if we treated the two like elements (the *b*'s) as distinct:

$$ b\ a\ b'\ c \quad \text{and} \quad b'\ a\ b\ c. $$

Similarly for all the other permutations. So, if x is the number of permutations with two elements alike, then $x \cdot 2! = 4!$,

i.e. $$x = \frac{4!}{2!} = 12.$$

In general, then, if we have n elements of which p are alike, the number of possible permutations taken n at a time is $n!/p!$.

Suppose now that we have n elements of which p are alike of one kind and q are alike of another kind. We list all the possible permutations of n elements and consider any one of them; treating temporarily the p elements as distinct, we are able to form $p!$ permutations; treating temporarily the q elements as distinct, we are able to form $q!$ *permutations from each of the $p!$ permutations.* So, treating both the p elements and q elements as distinct, we can form $p! \, q!$ permutations from our arbitrarily chosen permutation from the list. Thus if x is the number of permutations with p elements alike of one kind and q elements alike of another kind, then,

$$x \, p! \, q! = n!,$$

i.e. $$x = \frac{n!}{p! \, q!}.$$

In general, if we have n elements of which p are alike of one kind, q are alike of another kind, r are alike of still another kind, etc., then the number of permutations of n elements taken at a time is given by:

$$x = \frac{n!}{p! \, q! \, r! \ldots},$$

where $(p + q + r + \ldots) \leqslant n$, and $p, q, r, \ldots$ each > 1.

EXAMPLES

1. $^{n}C_{n-r} = {}^{n}C_{r}$.

   Proof. Writing $(n - r)$ for r in the formula for $^{n}C_{r}$, we have,

   $$^{n}C_{n-r} = \frac{n!}{[n-(n-r)]! \, (n-r)!} = \frac{n!}{r! \, (n-r)!} = {}^{n}C_{r}.$$

2. $^nC_{r-1} + {}^nC_r = {}^{n+1}C_r$, $n \geqslant r \geqslant 1$.

Proof. L.H.S. $= \dfrac{n!}{[n-(r-1)]!\,(r-1)!} + \dfrac{n!}{(n-r)!\,r!}$

$$= \dfrac{n!\,r+n!\,(n-r+1)}{(n-r+1)!\,r!} = \dfrac{n!\,r+(n+1)!-n!\,r}{(n-r+1)!\,r!}$$

$$= \dfrac{(n+1)!}{(n-r+1)!\,r!} = {}^{n+1}C_r.$$

3. If there are three ways of going from A to B, and five ways of going from B to A, how many ways are there of going from A to B and back?

For each of the three ways of going from A to B there are five ways of coming back from B to A. Therefore, the total number of ways of going from A to B and back is fifteen.

4. In how many ways can n people be arranged in a row so that two particular people are next to one another?

Firstly, consider just four people a_1, a_2, a_3 and a_4. Suppose that a_1 and a_2 are to sit next to each other, then there will be $(4-1) = 3$ positions for them to sit in:

	1	2	3	4
	a_1	a_2	–	–
or	–	a_1	a_2	–
or	–	–	a_1	a_2

For *each* of these positions there are $(4-2)! = 2!$ ways of arranging the remaining two people. Therefore, the number of ways of arranging the four people $= 3 \times 2!$; this is keeping a_1 and a_2 next to each other in that order (from left to right say). If now a_1 and a_2 interchange, there will be a further $3 \times 2!$ ways of arranging the four people. Thus the *total* number of ways of arranging the four people is $2 \times (3 \times 2!) = 12$. Generally then, the number of ways of arranging n people so that two particular people are next to one another is $2 \times [(n-1) \times (n-2)!] = 2(n-1)!$. (Strictly speaking this proof should be completed using the principle of induction; however, it is generally agreed upon that in problems such as the above, proof by induction is omitted for the sake of brevity.)

5. In how many ways can the letters of the word "college" be arranged?

In how many of these arrangements are both end positions occupied by vowels?

Since there are seven letters including two l's, and two e's, then the number of arrangements of "college" is:

$$\frac{7!}{2!\,2!} = 1260.$$

The following are the possible end positions for occupation by vowels:

$$e - - - - - e$$
$$o - - - - - e$$
$$e - - - - - o$$

The remaining five letters in *each* case contain two l's, and permuting these gives $5!/2!$ arrangements. Thus the total number of arrangements is

$$3 \times \frac{5!}{2!} = 180.$$

6. Four people draw simultaneously a card each from an ordinary pack of 52 cards. In how many different cases can the draw result in four cards of the same suit?

The number of cards in any suit is 13, and the number of ways of selecting any 4 out of the 13 is

$$^{13}P_4 = \frac{13!}{9!} = 17,160.$$

Since there are 4 suits to choose from, the total number of ways of selecting $= 4 \times {}^{13}P_4 = 68,640.$

7. A board consists of 10 men and 4 women. Find the number of ways of choosing a committee of 3 members, so as to contain

at least 1 woman. How many such committees will (a) contain more women than men, and (b) contain a particular woman?

The *total* number of ways of choosing a committee is $^{14}C_3$. The number of ways of choosing a committee containing men only is $^{10}C_3$. Therefore, the number of committees that contain at least one woman is $^{14}C_3 - {}^{10}C_3 = 244$.

The number of committees containing 3 women $= {}^4C_3 = 4$. The number of committees containing 2 women, and therefore 1 man, $= {}^{10}C_1 \times {}^4C_2 = 60$. Therefore the total number of committees that contain more women than men $= 60 + 4 = 64$. The number of committees containing a particular woman is equal to the number of ways of choosing 2 other people from the remaining 13 people (in order to make 3 members in the committee) $= {}^{13}C_2 = 78$.

8. In how many ways can 3 balls be drawn from a bag containing 3 red, 4 white, and 5 black balls, when the 3 balls are (i) all black, (ii) one red, one white and one black?

(i) The number of ways of picking 3 black balls is $^5P_3 = 60$. It should be noted that we cannot distinguish any one way from another, since the balls themselves are indistinguishable; therefore *in practice*, 60 is the *maximum possible number of ways* of picking the 3 black balls (i.e. we might well pick 3 black balls in less than 60 ways and think we had exhausted all possibilities).

(ii) There are 3! = 6 *orders* of choosing one red, one white and one black ball. Consider any one of these orders, say white first, black second, and red third; there are 4 ways of choosing the white ball, 5 ways of choosing the black, and 3 ways of choosing the red ball. So, for any one order, there are $3 \times 4 \times 5$ ways of choosing 3 balls (one of each colour). Therefore, the total number of ways $= 6 \times (3 \times 4 \times 5) = 360$.

EXERCISES 3b

1. Prove that $^nP_r = n \cdot {}^{n-1}P_{r-1}$.

2. Prove that $^nC_r + {}^nC_{r-1} = \dfrac{n+1}{r}\,{}^nC_{r-1}$.

3. Investigate when $^nP_r = {}^nC_r$.

4. Prove that $^nP_r = n(n-1)(n-2)\ldots(n-r+1)$ using the principle of mathematical induction.

5. In how many ways can n people be seated at a round table? (Two arrangements are considered the same if they are in the same cyclic order.)

6. In how many ways can n people be seated at a round table (i) if two particular people must be next to one another, (ii) if two particular people must not be next to one another?

7. In how many ways can the letters of the word "addresses" be arranged? In how many of these arrangements are both end positions occupied by vowels?

8. Prove that the number of combinations of n different things, taken one or more at a time is $2^n - 1$.

9. Find the number of combinations of $(x+y)$ elements, x of which are alike and the remaining y all different.

10. In a certain room there are n people. What is the total number of possibilities for their birthdays if (i) no two people have the same birthday, (ii) at least two people have the same birthday?

11. A group (i.e. a combination) of 7 men, including 2 particular men, is chosen from 12 men. In how many ways may this be done?

12. In how many ways can m balls be drawn from a bag containing p blue, q white, r pink and s brown balls when the m balls are (i) all white, (ii) one blue, one white, one pink and one brown. ($m \leqslant p, q, r$ and s.)

3.4. Binomial theorem

As the section title suggests, we are going to discuss a theorem concerning any two real numbers; to be more precise, we are to expand the nth power of the sum of any two real numbers a and x, i.e. to find the expansion for $(a+x)^n$. We will show that $(a+x)^n$ can be written in the form

$$c_0 a^n + c_1 a^{n-1}x + c_2 a^{n-2}x^2 + \ldots + c_r a^{n-r}x^r + \ldots + c_n x^n,$$

where c_r, $r = 0, 1, 2, \ldots, n$, are constants. We limit our attention to the case where n is any positive integer.

To show that $(a+x)^n$ can be written in the above form, we note the following expansions for the cases $n = 1, 2, 3$ and 4, obtained by multiplying $(a+x)$ by itself the requisite number of times:

$$(a+x)^1 = a+x$$
$$(a+x)^2 = a^2 + 2ax + x^2$$
$$(a+x)^3 = a^3 + 3a^2x + 3ax^2 + x^3$$
$$(a+x)^4 = a^4 + 4a^3x + 6a^2x^2 + 4ax^3 + x^4$$

Take $n = 3$ for example, then $c_0 = 1$, $c_1 = 3$, $c_2 = 3$, and $c_3 = 1$. It is left as an exercise to the reader to prove that $(a+x)^n$ can be written in the above form (use the principle of mathematical induction). We determine the constant terms by differentiating as follows:

Let $f(x) = (a+x)^n$

$$= c_0 a^n + c_1 a^{n-1} x + c_2 a^{n-2} x^2 + \ldots + c_r a^{n-r} x^r + \ldots + c_n x^n,$$

then $f'(x) = n(a+x)^{n-1}$

$$= c_1 a^{n-1} + 2c_2 a^{n-2} x + 3c_3 a^{n-3} x^2 + \ldots + r c_r a^{n-r} x^{r-1} + \ldots + n c_n x^{n-1}$$

$f''(x) = n(n-1)(a+x)^{n-2}$

$$= 2c_2 a^{n-2} + 3.2c_3 a^{n-3} x + \ldots + r(r-1) c_r a^{n-r} x^{r-2} + \ldots + n(n-1) c_n x^{n-2}$$

$$\cdot \qquad\qquad \cdot \qquad\qquad \cdot$$
$$\cdot \qquad\qquad \cdot \qquad\qquad \cdot$$
$$\cdot \qquad\qquad \cdot \qquad\qquad \cdot$$

$f^r(x) = n(n-1)(n-2) \ldots (n-r+1)(a+x)^{n-r}$

$$= r(r-1)(r-2) \ldots 3.2.1. \; c_r a^{n-r} + \ldots + n(n-1)(n-2) \ldots (n-r+1) \; c_n x^{n-r}$$

$$\cdot \qquad\qquad \cdot \qquad\qquad \cdot$$
$$\cdot \qquad\qquad \cdot \qquad\qquad \cdot$$
$$\cdot \qquad\qquad \cdot \qquad\qquad \cdot$$

$f^n(x) = [n(n-1)(n-2) \ldots 3.2.1](a+x)^{n-n}$

$$= n!$$
$$= [n(n-1)(n-2) \ldots 3.2.1] c_n x^{n-n}$$
$$= n! \, c_n.$$

Putting $x = 0$ into each of the above identities,

$$f(0) = a^n = c_0 a^n \Rightarrow \underline{c_0 = 1}$$

$$f'(0) = na^{n-1} = c_1 a^{n-1} \Rightarrow \underline{c_1 = n}$$

$$f''(0) = n(n-1)a^{n-2} = 2c_2 a^{n-2} \Rightarrow \underline{c_2 = \frac{n(n-1)}{2}}$$

$$\cdot \qquad \cdot \qquad \cdot$$
$$\cdot \qquad \cdot \qquad \cdot$$
$$\cdot \qquad \cdot \qquad \cdot$$

$$f^r(0) = [n(n-1)(n-2)\ldots(n-r+1)]a^{n-r}$$
$$= r!\, c_r a^{n-r} \Rightarrow \underline{c_r = {}^n C_r}$$

$$\cdot \qquad \cdot \qquad \cdot$$
$$\cdot \qquad \cdot \qquad \cdot$$
$$\cdot \qquad \cdot \qquad \cdot$$

$$f^n(0) = n! = n!c_n \Rightarrow \underline{c_n = 1}$$

Thus,

$$\underline{(a+x)^n = {}^n C_0 a^n + {}^n C_1 a^{n-1}x + {}^n C_2 a^{n-2}x^2 + \ldots}$$
$$\underline{+ {}^n C_r a^{n-r}x^r + \ldots + {}^n C_n x^n.}$$

Since ${}^n C_r = {}^n C_{n-r}$, the coefficients in the binomial expansion which are symmetrically placed about the middle term(s) are equal in value. If n is odd there are two middle terms, and if n is even there is one middle term. The coefficients can be arranged as follows:

$$
\begin{array}{ccccccccc}
 & & & & 1 & & 1 & & & & (n=1) \\
 & & & 1 & & 2 & & 1 & & & (n=2) \\
 & & 1 & & 3 & & 3 & & 1 & & (n=3) \\
 & 1 & & 4 & & 6 & & 4 & & 1 & (n=4) \\
1 & & 5 & & 10 & & 10 & & 5 & & 1 \quad (n=5)
\end{array}
$$

$$\cdot \qquad \cdot \qquad \cdot$$

This arrangement is known as **Pascal's triangle** after the French mathematician, Blaise Pascal (1623–62). In each row, each coefficient except the first and the last is the sum of two consecutive coefficients in the previous row; this illustrates the property $^nC_{r-1} + {}^nC_r = {}^{n+1}C_r$.

EXERCISES 3c

1. Prove the binomial theorem from first principles, i.e. by noting that $(a+x)^n$ is the sum of all products which can be formed by multiplying together one term from each factor.

2. Prove the binomial theorem using the principal of mathematical induction.

3. Prove that the total number of subsets that can be formed from a set of order n is 2^n.

ELEMENTARY PROBABILITY THEORY

3.5. In everyday usage of language one often hears statements or propositions of the kind: "It is likely that it will rain today", or "There is a good chance of winning some money", or "I stand a fair chance of passing the examination". In each case one is not sure of the outcome, but states with a certain degree of confidence that the prediction will be true. In mathematics there are several approaches to the subject of probability; the most common approach nowadays, the one adopted in this book, is to concentrate on the set corresponding to a proposition (see Chapter 2 on isomorphism) rather than directly concentrating on the proposition itself. The set corresponding to a proposition is called the **truth set** of the proposition; e.g. the truth set of the proposition "The number that will turn up if a single die is thrown is less than 5" is $\{1, 2, 3, 4\}$.

The basic problem in hand, then, is to *calculate* the probability or chance of an **event** happening. Clearly, if we are to calculate the probability of an event happening in a particular situation, we must be given sufficient information which will enable us to find the total number of possibilities for *this event* to happen and compare this with the total number of possibilities for *any event* to happen. The set of all possibilities for any event to happen is

called, naturally enough, the **set of all logical possibilities** and is
denoted by U (the same symbol used for universal set). In this
book we confine our attention to those cases where U is finite, i.e.
to those situations where it is possible to have only a finite number
of outcomes (events).

We exemplify what has been said so far as follows:

Two dice are thrown and the difference of the numbers facing
upwards is noted; there are $6 \times 6 = 36$ distinct possibilities (i.e.
$n(U) = 36$) tabulated below:

Case	n_1	n_2	d	Case	n_1	n_2	d	Case	n_1	n_2	d	Case	n_1	n_2	d
1	1	1	0	10	2	4	2	19	4	1	-3	28	5	4	-1
2	1	2	1	11	2	5	3	20	4	2	-2	29	5	5	0
3	1	3	2	12	2	6	4	21	4	3	-1	30	5	6	1
4	1	4	3	13	3	1	-2	22	4	4	0	31	6	1	-5
5	1	5	4	14	3	2	-1	23	4	5	1	32	6	2	-4
6	1	6	5	15	3	3	0	24	4	6	2	33	6	3	-3
7	2	1	-1	16	3	4	1	25	5	1	-4	34	6	4	-2
8	2	2	0	17	3	5	2	26	5	2	-3	35	6	5	-1
9	2	3	1	18	3	6	3	27	5	3	-2	36	6	6	0

In the above table, the first and second numbers are denoted by
n_1 and n_2 respectively (it being agreed, say, that one die is thrown
just before the other one), and $d =$ difference between n_1 and
$n_2 = n_2 - n_1$. If the dice are perfectly symmetrical, then we can
agree that each of the outcomes have the same **weight** $(\frac{1}{36})$, i.e.
all are equally likely. Consider the proposition a: "The difference
in the numbers is 2." Then since there are four possibilities where
$d = 2$, the probability that a is true, written P(a), is given by,

$$P(a) = \frac{1}{36} + \frac{1}{36} + \frac{1}{36} + \frac{1}{36} = \frac{4}{36},$$

i.e.
$$P(a) = \frac{1}{9}.$$

Consider, on the other hand, the proposition b: "The difference in the numbers is 1 or 5." Since there are five possibilities where $d = 1$, and one possibility where $d = 5$, we have,

$$P(b) = \left(\frac{1}{36}\right) + \left(\frac{1}{36} + \frac{1}{36} + \frac{1}{36} + \frac{1}{36} + \frac{1}{36}\right) = \frac{6}{36},$$

i.e. $\quad P(b) = \frac{1}{6}$.

In each case, the probability of a proposition is equal to the sum of the weights of the elements in the truth set of the proposition; this sum of the weights is called the **measure** of the truth set.

We can write U, the set of all logical possibilities, as $\{1, 2, 3, \ldots, 36\}$, where the weight of each possibility is $\frac{1}{36}$ and the measure of U, denoted by $\mu(U)$, is 1 (this means, of course, that the probability of any of the thirty-six possibilities occurring is 1, i.e. a certainty). The truth set A of the proposition a is $\{3, 10, 17, 24\}$, and the truth set B of the proposition b is $\{2, 6, 9, 16, 23, 30\}$.

There is no unique way of analysing all the logical possibilities; the table above gives a fine analysis, whereas the following table gives a rough analysis.

d	-5	-4	-3	-2	-1	0	1	2	3	4	5
Weight	$\frac{1}{36}$	$\frac{2}{36}$	$\frac{3}{36}$	$\frac{4}{36}$	$\frac{5}{36}$	$\frac{6}{36}$	$\frac{5}{36}$	$\frac{4}{36}$	$\frac{3}{36}$	$\frac{2}{36}$	$\frac{1}{36}$

Here, $U = \{-5, -4, -3, -2, -1, 0, 1, 2, 3, 4, 5\}$, and $n(U) = 11$.

Of course,

$$\mu(U) = 1 = 2\left(\frac{1}{36} + \frac{2}{36} + \frac{3}{36} + \frac{4}{36} + \frac{5}{36}\right) + \frac{6}{36}.$$

The outcomes certainly do not each have the same weight. The truth set A is now $\{2\}$, and the truth set B is $\{1, 5\}$; thus,

$$P(a) = \mu(A) = \frac{4}{36} = \frac{1}{9} \quad \text{(as before)},$$

and $\qquad$ $P(b) = \mu(B) = \dfrac{5}{36} + \dfrac{1}{36} = \dfrac{1}{6}$ $\qquad$ (as before).

A formal development of the subject will now be given.

3.6. Definitions

(i) *Weight* (μ_r)

A positive number μ_r assigned to each element r of U (a set of n elements) such that,

$$\sum_{r=1}^{n} \mu_r = \mu_1 + \mu_2 + \ldots + \mu_n = 1.$$

(ii) *Set measure* $[\mu(A)]$

The measure $\mu(A)$ of any subset A of U is given by,

$$\mu(A) = \sum_{A} \mu_r,$$

where $\sum\limits_{A}$ is summation over the elements of A.

(iii) *Probability measure (i.e. probability)* $[P(a)]$

The probability $P(a)$ of the proposition a is given by,

$$P(a) = \mu(A),$$

where A is the truth set of a.

Fundamental properties of set measure

(i) $\mu(A) = 1$ if and only if $A = $ U. This follows immediately from definitions (i) and (ii).

(ii) $\mu(A) = 0$ if and only if $A = \varnothing$. We prove this below (just because $\varnothing$ has no elements, and therefore no weights are assigned, does not justify the conclusion that $\mu(\varnothing) = 0$).

(iii) $0 \leqslant \mu(A) \leqslant 1$ for any set A.

Proof. Since for any set A, $\varnothing \subseteq A \subseteq $ U, then,

$$\mu(\varnothing) \leqslant \mu(A) \leqslant \mu(\text{U}),$$

i.e. $\qquad\qquad 0 \leqslant \mu(A) \leqslant 1,$

from properties (i) and (ii).

(iv) (a) $\mu(A \cup B) = \mu(A) + \mu(B)$ if and only if A and B are disjoint, i.e. $A \cap B = \emptyset$.

(b) $\mu(A \cup B) = \mu(A) + \mu(B) - \mu(A \cap B)$ for any two sets A and B.

Proof. (a) $\mu(A) + \mu(B) = \sum_A \mu_r + \sum_B \mu_r$, i.e. the sum of the weights of the elements in A and the weights of the elements in B. If A and B are disjoint, then the weight of every element in $A \cup B$ is added once and only once. Thus,

$$\sum_A \mu_r + \sum_B \mu_r = \sum_{A \cup B} \mu_r,$$

i.e. $\qquad\qquad \mu(A \cup B) = \mu(A) + \mu(B)$.

Proof. (b) If $A \cap B \neq \emptyset$, then the weights of the elements in both A *and* B, i.e. in $A \cap B$, are added twice in the sum

$$\sum_A \mu_r + \sum_B \mu_r.$$

Thus, $\qquad\qquad \sum_{A \cup B} \mu_r = \sum_A \mu_r + \sum_B \mu_r - \sum_{A \cap B} \mu_r,$

i.e. $\qquad\qquad \mu(A \cup B) = \mu(A) + \mu(B) - \mu(A \cap B)$.

Since each of the weights μ_r are positive by definition, then,

$$\mu(A \cup B) < \mu(A) + \mu(B).$$

We are now in a position to prove property (ii): for any set A,

$$A = A \cup \emptyset,$$

$$\therefore \quad \mu(A) = \mu(A \cup \emptyset),$$

and since A and $\emptyset$ are disjoint, we have from property (iv) (a),

$$\mu(A \cup \emptyset) = \mu(A) + \mu(\emptyset).$$

Thus, $\qquad\qquad \mu(A) = \mu(A) + \mu(\emptyset),$

and therefore, $\qquad\qquad \mu(\emptyset) = 0.$

From definition (iii) and the above properties of set measure, we immediately deduce the following.

Fundamental properties of probability measure

   (i) $P(a) = 1$ if and only if a is logically true.
   (ii) $P(a) = 0$ if and only if a is logically false.
   (iii) $0 \leqslant P(a) \leqslant 1$, for any proposition a.
   (iv) (a) $P(a \vee b) = P(a) + P(b)$, if and only if a and b are exclusive, i.e. $a \wedge b$ is logically false.
   (b) $P(a \vee b) = P(a) + P(b) - P(a \wedge b)$ for any two propositions a and b.
   Also, $P(a \vee b) \leqslant P(a) + P(b)$.

Some further properties of probability measure

   (v) $P(\bar{a}) = 1 - P(a)$.

Proof. Since a and $\bar{a}$ are exclusive, then,

$$P(\bar{a} \vee a) = P(\bar{a}) + P(a),$$

but $(\bar{a} \vee a)$ is logically true,

$$\therefore \quad P(\bar{a} \vee a) = 1 = P(\bar{a}) + P(a),$$

i.e. $$P(\bar{a}) = 1 - P(a).$$

   (vi) $P(a_1) + P(a_2) + \ldots + P(a_i) + \ldots + P(a_n) = 1$, if and only if a_i $(i = 1, 2, \ldots, n)$ are exclusive and exhaustive.

Proof. a_i $(i = 1, 2, \ldots, n)$ are exclusive if $a_i \wedge a_j$ $(i \neq j)$ is logically false, and are exhaustive if $(a_1 \vee a_2 \vee \ldots \vee a_i \vee \ldots a_n)$ is logically true. Thus,

$$P(a_1 \vee a_2 \vee \ldots \vee a_i \vee \ldots \vee a_n)$$
$$= P(a_1) + P(a_2) + \ldots + P(a_i) + \ldots + P(a_n) = 1.$$

If some of the a_i are not exclusive, although all the a_i are still exhaustive, then,

$$P(a_1 \vee a_2 \vee \ldots \vee a_n) = 1 < P(a_1) + P(a_2) + \ldots + P(a_n).$$

This follows from (iv) (b).

3.7. Conditional probability

When we calculate the probability $P(a_1)$ of a proposition a_1 we assign weights μ_r $(r = 1, 2, \ldots, n)$ to the elements of the set U of all logical possibilities, and then determine the measure $\mu(A_1)$ of the truth set A_1. Thus,

$$P(a_1) = \mu(A_1) = \sum_{A1} \mu_r.$$

Suppose now, we are given that a certain proposition a_2 is true; we want to find out how this information affects the value of $P(a_1)$. For example, suppose that in considering a pack of ordinary playing cards, a_1 is the proposition "This card is the ace of spades" and a_2 is the proposition "This card is a spade"; U is the pack of 52 cards. Since each card is equally likely to be chosen from the pack, we assign an equal weight $(\mu_r = 1/52)$ to each element of U. Thus,

$$P(a_1) = \mu(A_1) = \sum_{A1} \mu_r = \frac{1}{52},$$

and

$$P(a_2) = \mu(A_2) = \sum_{A2} \mu_r = \frac{13}{52}.$$

If we are told that the chosen card is a spade, i.e. $P(a_2) = 1$, then, of course, we should stand a better chance of the card being the ace of spades; all we have to do is to choose 1 card (the ace of spades) from 13 cards (the suit of spades). Clearly, the probability of choosing the ace of spades, given that the card chosen is a spade, is $1/13$. We call this type of probability the **conditional probability of a_1 given a_2** and is written $P(a_1|a_2)$. Since we are given a_2, then $P(a_2) = 1$; but, assigning the weights $(\mu_r = 1/52)$ to each element of U gives $P(a_2) = 13/52$. Therefore we must assign new weights (μ_r'), so that taking A_2 as the set of all logical possibilities, the new measure μ' is given by:

$$\mu'(A_2) = \sum_{A2} \mu_r' = 1 \qquad\qquad \text{(i)}$$

D

But, $\qquad \mu(A_2) = \sum_{A_2} \mu_r = \dfrac{13}{52},$

i.e. $\qquad \dfrac{52}{13} \sum_{A_2} \mu_r = 1,$

i.e. $\qquad \sum_{A_2} \left(\dfrac{52}{13} \mu_r \right) = 1,$ $\hspace{3cm}$ (ii)

therefore from (i) and (ii),

$$\sum_{A_2} \mu_r{}' = \sum_{A_2} \left(\dfrac{52}{13} \mu_r \right),$$

i.e. $\qquad \mu_r{}' = \dfrac{52}{13} \mu_r.$

Thus,

$$P(a_1 \,|\, a_2) = \sum_{A_1} \mu_r{}' = \sum_{A_1} \left(\dfrac{52}{13} \right) \mu_r,$$

i.e. $\qquad P(a_1 \,|\, a_2) = \dfrac{52}{13} \sum_{A_1} \mu_r = \dfrac{52}{13} \mu(A_1) = \dfrac{52}{13} \, P(a_1),$

i.e. $\qquad P(a_1 \,|\, a_2) = \dfrac{52}{13} \times \dfrac{1}{52} = \dfrac{1}{13}$ (as was made clear above).

In the above example, $A_1 \subset A_2$, and we found that,

$$P(a_1 \,|\, a_2) = \dfrac{52}{13} \times \dfrac{1}{52} = \dfrac{P(a_1)}{P(a_2)}.$$

We will now show, that in general where $A_1 \subseteq A_2$ (note that we include the possibility $A_1 = A_2$), we have,

$$P(a_1 \,|\, a_2) = \dfrac{P(a_1)}{P(a_2)}.$$

THEOREM. If the truth sets A_1 and A_2 of the propositions a_1 and a_2 are such that $A_1 \subseteq A_2$, then,

$$P(a_1 \,|\, a_2) = \dfrac{P(a_1)}{P(a_2)}.$$

Proof. Let U be the set of all logical possibilities, then, $A_1 \subseteq A_2 \subseteq U$, and,

$$P(U) = \mu(U) = \sum_U \mu_r = 1$$

$$P(a_1) = \mu(A_1) = \sum_{A_1} \mu_r$$

$$P(a_2) = \mu(A_2) = \sum_{A_2} \mu_r.$$

If a_2 is given (i.e. a_2 true, and $\bar{a}_2$ false), then,

$$P'(a_2) = \mu'(A_2) = \sum_{A_2} \mu_r' = 1,$$

where P', μ' and μ_r' are the new probability, measure and weight respectively. Therefore, since

$$\mu(A_2) = \sum_{A_2} \mu_r = P(a_2),$$

i.e.

$$\sum_{A_2} \left(\frac{\mu_r}{P(a_2)} \right) = 1,$$

we have

$$\sum_{A_2} \mu_r' = \sum_{A_2} \left(\frac{\mu_r}{P(a_2)} \right) = 1,$$

i.e.

$$\mu_r' = \frac{\mu_r}{P(a_2)},$$

therefore

$$P(a_1 | a_2) = \mu'(A_1) = \sum_{A_1} \mu_r' = \frac{1}{P(a_2)} \sum_{A_1} \mu_r,$$

i.e.

$$P(a_1 | a_2) = \frac{P(a_1)}{P(a_2)}.$$

So, for *any two* propositions a_1 and a_2, i.e. $A_1 \cap A_2 \subseteq A_2$,

$$P(a_1 | a_2) = \frac{P(a_1 \wedge a_2)}{P(a_2)}.$$

Venn diagrams in Fig. 3.2 illustrate this.

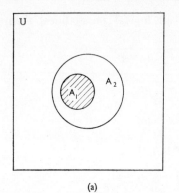 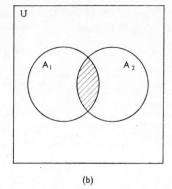

(a)

(b)

Fig. 3.2.

$$\text{(a) } P(a_1 | a_2) = \frac{P(a_1)}{P(a_2)}. \qquad \text{(b) } P(a_1 | a_2) = \frac{P(a_1 \wedge a_2)}{P(a_2)}.$$

If the value for $P(a_1)$ is not affected by the information given by a_2, then

$$P(a_1 | a_2) = P(a_1),$$

i.e.

$$P(a_1) = P(a_1 | a_2) = \frac{P(a_1 \wedge a_2)}{P(a_2)},$$

i.e.

$$P(a_1 \wedge a_2) = P(a_1)P(a_2).$$

If, on the other hand, the value for $P(a_2)$ is not affected by the information given by a_1, then

$$P(a_2 | a_1) = P(a_2),$$

i.e.

$$P(a_2) = P(a_2 | a_1) = \frac{P(a_2 \wedge a_1)}{P(a_1)},$$

i.e.

$$P(a_1 \wedge a_2) = P(a_1)P(a_2) \qquad \text{(as before)}.$$

We therefore have the following definition:

Definition. Two propositions a_1 and a_2 are said to be **independent** if and only if,

$$P(a_1 \wedge a_2) = P(a_1)P(a_2).$$

3.8. Bayes's theorem (*a-posteriori* probability)

We now consider a special type of conditional probability. Suppose we have the following problem to solve:

In England the roads are wet for 15% of the time. A certain car driver reckons on having at least one skid on a journey for 60% of the journeys he makes on wet roads, and at least one skid on a journey for 10% of the journeys he makes on dry roads. On a particular journey the driver skidded. What is the probability that the roads were dry on that journey?

Let U be the set of all journeys (on which the roads are wet or dry), a_1 be the proposition "The roads are wet", a_2 be the proposition "The roads are dry", and a be the proposition "The driver skidded". The Venn diagram, Fig. 33, illustrates the truth sets, A_1, A_2 and A.

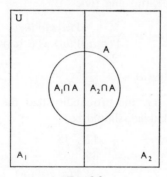

FIG. 3.3.

We are given that

$$P(a_1) = \frac{3}{20} \qquad P(a_2) = \frac{17}{20}$$

$$P(a|a_1) = \frac{3}{5} \qquad P(a|a_2) = \frac{1}{10}$$

and we wish to find $P(a_2|a)$.

Now
$$P(a_2 | a) = \frac{P(a_2 \wedge a)}{P(a)} \qquad \text{(i)}$$

and
$$P(a_2 \wedge a) = P(a | a_2)P(a_2) = \frac{1}{10} \times \frac{17}{20}. \qquad \text{(ii)}$$

To calculate $P(a)$, we note that $A = (A_1 \cap A) \cup (A_2 \cap A)$, i.e. A = the union of two disjoint subsets. Thus the corresponding propositional relation is

$$a = (a_1 \wedge a) \vee (a_2 \wedge a),$$

and therefore,
$$P(a) = P(a_1 \wedge a) + P(a_2 \wedge a). \qquad \text{(iii)}$$

We found the right-hand term in the right-hand side of (iii) in (ii). Similarly,

$$P(a_1 \wedge a) = P(a | a_1)P(a_1) = \frac{3}{5} \times \frac{3}{20}. \qquad \text{(iv)}$$

Thus, from (i), (ii), (iii) and (iv),

$$P(a_2 | a) = \frac{P(a | a_2)P(a_2)}{P(a | a_1)P(a_1) + P(a | a_2)P(a_2)},$$

i.e.
$$P(a_2 | a) = \frac{\frac{1}{10} \times \frac{17}{20}}{\left(\frac{3}{5} \times \frac{3}{20}\right) + \left(\frac{1}{10} \times \frac{17}{20}\right)} = \frac{17}{35}.$$

Check. $P(a_1 | a)$, i.e. the probability that the roads were wet when the driver skidded, should be

$$1 - \frac{17}{35} = \frac{18}{35}.$$

Now,
$$P(a_1 | a) = \frac{P(a | a_1)P(a_1)}{P(a | a_2)P(a_2) + P(a | a_1)P(a_1)},$$

i.e.
$$P(a_1 | a) = \frac{\frac{3}{5} \times \frac{3}{20}}{\left(\frac{1}{10} \times \frac{17}{20}\right) + \left(\frac{3}{5} \times \frac{3}{20}\right)} = \frac{18}{35}.$$

$$\therefore \ P(a_2 | a) + P(a_1 | a) = 1.$$

The generalization of the formula above for $P(a_2 | a)$ is called Bayes's theorem, after the English mathematician, Thomas Bayes (d. 1761). It connects the *a-posteriori probability* $P(a_2 | a)$ with the *a-priori probabilities* $P(a_1)$ and $P(a_2)$.

BAYES'S THEOREM. If $a_1, a_2, \ldots, a_n$ are exlusive and exhaustive propositions, i.e. $P(a_1 \vee a_2 \vee \ldots \vee a_n) = 1$, $a_i \wedge a_j (i \neq j)$ logically false, then for any one of these propositions a_r,

$$P(a_r \mid a) = \frac{P(a_r)P(a \mid a_r)}{\sum\limits_{i=1}^{n} P(a_i)P(a \mid a_i)}$$

where proposition a is given.

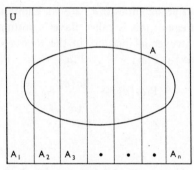

FIG. 3.4.

Proof. $A_1, A_2, \ldots, A_n$ and A are the corresponding truth sets of the propositions and are illustrated in Fig. 3.4. We assume that we are given $P(a_1), P(a_2), \ldots, P(a_n)$, and $P(a \mid a_1), P(a \mid a_2), \ldots, P(a \mid a_n)$.

Now, $P(a_r \mid a) = \dfrac{P(a_r \wedge a)}{P(a)}$ (i)

and, $P(a_r \wedge a) = P(a \mid a_r)P(a_r)$ (ii)

$$A = (A_1 \cap A) \cup (A_2 \cap A) \cup \ldots \cup (A_n \cap A),$$

i.e. $a = (a_1 \wedge a) \vee (a_2 \wedge a) \vee \ldots \vee (a_n \wedge a),$

and therefore,

$$P(a) = P(a_1 \wedge a) + P(a_2 \wedge a) + \ldots + P(a_n \wedge a) \quad \text{(iii)}$$

but,

$P(a_i \wedge a) = P(a \mid a_i)P(a_i), \quad i = 1, 2, \ldots, n$ (iv)

therefore from (iii) and (iv),

$$P(a) = \sum_{i=1}^{n} P(a|a_i)P(a_i),$$

and using this last expression for $P(a)$ together with (i) and (ii), we have,

$$P(a_r|a) = \frac{P(a|a_r)P(a_r)}{\sum\limits_{i=1}^{n} P(a_i)P(a|a_i)}.$$

When the *a-priori* probabilities $P(a_i)$ are not known then we assume that they are all equal; this is called Bayes's postulate, and is one of the most controversial matters in the theory of probability. Thus setting $P(a_1) = P(a_2) = \ldots = P(a_r) = \ldots = P(a_n)$, we have,

$$P(a_r|a) = \frac{P(a|a_r)}{\sum\limits_{i=1}^{n} P(a|a_i)}.$$

EXAMPLES

1. Two bags each contain 10 coins. What is the probability that a specified coin will appear in a combination of 8 coins obtained by drawing 4 coins from each bag?

Firstly, we determine precisely the set U of all possibilities, namely the total number of ways of drawing any 8 coins, 4 from each bag.

The number of ways of drawing a combination of 4 coins from one of the bags is $^{10}C_4$ and for each of these ways there are $^{10}C_4$ ways of drawing a combination of 4 coins from the remaining bag. There are, therefore, $(^{10}C_4)^2$ ways of drawing the 8 coins. Assuming that each of these ways is equally likely, then we assign the equal weight $1/(^{10}C_4)^2$ to each element of U = {all ways of drawing 8 coins}.

We now determine the truth set of the proposition "A specified coin will appear in a combination of 8 coins": Having chosen the specified coin, there are $^{9}C_3$ ways of choosing the other 3 coins from one of the bags and for each of these ways there are $^{10}C_4$

ways of drawing 4 coins from the other bag. So, there are $^9C_3 \times {}^{10}C_4$ ways of drawing 8 coins containing a specified coin. Thus the truth set of the proposition is {all ways of drawing 8 coins including a specified coin} and the number of elements in this set is $^9C_3 \times {}^{10}C_4$. Therefore the sum of the weights of the elements in the truth set

$$= \frac{^9C_3 \times {}^{10}C_4}{(^{10}C_4)^2} = \frac{2}{5},$$

which is equal to the probability of the proposition.

In practice the above explanations are much abbreviated; full explanations are given here to make quite sure that the reader understands what has been said in the foregoing theory.

2. What is the probability that out of a group of r people at least two have the same birthday (ignoring the year)?

Number of possible birthdays for any one person is 365 (discounting leap years), and for each of these possibilities there are 365 possible birthdays for any one other person (including the possibility of both birthdays being the same). Thus for any two people, there are 365^2 possible birthdays, and in general for r people, there are 365^r possible birthdays. Now consider the number of possible birthdays for r people where *no two birthdays are the same*: The number of possible birthdays for any one person is 365, and for each of the possibilities there remain 364 possible birthdays for any one other person. Therefore, for r people the number of birthdays such that no two are the same is $365 \times 364 \times \ldots \times (365 - r + 1)$. The probability P that no two birthdays are the same is therefore given by:

$$P = \frac{365 \times 364 \times \ldots \times (365 - r + 1)}{365^r},$$

and the probability *that at least two birthdays are the same*

$$= (1 - P) = 1 - \frac{365 \times 364 \times \ldots \times (365 - r + 1)}{365^r}.$$

If $r = 23$, $(1 - P) \sim 0.51$; this is a surprisingly high probability for so few people.

3. What is the probability that a card drawn at random from a pack of 52 cards, is an ace or a spade?

Let a be the proposition "The card is an ace".

Let b be the proposition "The card is a spade".

Then $P(a \vee b) = P(a) + P(b) - P(a \wedge b)$, where $(a \wedge b)$ is "The card is the ace of spades".

Now,

$$P(a) = \frac{4}{52} = \frac{1}{13},$$

$$P(b) = \frac{13}{52} = \frac{1}{4},$$

and
$$P(a \wedge b) = \frac{1}{52}.$$

Therefore
$$P(a \vee b) = \frac{1}{13} + \frac{1}{4} - \frac{1}{52},$$

i.e.
$$P(a \vee b) = \frac{4}{13}.$$

4. Generalizing $P(a_1 \vee a_2) = P(a_1) + P(a_2) - P(a_1 \wedge a_2)$, where a_1 and a_2 are any two propositions, we have

$$P(a_1 \vee a_2 \vee \ldots \vee a_n) = \sum_i^n P(a_i) - \sum_{i<j}^n P(a_i \wedge a_j)$$
$$+ \sum_{i<j<k}^n (a_i \wedge a_j \wedge a_k) - \ldots + (-1)^{n+1} P(a_1 \wedge a_2 \wedge \ldots \wedge a_n),$$

where a_i $(i = 1, 2, \ldots, n)$, are any propositions (i.e. not mutually exclusive).

Similarly, for the number of elements in non-disjoint sets,

$$n(A_1 \cup A_2 \cup \ldots \cup A_n) = \sum_i^n n(A_i) - \sum_{i<j}^n n(A_i \cap A_j)$$
$$+ \sum_{i<j<k}^n n(A_i \cap A_j \cap A_k) - \ldots + (-1)^{n+1} n(A_1 \cap A_2 \cap \ldots \cap A_n).$$

The proofs for both cases are exactly similar, namely by induction on n, and we give here a proof for the probabilities (this may be omitted on a first reading).

Proof. (i) $n = 1$.

Putting $n = 1$ into the above formula we obtain

$$P(a_1) = P(a_1),$$

which is clearly true.

(ii) We now show that the truth of the formula for $n = r$ implies the truth of the formula for $n = r + 1$.

Now,

$$P(a_1 \vee a_2 \vee \ldots \vee a_{r+1}) = P[(a_1 \vee a_2 \vee \ldots \vee a_r) \vee a_{r+1}]$$

$$= P(a_1 \vee a_2 \vee \ldots \vee a_r) + P(a_{r+1}) - P[(a_1 \vee a_2 \vee \ldots \vee a_r) \wedge a_{r+1}]$$

$$= \sum_i^r P(a_i) - \sum_{i<j}^r P(a_i \wedge a_j) + \ldots + (-1)^{r+1} P(a_1 \wedge a_2 \wedge \ldots \wedge a_r)$$

$$+ P(a_{r+1}) - P[(a_1 \wedge a_{r+1}) \vee (a_2 \wedge a_{r+1}) \vee \ldots \vee (a_r \wedge a_{r+1})]$$

$$= \sum_i^{r+1} P(a_i) - \sum_{i<j}^r P(a_i \wedge a_j) + \ldots + (-1)^{r+1} P(a_1 \wedge a_2 \wedge \ldots \wedge a_r)$$

$$- P[(a_1 \wedge a_{r+1}) \vee (a_2 \wedge a_{r+1}) \vee \ldots \vee (a_r \wedge a_{r+1})]. \tag{1}$$

But,

$$P[(a_1 \wedge a_{r+1}) \vee (a_2 \wedge a_{r+1}) \vee \ldots \vee (a_r \wedge a_{r+1})]$$

$$= \sum_i^r P(a_i \wedge a_{r+1}) - \sum_{i<j}^r P[(a_i \wedge a_{r+1}) \wedge (a_j \wedge a_{r+1})] + \ldots$$

$$+ (-1)^{r+1} P(a_1 \wedge a_2 \wedge \ldots \wedge a_{r+1})$$

$$= \sum_i^r P(a_i \wedge a_{r+1}) - \sum_{i<j}^r P(a_i \wedge a_j \wedge a_{r+1}) + \ldots$$

$$- (-1)^{r+2} P(a_1 \wedge a_2 \wedge \ldots \wedge a_{r+1}). \tag{2}$$

Therefore from (1) and (2) we have,

$$P(a_1 \vee a_2 \vee \ldots \vee a_{r+1})$$

$$= \sum_i^{r+1} P(a_i) - \left\{ \sum_{i<j}^r P(a_i \wedge a_j) + \sum_i^r P(a_i \wedge a_{r+1}) \right\}$$

$$+ \left\{ \sum_{i<j<k}^{r} P(a_i \wedge a_j \wedge a_k) + \sum_{i<j}^{r} P(a_i \wedge a_j \wedge a_{r+1}) \right\}$$

$$- \quad . \quad . \quad .$$

$$+ \left\{ (-1)^{r+1} P(a_1 \wedge a_2 \wedge \ldots \wedge a_r) \right.$$

$$\left. + \sum_{i<j<\cdots<s}^{r} P(a_i \wedge a_j \wedge \ldots \wedge a_s \wedge a_{r+1}) \right\}$$

$$+ (-1)^{r+2} P(a_1 \wedge a_2 \wedge \ldots \wedge a_{r+1}). \qquad (3)$$

Now,

$$\sum_{i<j}^{r} P(a_i \wedge a_j) + \sum_{i}^{r} P(a_i \wedge a_{r+1})$$

$$= P(a_1 \wedge a_2) + P(a_1 \wedge a_3) + \ldots + P(a_1 \wedge a_r) + P(a_1 \wedge a_{r+1})$$

$$+ P(a_2 \wedge a_3) + P(a_2 \wedge a_4) + \ldots + P(a_2 \wedge a_r) + P(a_2 \wedge a_{r+1})$$

$$+ \quad . \quad . \quad .$$

$$+ P(a_{r-1} \wedge a_r) + P(a_{r-1} \wedge a_{r+1})$$

$$+ P(a_r \wedge a_{r+1})$$

$$= \sum_{i<j}^{r+1} P(a_i \wedge a_j).$$

Similarly,

$$\sum_{i<j<k}^{r} P(a_i \wedge a_j \wedge a_k) + \sum_{i<j}^{r} P(a_i \wedge a_j \wedge a_{r+1})$$

$$= \sum_{i<j<k}^{r+1} P(a_i \wedge a_j \wedge a_k),$$

and so on.

Thus, substituting into (3),

$$P(a_1 \vee a_2 \vee \ldots \vee a_{r+1}) = \sum_{i}^{r+1} P(a_i) - \sum_{i<j}^{r+1} P(a_i \wedge a_j) + \ldots$$

$$+ (-1)^{r+2} P(a_1 \wedge a_2 \wedge \ldots \wedge a_{r+1}).$$

We have now completed the proof.

5. n different letters are to be sent to n different addresses. If the letters are placed at random, one in each envelope, show that the probability P that every letter is in a wrong envelope is given by:

$$P = \frac{1}{2!} - \frac{1}{3!} + \frac{1}{4!} - \ldots + (-1)^n \frac{1}{n!}.$$

Number both the letters and envelopes $1, 2, \ldots, n$, so that if the ith letter is placed into the ith envelope then it is correctly placed. Suppose now, that the letters are placed at random in one row, and the envelopes are placed at random in another row adjacent to the letters so that there is a one–one correspondence between the letters and envelopes. Consider the proposition a_i "The letter numbered i corresponds to the envelope numbered i". The number of ways of rearranging the $(n-1)$ envelopes is $(n-1)!$, and the number of ways of rearranging all n envelopes is $n!$, and therefore,

$$P(a_i) = \frac{(n-1)!}{n!} = \frac{1}{n},$$

assuming each arrangement to be equally likely. Similarly,

$$P(a_i \wedge a_j) = \frac{1}{n(n-1)},$$

and

$$P(a_i \wedge a_j \wedge a_k) = \frac{1}{n(n-1)(n-2)},$$

and so on until,

$$P(a_1 \wedge a_2 \wedge \ldots \wedge a_n) = \frac{1}{n!}$$

Thus,

$$P(a_1 \vee a_2 \vee \ldots \vee a_n) = \sum_i^n P(a_i) - \sum_{i<j}^n P(a_i \wedge a_j)$$
$$+ \sum_{i<j<k}^n P(a_i \wedge a_j \wedge a_k) - \ldots + (-1)^{n+1} P(a_1 \wedge a_2 \wedge \ldots \wedge a_n)$$
$$= n\frac{1}{n} - {}^nC_2\frac{1}{n(n-1)} + {}^nC_3\frac{1}{n(n-1)(n-2)} - \ldots + (-1)^{n+1}\frac{1}{n!}$$
$$= 1 - \frac{1}{2!} + \frac{1}{3!} - \ldots + (-1)^{n+1}\frac{1}{n!}.$$

Therefore, the probability P that every letter is in a wrong envelope is given by:

$$P = 1 - P(a_1 \vee a_2 \vee \ldots \vee a_n),$$

i.e. $$P = \frac{1}{2!} - \frac{1}{3!} + \frac{1}{4!} - \ldots + (-1)^n \frac{1}{n!}.$$

As $n \to \infty$, $P \to 1/e \sim 0.3679$; indeed if n is as small as 7, $P = 0.3679$ (to 4 sig. fig.), which shows that P is practically independent of n—an incredible result (intuitively).

6. Show that if two propositions a and b are independent then a and $\bar{b}$ are independent and hence $\bar{a}$ and $\bar{b}$ are independent.

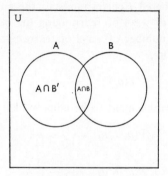

FIG. 3.5.

The Venn diagram in Fig. 3.5 illustrates the truth sets A and B of the propositions a and b. It is clear that,

$$A = (A \cap B) \cup (A \cap B'),$$

and the corresponding propositional expression is,

$$a = (a \wedge b) \vee (a \wedge \bar{b}).$$

Thus

$$P(a) = P(a \wedge b) + P(a \wedge \bar{b}),$$

since $(a \wedge b)$ and $(a \wedge \bar{b})$ are exclusive. But, since $P(a \wedge b) = P(a)P(b)$, because a and b are independent, it follows that,

$$P(a) = P(a)P(b) + P(a \wedge \bar{b}),$$

i.e. $$P(a \wedge \bar{b}) = P(a)[1 - P(b)] = P(a)P(\bar{b}),$$

and therefore and a and $\bar{b}$ are independent.

7. There is a 10% chance that student A passes the examination, and a 20% chance that student B passes the same examination. Find the probability that (a) at least one student passes, (b) both students pass, (c) only student A passes.

Let a be the proposition "Student A passes the examination", and b be the proposition "Student B passes the examination". Then, we are given that,

$$P(a) = \frac{1}{10} \qquad \therefore P(\bar{a}) = \frac{9}{10},$$

and $$P(b) = \frac{1}{5} \qquad \therefore P(\bar{b}) = \frac{4}{5}.$$

(a) $$P(a \vee b) = P(a) + P(b) - P(a \wedge b)$$
$$= \frac{1}{10} + \frac{1}{5} - P(a \wedge b).$$

Assuming a and b are independent (realistic!),

$$P(a \wedge b) = P(a)P(b) = \frac{1}{10} \times \frac{1}{5} = \frac{1}{50}.$$

Hence,

$$P(a \vee b) = \frac{1}{10} + \frac{1}{5} - \frac{1}{50} = \frac{7}{25} = 0 \cdot 28.$$

(b) $$P(a \wedge b) = \frac{1}{50} = 0 \cdot 02 \text{ from (a).}$$

(c) $$P(a \wedge \bar{b}) = P(a)P(\bar{b}), \text{ since } a \text{ and } b \text{ are independent.}$$

Therefore $$P(a \wedge \bar{b}) = \frac{1}{10} \times \frac{4}{5} = \frac{4}{50} = 0 \cdot 08.$$

Exercises 3d

1. The faces of each of two dice are numbered from one to six. If the dice are thrown on a table, find the probability that the sum of the numbers on the uppermost faces of the two dice will be greater than eight.

2. If ten people are seated at a circular table at random, what is the probability that a particular pair of people are seated next to each other?

3. A word is chosen at random from the set of words {Pen, House, Mathematics, Problem, Table}. Let a and b be the propositions: "The word contains two vowels", "The first letter of the word is P", respectively. Find the probability of the following propositions:

(i) a (ii) b (iii) $a \lor b$ (iv) $a \land b$ (v) $a \to b$.

4. Show that out of a group of n people, the probability that only one pair of people have the same birthday is given by:

$$P = {}^nC_2 \frac{365 \cdot 364 \ldots (365 - n + 2)}{365^n}.$$

5. In a game of snap played with 52 playing cards, find the probability that no pair of cards match.

6. Prove that for any three propositions a, b and c,

$$P(a \land b \land c) = P(a)P(b|a)P[c|(a \land b)].$$

7. Three propositions, a, b and c, are said to be independent if they are pairwise independent and,

$$P(a \land b \land c) = P(a)P(b)P(c).$$

If a, b and c are independent, prove that the following are also independent:

(i) a and $(b \land c)$.

(ii) $\bar{a}$, b and c.

(iii) a and $(b \lor c)$.

8. There is a 20% chance that any car tyre will have a puncture in any one year. Find the probability that in a period of two consecutive years, a motor car will have exactly one puncture.

CHAPTER 4

Relations and Functions

4.1. Cartesian Product [after the French mathematician and philosopher, René Descartes (1596–1650)]

The **Cartesian product** of two sets A and B, denoted by $A \times B$, is the set of all **ordered pairs** given by:

$$A \times B = \{(a,b): a \in A,\ b \in B\}.$$

For example, if $A = \{1, 2, 3\}$, and $B = \{a, b\}$, then

$$A \times B = \{(1, a),\ (1, b),\ (2, a),\ (2, b),\ (3, a),\ (3, b)\},$$

and $\quad B \times A = \{(a, 1),\ (b, 1),\ (a, 2),\ (b, 2),\ (a, 3),\ (b, 3)\}.$

In general, $A \times B \neq B \times A$; in fact, $A \times B = B \times A$ only if $A = B$, or either A or B (or both) $= \varnothing$. If set A has m elements and set B has n elements, then $A \times B$ has mn elements. The Cartesian plane is a geometrical example of a Cartesian product, namely $R^* \times R^*$; each point in the plane is represented by a number pair (x, y) where $x, y \in R^*$ (see Fig. 4.1).

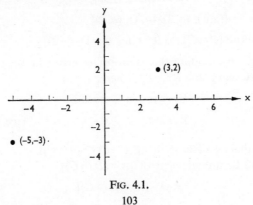

Fig. 4.1.

EXAMPLES

1. Illustrate graphically $A \times B$, where $A = (2, 3, 4)$ and $B = (a, b)$.

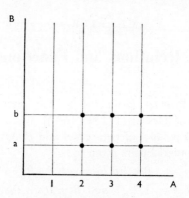

FIG. 4.2. $A \times B$.

2. If $A = \{\alpha, \beta\}$, $B = \{\alpha, a\}$, and $C = \{1, 2\}$, find (i) $A \times (B \cup C)$ and (ii) $(A \times C) \cap (B \times C)$.

(i) $B \cup C = \{\alpha, a, 1, 2\}$

therefore $A \times (B \cup C) = \{(\alpha, \alpha), (\alpha, a), (\alpha, 1), (\alpha, 2), (\beta, \alpha), (\beta, a), (\beta, 1), (\beta, 2)\}$

(ii) $A \times C = \{(\alpha, 1), (\alpha, 2), (\beta, 1), (\beta, 2)\}$

$B \times C = \{(\alpha, 1), (\alpha, 2), (a, 1), (a, 2)\}$

therefore $(A \times C) \cap (B \times C) = \{(\alpha, 1), (\alpha, 2)\}$.

3. Sketch, by shading the appropriate area, the set $(X) \times (Y)$ on the Cartesian plane $R^* \times R^*$, where,

$$X = \{x : -1 \leqslant x < 3\}$$
$$Y = \{y : -2 \leqslant y \leqslant 4\} \qquad \text{(see Fig. 4.3)}$$

4. Prove that $[A \times (B \cap C)] \subseteq [(A \times B) \cap (A \times C)]$.

Let (x, y) be any element of $[A \times (B \cap C)]$,

i.e. $\qquad\qquad (x, y) \in [A \times (B \cap C)]$

$\Rightarrow x \in A$ and $y \in (B \cap C)$ (definition of Cartesian product)

$\Rightarrow x \in A$ and $y \in B$ and $y \in C$ (definition of intersection)

$\therefore \qquad (x, y) \in (A \times B)$ (definition of Cartesian product)

and $\qquad (x, y) \in (A \times C)$ (definition of Cartesian product)

Hence, $(x, y) \in [(A \times B) \cap (A \times C)]$ (definition of intersection)

i.e. $\qquad [A \times (B \cap C)] \subseteq [(A \times B) \cap (A \times C)]$.

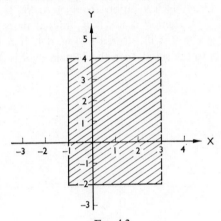

Fig. 4.3.

Exercises 4a

1. Illustrate the following graphically:

(i) $\{x: x > 0\} \times \{x: x \leqslant 2\}$ where $x \in R^*$

(ii) $\{a: 1 > a \geqslant 3\} \times \{b: -1 \leqslant b < 2\}$ where $a, b \in R^*$

(iii) $A \times B$ where $A = \{h, k\}$ and $B = \{u, v, w\}$.

2. Prove that $(A \subseteq B) \wedge (C \subseteq D) \Leftrightarrow (A \times C) \subseteq (B \times D)$.

3. Prove that $[(A \times B) \cap (A \times C)] \subseteq [A \times (B \cap C)]$ and use the result of example 4 to prove that $A \times (B \cap C) = (A \times B) \cap (A \times C)$.

4. Using the method of number 3, prove the following:

(i) $(A \cup B) \times C = (A \times C) \cup (B \times C)$

(ii) $(A \cap B) \times C = (A \times C) \cap (B \times C)$

(iii) $A \times (B \cup C) = (A \times B) \cup (A \times C)$.

4.2. Relations

A **relation** R from the set A to the set B is any subset of $A \times B$. A relation R from A to B is often denoted by "bRa", where $a \in A$ and $b \in B$, to signify that the ordered pair (a, b) is a member of R. bRa is read "b is related to a". In a more detailed discussion, R would be called a **binary relation** since it deals with ordered *pairs*. For example if $A = \{1, 2, 3\}$ and $B = \{a, b\}$, then $R = \{(1, a), (1, b), (2, b), (3, a)\}$ is a relation from A to B. If $R = \{(x, y): y \geqslant x^2, x, y \in R^*\}$, then R is a set of ordered pairs (x, y), i.e. a subset of $R^* \times R^*$; R is illustrated in Fig. 4.4. If R is a relation from the set A to the set B, then the **domain** of R is defined to be

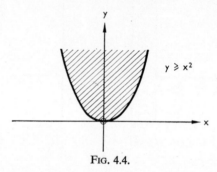

FIG. 4.4.

the set of all first elements of the ordered pairs which belong to R, i.e. domain $= \{a: a \in A, (a, b) \in R\}$. The **range** of R is defined to be the set of all second elements of the ordered pairs which belong to R, i.e. range $= \{b: b \in B, (a, b) \in R\}$. So, in the first of the above examples, the domain $= \{1, 2, 3\}$, and the range $= \{a, b\}$, and in the second example, the domain $= \{x: |x| \leqslant +\sqrt{y}, x, y \in R^*\}$ and the range $= \{y: y \geqslant x^2, x, y \in R^*\}$.

Inverse relations

Every relation R from A to B has an inverse relation R^{-1} from B to A which is defined by,

$$R^{-1} = \{(b, a) : (a, b) \in R\}.$$

Thus the domain of R is the range of R^{-1}, and the range of R is the domain of R^{-1}. For example, if $A = \{u, v, w\}$ and $B = \{a, b\}$, then $R = \{(u, b), (v, a), (w, a), (w, b)\}$ is a relation from A to B, and $R^{-1} = \{(b, u), (a, v), (a, w), (b, w)\}$, is the inverse relation from B to A. On the other hand, suppose we have the following relation in the set $S = \{1, 2, 3, 4, 5, 6\}$,

$$R = \{(1, 2), (1, 3), (1, 4), (5, 6)\},$$

then the inverse relation R^{-1} in S is given by,

$$R^{-1} = \{(2, 1), (3, 1), (4, 1), (6, 5)\}.$$

Reflexive relations

Let R be a subset of $A \times A$, then R is called a **reflexive relation** if, for every $a \in A$, $(a, a) \in R$. So, R is reflexive if every element in A is related to itself, i.e. aRa. For example, the relation "is similar to" in the set of all triangles is reflexive, since any one triangle is similar to itself. Suppose we consider the relation $R = \{(1, 1), (2, 4), (2, 2), (4, 1), (3, 3), (4, 4)\}$ in the set $A = \{1, 2, 3, 4\}$; then R is reflexive since for every $a \in A$, we have $(a, a) \in R$. Consider, on the other hand, the relation $R = \{(a, a), (b, c), (c, a), (c, c)\}$ in the set $B = \{a, b, c\}$; then R is *not* reflexive since $(b, b) \notin R$.

Symmetric relations

If R is a relation in A, then it is called a **symmetric relation** if, for $a, b \in A$, $(a, b) \in R \Rightarrow (b, a) \in R$, i.e. $bRa \Rightarrow aRb$. For example, the relation "is similar to" in the set of all triangles is a symmetric relation, since if triangle a is similar to triangle b, then it is clear that triangle b is similar to triangle a. On the other hand, the relation "is divided by" in the set J^+, is *not* symmetric, since (to produce a single counterexample) 6 is divided by 3, but 3 is not divided by 6, i.e. $(6, 3) \in R$ but $(3, 6) \notin R$.

Since R^{-1} is the inverse of R if $(b, a) \in R^{-1}$ where $(a, b) \in R$, then it immediately follows that R is symmetric only if $R = R^{-1}$.

Transitive relations

If R is a relation in A, then it is called a **transitive relation** if, for a, b, $c \in A$, $(a, b) \in R$ and $(b, c) \in R \Rightarrow (a, c) \in R$, i.e. $bRa \wedge cRb \Rightarrow cRa$, or $cRb \wedge bRa \Rightarrow cRa$. For example, the relation "is less than" in the set J^+ is transitive; for if a, b, $c \in J^+$, then $(a < b) \wedge (b < c) \Rightarrow a < c$. However, if we consider the relation $R = \{(1, 2), (2, 3), (1, 3), (2, 1), (1, 1)\}$ in the set $V = \{1, 2, 3\}$, then R is *not* transitive since $(2, 1) \in R \wedge (1, 2) \in R \nRightarrow (2, 2) \in R$ since $(2, 2) \notin R$.

Equivalence relations

An equivalence relation is one which is

(a) reflexive,
(b) symmetric,
(c) transitive.

One of the most important examples of an equivalence relation is that of "equality":

For any a, b, $c \in S$,

(a) $a = a$ (Reflexive)
(b) $a = b \Rightarrow b = a$ (Symmetric)
(c) $(a = b) \wedge (b = c) \Rightarrow a = c$ (Transitive).

The relation "is similar to" in the set of all triangles is an equivalence relation.

EXAMPLES

1. Illustrate the following relations graphically; in each case x, $y \in R^*$.

(a) $y = x^3$ (b) $y \leqslant x^3$ (c) $y \geqslant \sin x$ (d) $x^2 + y^2 \leqslant 16$ (e) $xy > 1$.

Note that the curve is drawn with dashes if the points on it do not belong to the relation.

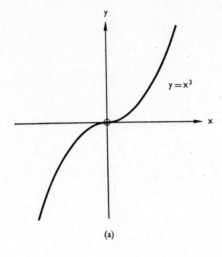

(a)

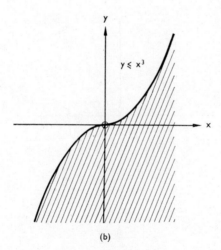

(b)

Fig. 4.5.

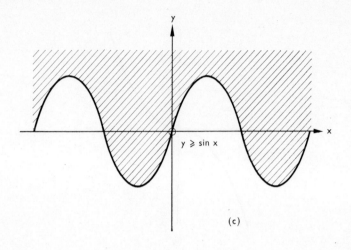

$y \geqslant \sin x$

(c)

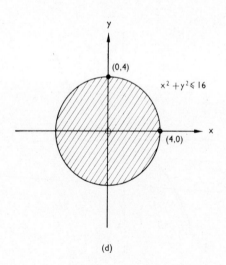

(0,4)

$x^2 + y^2 \leqslant 16$

(4,0)

(d)

Fig. 4.5—cont.

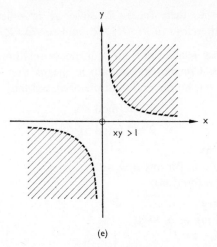

(e)

FIG. 4.5—*cont.*

2. Let R be the relation $3x + y = 12$ in the set J^+ of natural numbers, i.e. let $R = \{(x, y): x, y \in J^+, 3x + y = 12\}$. Find the domain and range of (a) R and (b) R^{-1}.

Note first that the solution set of $3x + y = 12$ in the set of natural numbers is $\{(1, 9), (2, 6), (3, 3)\}$. Thus $R = \{(1, 9), (2, 6), (3, 3)\}$, and $R^{-1} = \{(9, 1), (6, 2), (3, 3)\}$.

(a) Domain of $R = \{1, 2, 3\}$
    range of $R = \{9, 6, 3\}$.
(b) domain of $R^{-1} = \{9, 6, 3\}$
    range of $R^{-1} = \{1, 2, 3\}$.

3. Let R and R' be relations in a set A. Prove each of the following statements:

(a) If R and R' are both symmetric, then $R \cup R'$ is symmetric.

(b) If R is reflexive and R' is any relation, then $R \cup R'$ is reflexive.

(a) Let $(a, b) \in R \cup R'$, then $(a, b) \in R \lor (a, b) \in R'$ and since both R and R' are symmetric, then $(b, a) \in R$ or $(b, a) \in R'$, i.e. $(b, a) \in R \cup R'$. Therefore $R \cup R'$ is symmetric.

(b) Let $a \in A$, then $(a, a) \in R$, since R is reflexive. Now, $R \subseteq R \cup R'$, therefore $(a, a) \in R \cup R'$, and so $R \cup R'$ is reflexive.

4. **Congruence modulo m** is an equivalence relation in the set J of all integers. Congruence modulo m means that for integers a, b, $m \in J$, $a - b$ is an integral multiple of m, written:

$$a \equiv b \pmod{m}.$$

For example, $2 \equiv 7 \pmod 5$.

(i) **Reflexivity**

Now, $a - a = 0 \times m$ for any a, $m \in J$.
Therefore $a \equiv a \pmod m$.

(ii) **Symmetry**

If $a \equiv b \pmod m$, a, b, $m \in J$,
i.e. $a - b = km$, $k \in J$,
then $b - a = (-k)m$,
i.e. $b \equiv a \pmod m$.

(iii) **Transitivity**

If $a \equiv b \pmod m$ and $b \equiv c \pmod m$, a, b, c, $m \in J$,
i.e. $a - b = k_1 m$ and $b - c = k_2 m$, k_1, $k_2 \in J$, then adding,

$$(a - c) = (k_1 + k_2)m,$$

i.e. $a \equiv c \pmod m$.

EXERCISES 4b

1. Let R be the relation from $A = \{5, 6, 7, 8\}$ to $B = \{5, 7, 9\}$ defined by $a < b$, where $a \in A$, and $b \in B$. Write R as a set of ordered pairs and plot R on a coordinate diagram of $A \times B$.

2. Let R be the relation from $A = \{1, 2, 3, 4\}$ to $B = \{5, 6, 7, 8, 9\}$ defined by "a divides b", where $a \in A$ and $b \in B$. Write R as a set of ordered pairs and plot R on a coordinate diagram of $A \times B$.

3. Illustrate the following relations graphically; in each case x, $y \in R^*$.

(a) $y = x^2$ (b) $y \geqslant x^3 - 4$ (c) $y < -x^3$ (d) $x^2 - 4y^2 > 9$ (e) $y \leqslant 5 - x$.

4. Prove that for any set A, the relation $R = A \times A$ is reflexive.

5. Prove that if R and R' are relations in a set A, then:
(a) $R \cap R'$ is symmetric if R and R' are both symmetric.
(b) If R is transitive, then R^{-1} is transitive.

6. The relation R in the set J of integers, is defined by "x and y are both even". What sort of relation is R? If, on the other hand, R is defined by "x and y are both odd", what sort of relation is R now?

7. In the case of an equivalence relation, is it possible to deduce the property of reflexivity from the properties of symmetry and transitivity? Illustrate using the two examples in question 6 above. (*Hint:* use only two elements x and y (say) when considering the equivalence relation.)

8. If $a \equiv b \pmod{m}$ and $c \equiv d \pmod{m}$, then prove that $a + c \equiv b + d \pmod{m}$, $a - c \equiv b - d \pmod{m}$ and, $ac \equiv bd \pmod{m}$.

9. Prove that logical equivalence (see Chapter 1) is an equivalence relation, thereby showing that the terminology is consistent.

4.3. Equivalence classes. Partitions

If R is an equivalence relation in a set A and a is any element of A, then the **equivalence class** S_a is defined to be the subset of all elements $b \in A$ such that bRa. For example, the equivalence relation R defined by "$x \equiv y \pmod{5}$" in the set of integers J leads to the equivalence classes listed:

Equivalence classes	Element a
$J_0 = \{\ldots -5, 0, 5, 10 \ldots\}$	0
$J_1 = \{\ldots -4, 1, 6, 11 \ldots\}$	1
$J_2 = \{\ldots -3, 2, 7, 12 \ldots\}$	2
$J_3 = \{\ldots -2, 3, 8, 13 \ldots\}$	3
$J_4 = \{\ldots -1, 4, 9, 14 \ldots\}$	4

The element a is typical of a particular equivalence class; thus in the above example, $a = 1$ is typical of J_1—although, of course, any other element in J_1 would be equally as typical. These typical elements are called **canonical forms.** Put another way, each canonical form uniquely determines an equivalence class. That an equivalence class is unique follows immediately from the definition: suppose $b \in S_b$, then all elements in S_b are related to b; but $a \in S_b$, and so all elements are also related to a; the equivalence class S_b could therefore be written S_a, or in other words $S_a = S_b$. So we could view an equivalence relation in a set as a relation splitting the set into exhaustive and disjoint subsets; each subset being an equivalence class, and a particular splitting (as determined by a particular equivalence relation) is called a **partition**. Thus, in the above example, $J = \{J_0, J_1, J_2, J_3, J_4\}$ is one partition of J; another partition of J is given by: $J = \{J_0, J_1\}$ where $J_0 = \{x: x = 2y, x, y \in J\}$ and $J_1 = \{x: x = 2y+1, x, y \in J\}$, i.e. J_0 is the set of even integers, and J_1 is the set of odd integers—the equivalence relation being defined by "congruence modulo 2".

EXERCISES 4c

1. There are three possible types of order in a set S of numbers:

    (i) *Complete ordering.*
        For any $a, b \in S$, either $a < b$ or $b < a$.
    (ii) *Partial ordering.*
        For any $a, b \in S$, either $a < b$ or $a = b$ or $b > a$.
    (iii) *Weak ordering.*
        For any $a, b \in S$, either $a < b$ or $a = b$ or $b > a$ or a and b not comparable.

Taking the order relation in S to be $<$ in case (i) and $\leqslant$ in both cases (ii) and (iii), show that a completely ordered set is partitioned into equivalence classes—each class containing *only one* element; that partially and weakly ordered sets are partitioned into equivalence classes—each class containing *at least one* element. Show, further, that the equivalence classes in completely and partially ordered sets can themselves be completely ordered; whereas in a weakly ordered set, the equivalence classes cannot be completely ordered.

2. Referring to the question above and writing R for the order relation, then if for any $a, b \in S$, we have either aRb or bRa, then R is called **complete**. Show that a complete ordering is irreflexive (i.e. not reflexive), antisymmetric (i.e. not symmetric), transitive and complete; that a partial ordering is reflexive, can be symmetric—in which case $a = b$, transitive and complete; that a weak ordering is reflexive, can be symmetric—in which case $a = b$, transitive and incomplete.

3. Write out the equivalence classes and their canonical forms formed by the equivalence relation "$x \equiv y \pmod 4$" in the set of integers J. Show also that $x \equiv y \pmod 4 \Leftrightarrow x \equiv y \pmod{-4}$, and that in general, $x \equiv y \pmod m$ $\Leftrightarrow x \equiv y \pmod{-m}$.

4. Prove that the following relations each form a partition in the set of integers J:

    (a) $(a,b)\, R\, (c,d)$, $a, b, c, d \in J$, where R is defined by $a+d = b+c$.
    (b) $(a,b)\, R\, (c,d)$, $a, b, c, d \in J$, where R is defined by $ad = bc$.

5. List the equivalence classes formed in question 1, Exercises 2c in Chapter 2. What is the equivalence relation here?

4.4. Order relations

The concept of a relation provides a more general framework for investigating the properties of order. Ordering of a set of numbers is dealt with in the section on number systems in Chapter 6, and relevant questions to this section (4.4) have been set in exercises 4c (nos. 1 and 2). If one is to attempt a general definition of order in a set, the relations denoted by $<$ and $\leqslant$ cannot be used to indicate the *relative magnitudes* of the elements; for, in a set S of numbers, $a < b$ means $b - a$ positive, and for *any set a* and b can be anything we care to choose; magnitude, then, becomes a meaningless concept in general. However, there are certain properties of ordered sets of numbers that can be used as definitions of order in sets in general; these properties for the three possible types of ordering have been stated in the questions 1 and 2 mentioned above. These properties do not rely upon the concept of magnitude and are tabulated for reference:

For any a, b, $c \in S$

(i) *Complete ordering*
  Irreflexive ($a\mathcal{R}a$)
  Antisymmetric ($aRb \not\Rightarrow bRa$)
  Transitive ($aRb \wedge bRc \Rightarrow aRc$)
  Complete ($a\mathcal{R}b \Rightarrow bRa$).

(ii) *Partial ordering*
  Reflexive (aRa)
  Equivalent ($aRb \wedge bRa \Rightarrow a = b$)
  Transitive ($aRb \wedge bRc \Rightarrow aRc$)
  Complete ($a\mathcal{R}b \Rightarrow bRa$).

(iii) *Weak ordering*
  Reflexive (aRa)
  Equivalent ($aRb \wedge bRa \Rightarrow a = b$)
  Transitive ($aRb \wedge bRc \Rightarrow aRc$)
  Incomplete ($a\mathcal{R}b \Rightarrow bRa$ or $a\mathcal{R}b \not\Rightarrow bRa$, i.e. a and b may or may not be related either way).

For example, in a Boolean algebra the order relation denoted by $\leqslant$ is a weak one; the proof is left as an exercise to the reader [see Chapter 2, Exercises 2b, no. 12 and note that $(a+b \neq b)$ $\not\Rightarrow (a+b = a)$ in general].

4.5. Functions

A **function** f is defined to be a relation from a set X to a set Y such that for any $x \in X$, we have $y \in Y$ uniquely determined. Thus, $f \subset \{(x,y): x \in X, y \in Y \wedge y \text{ unique}\}$. Just as a relation R from A to B is often denoted by bRa, where $a \in A$ and $b \in B$, we denote a function f from X to Y by yfx or $y = f(x)$ (read "y equals f of x"). More strictly we should call f a **single-valued function** since each $x \in X$ determines one and only one $y \in Y$; in other words each first element x in the number pairs (x,y) occur only once in f. As an example of a function, consider $y = x^2$ whose graph is shown in Fig. 4.6.

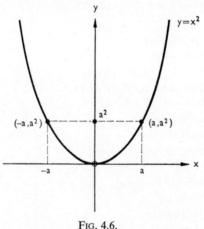

FIG. 4.6.

Here $X = R^*$ and $Y = R_0^{*+}$, where R^* and R_0^{*+} are the sets of all real numbers and all non-negative real numbers respectively. Two ordered pairs of the function are shown: (a, a^2) and $(-a, a^2)$; although $y = a^2$ corresponds to either $x = a$ or $x = -a$, each x corresponds to one and only one y.

Consider on the other hand, the relation defined by $y^2 = x$; this relation is not a function, or more strictly a single-valued function, since each y corresponds to two x's. However, the relations defined by $(y^2 = x) \wedge (y \geqslant 0)$ and $(y^2 = x) \wedge (y \leqslant 0)$ are single-valued functions, and their graphs are shown in Figs. 4.7 and 4.8.

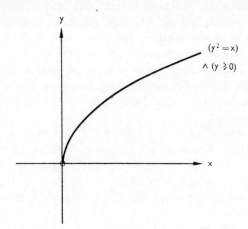

FIG. 4.7.

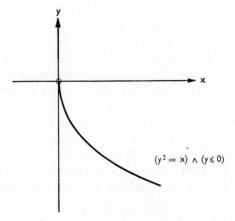

FIG. 4.8.

So, the relation $y^2 = x$ may be considered to be the union of two single-valued functions, i.e.

$$(y^2 = x) \Leftrightarrow [(y^2 = x) \wedge (y \geqslant 0)] \cup [(y^2 = x) \wedge (y \leqslant 0)].$$

In general though, a relation cannot be considered as the union of n single-valued functions (n integral); this follows from the definitions of relation and function. However, when a relation is the union of n single-valued functions, we call the relation an **n-valued function.** Thus the above example ($y^2 = x$) is a two-valued function. The essential features of an n-valued function may therefore be studied by concentrating in turn on each of its single-valued functions; we accordingly limit our discussion to single-valued functions.

The **domain** of a function is the *set* X such that for any $x \in X$, $y = f(x)$ exists. The **range** of a function is a *subset* of Y such that for any $y \in Y$, $y = f(x)$ exists. So in the above examples, the domains of $y = x^2$, $(y^2 = x) \wedge (y \geqslant 0)$, and $(y^2 = x) \wedge (y \leqslant 0)$ are R^*, R_0^{*+} and R_0^{*+}, respectively; their ranges are R_0^{*+}, R_0^{*+} and R_0^{*-}, respectively.

Another definition of a function will now be given in terms of a **mapping:** the function $y = f(x)$ is a mapping from a set X to a set Y, denoted by $X \xrightarrow{f} Y$ such that to each $x \in X$ there is a unique **image** $y \in Y$. If the set Y is the range of the function, then we say that X **maps on to** Y; otherwise if the range of the function is a subset of Y, then we say that X **maps into** Y. This definition in terms of a mapping illustrates certain interesting aspects of a function; for example, take the function which maps the set $A = \{a, b, c, d, e\}$ into the set $B = \{1, 2, 3, 4, 5, 6, 7, 8\}$ as shown in Fig. 4.9. The function or mapping (same thing) can be written down as: $a \to 8$, $b \to 7$, $c \to 4$, $d \to 7$, $e \to 4$. The set A is mapped into set B, and the domain of the function is $\{a, b, c, d, e\}$ and the range is $\{4, 7, 8\}$. (Note that if any element in A had not been mapped into B, then $A \xrightarrow{f} B$ would *not* be a function, whereas any element in B need not be the image of an element in A for $A \xrightarrow{f} B$ to be a function.)

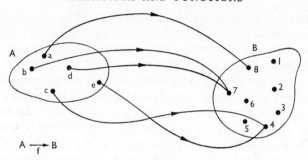

FIG. 4.9.

The notion that a function is a mapping illustrates very well what we mean by a **function of a function**; if a function f maps a set A into a set B and a function g maps the set B into a set C, then for any element $x \in A$ we have the image $f(x) \in B$, and the element $f(x) \in B$ has the image $g[f(x)] \in C$. We define, therefore, $g[f(x)]$ to be a function of a function and this is represented diagrammatically in Fig. 4.10. The domain of $B \underset{g}{\to} C$ is the range

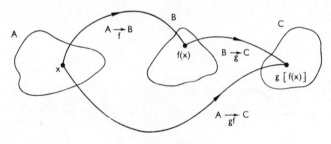

FIG. 4.10.

of $A \underset{f}{\to} B$. Another example of a function of a function is $y = \log_e \tan x$; here if one writes $v = f(x) = \tan x$, then $y = \log_e v = g(v)$ (say), and $f(x) = X \underset{f}{\to} V$, and $g(v) = V \underset{g}{\to} Y$, where $x \in X$, $y \in Y$.

We now define an **inverse function**. If we have a function f from a set X to a set Y, then the inverse function f^{-1}, *if it exists*,

E

is a function from the set Y to the set X, i.e. $f^{-1} \subset \{(y, x): y \in Y, x \in x \land x \text{ unique}\}$. Now, since $f \subset \{(x, y): x \in X, y \in Y \land y \text{ unique}\}$, the *necessary condition* for f^{-1} to exist is that the domain of f should be the range of f^{-1}, and the range of f should be the domain of f^{-1}. In terms of a mapping, since all $x \in X$ are uniquely determined and all $y \in Y$ are uniquely determined, X is mapped *on to* Y; furthermore, we have a one–one correspondence between the sets X and Y. If one draws graphs of a function and its inverse on the same diagram, then one graph is the reflection of the other in the line $y = x$ (itself a function, of course); this follows immediately from the definitions of a function and its inverse and the diagram in Fig. 4.11 illustrates the reflection of a typical point (x, y). (Note that the scales on each axis must be the same. For Q to be the reflection of P, $PT = TQ$, and PQ must be perpendicular to the line $y = x$.

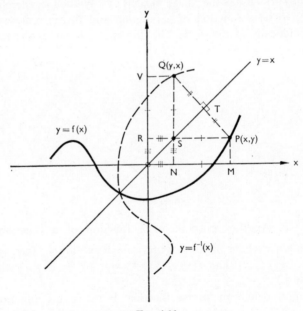

Fɪɢ. 4.11.

Now, $\triangle TPS \equiv \triangle TSQ \Rightarrow SP = SQ$,

and since $QN \parallel y$-axis and $PR \parallel x$-axis, $RSNO$ is a square.

Thus, $\qquad QN = QS + SN = RS + SP = x,$

and $\qquad VQ = ON = NS = y.$

Often a function or mapping is called a **transformation**, and is usually denoted by T. Thus, in the example $A \xrightarrow{f} B$ shown in Fig. 4.9, we would write $A \xrightarrow{T} B$, and $T(a) \to 8$, $T(b) \to 7$, $T(c) \to 4$, $T(d) \to 7$, and $T(e) \to 4$, and say that the elements a, b, etc., have been **transformed** into the elements 8, 7, etc. In the case $y = f(x)$ and its inverse $y = f^{-1}(x)$ illustrated in Fig. 4.11, we could write $T(x, y) \to (y, x)$ to show that all points $(x, y) \in f$ have been transformed into the points $(y, x) \in f^{-1}$; the transformation T reflects all points (x, y) in the line $y = x$. In general, a transformation T transforms an m-tuple $(x_1, x_2, \ldots, x_m)$ into an n-tuple $(y_1, y_2, \ldots, y_n)$; however, all that the reader is likely to encounter at this level are transformations of pairs into pairs or triples into triples. For example, the linear transformation $T(x_1, x_2, x_3) \to (y_1, y_2, y_3)$ given by the following equations:

$$y_1 = a_{11}x_1 + a_{12}x_2 + a_{13}x_3$$
$$y_2 = a_{21}x_1 + a_{22}x_2 + a_{23}x_3$$
$$y_3 = a_{31}x_1 + a_{32}x_2 + a_{33}x_3,$$

where a_{ij} ($i = 1, 2, 3$; $j = 1, 2, 3$) are constants, is dealt with in Chapter 5.

So, we have three terms—namely, function, mapping, and transformation, which all have the same meaning. These terms are used, then, when we wish to illustrate different aspects of the same concept: function in terms of number pairs, mapping in terms of an element and its image, and transformation as a special kind of mapping—that of a set of m-tuples into a set of n-tuples in general.

EXERCISES 4d

1. Let the domain of the function $f(x) = x^2 + 2$ be all the real values of x given by $-3 \leqslant x \leqslant 5$. Find the following:

(a) the range of $f(x)$,

(b) the values of $f(-1)$, $f(2)$, $f(u+2)$,

(c) the inequality which u must satisfy in the latter example in part (b).

Draw a graph of $f(x)$.

2. Let the function $R^* \underset{f}{\to} R^*$ be defined by

$$f(x) = \begin{cases} x^3 + 2x + 1 & \text{if } x \geqslant 1 \\ -3x + 3 & \text{if } -1 < x < 1 \\ x^2 + 5 & \text{if } x \leqslant -1 \end{cases}$$

Find the following:

(a) the domain and range of $f(x)$,

(b) the values of $f(3)$, $f(0)$, $f(-\frac{1}{2})$, $f(-5)$.

Draw a graph of $f(x)$.

3. If $A = \{1, 2\}$ and $B = \{\alpha, \beta, \gamma\}$, list all the possible functions from A to B and show that each is a subset of $A \times B$.

4. State the maximum possible domain and then determine the range for each of the following two functions to exist, where $x \in R^*$ and $y \in R^*$:

(a) $y = 1^x$ (b) $y = (-1)^x$.

5. Write down the inverse functions, where they exist, of the following functions:

(a) $y = \sin x$, where $x \in R^*$ and $y \in R^*$,

(b) $y = x^2$, where $x \in R^*$ and $y \in R^*$,

(c) $y = \dfrac{1}{x}$, where $x \in R^*$ and $y \in R^*$, except $x = 0$.

(d) $y = \sin\left(\dfrac{1}{x}\right)$, where $x \in R^*$ and $y \in R^*$, except $x = 0$.

(e) $A \underset{f}{\to} B$, where $A = \{a, b, c, d, e\}$, $B = \{1, 2, a, 5\}$, and

$f = \{(a, 1), (b, a), (c, 2), (d, 5), (e, 2)\}$.

(f) $X \underset{g}{\to} Y$, where $X = \{1, 2, 3\} = Y$, and $g = \{(1, 2), (2, 4), (3, 2), (4, 4)\}$.

(g) $S \underset{f}{\to} T$, where $S = \{1, 2, 3\}$, $T \subset J$ (set of integers), and

$f = \{(1, 2), (2, 5), (3, 9)\}$.

6. Draw diagrams to illustrate the functions and their inverses (where they exist) listed in question 5.

7. If $f(x) = x^3 - 2x + 2$ and $g(x) = 3x + 4$, find $f[g(x)]$ and $g[f(x)]$.

8. If T_1, T_2 and T_3 are transformations such that $T_1(A) \to B$, $T_2(B) \to C$, and $T_3(C) \to D$, where A, B, C and D are sets, prove that $(T_3 . T_2) . T_1 = T_3 . (T_2 . T_1)$ (**associative property**); where $T_i . T_j$ means first map according to T_j, then map according to T_i. Further, show that the operation of "function of a function" is exactly analogous to that of combining transformations as defined above.

9. Show that there exists an **identity transformation** I (defined by $IT = TI = T$) such that for any transformation T and its inverse T^{-1} (where it exists), $T^{-1}T = TT^{-1} = I$. Illustrate in the case of the transformation $T(x,y) \rightarrow (x',y')$ given by the linear equations:

$$x' = ax + by$$
$$y' = -bx + ay,$$

where $x, y, x', y', a, b \in R^*$ and a, b are constants.

10. Show that the transformation $T(x,y) \rightarrow (x',y')$ given in question 9, maps straight lines into straight lines in the Cartesian plane. Illustrate geometrically. Further, show that this transformation maps circles into circles. (*Hint*: consider any straight line $lx + my + n = 0$, or in the case of a circle $x^2 + y^2 + 2gx + 2fy + c = 0$, replace x and y by the linear expressions obtained for T^{-1} in question 9—this way one obtains equations with respect to the x', y' plane.)

11. Show that for any transformation T, the inverse transformation T^{-1} and the identity transformation I are both unique.

CHAPTER 5

Matrices

5.1. Definition of a matrix

One often encounters certain patterns in mathematics called **arrays**. For example the multiplication table below is an array of positive integers; it has 3 rows and 3 columns.

Multiplication table

×	1	2	4
1	1	2	4
2	2	4	8
4	4	8	16

Array

1	2	4
2	4	8
4	8	16

Consider on the other hand the coefficients of the four equations in three unknowns:

$$3x + y + 2z = 0$$
$$2x - 3y + 4z = 0$$
$$x + y - z = 0$$
$$5x - 2y + 7z = 0$$

We may *list* the coefficients of these equations in the form of an array:

3	1	2
2	-3	4
1	1	-1
5	-2	7

This array has 4 rows and 3 columns; note that we have written down the array in a particular **order,** i.e. the order in which the coefficients in the above equations appear is **preserved** in the array.

Patterns of this sort, or arrays, are to be met in many fields other than mathematics; for example, consider the four-terminal network shown in Fig. 5.1.

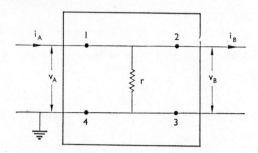

Fig. 5.1.

Here one has a box with four terminals 1, 2, 3 and 4 (the box may have an assortment of electrical components inside it, but we consider for simplicity a shunt resistance r only), an input current i_A, input potential (relative to earth) v_A, output current i_B, and an output potential (again relative to earth) v_B. Clearly, $v_A = v_B$, and since a current v_A/r (Ohm's law) leaks to earth, $i_B = i_A - (v_A/r)$. Now suppose the box contains a resistance r across the terminals 1 and 2 as shown in Fig. 5.2.

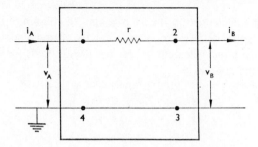

Fig. 5.2.

Here $i_A = i_B$, and $v_B = v_A - i_A r$ (Ohm's law). For the two simple cases considered, v_B and i_B are linearly dependent on v_A and i_A and are given by:

$$v_B = v_A + 0i_A$$

$$i_B = \frac{-v_A}{r} + i_A \qquad \text{for the shunt } r \text{ (Fig. 5.1)}$$

and

$$v_B = v_A - ri_A$$

$$i_B = 0v_A + i_A \qquad \text{for the series resistance } r \text{ (Fig. 5.2)}.$$

The coefficients of the two pairs of linear equations written as arrays are:

$$\begin{array}{cc} 1 & 0 \\[2mm] \dfrac{-1}{r} & 1 \end{array} \qquad \text{for the shunt } r$$

and

$$\begin{array}{cc} 1 & -r \\[2mm] 0 & 1 \end{array} \qquad \text{for the series resistance } r.$$

Linear circuits like those above are important in the design of electrical filters.

We now define a **matrix** as an array of the elements a_{ij} of a set; in general, the matrix has m rows and n columns and is written:

$$\begin{pmatrix} a_{11} & a_{12} & \cdots & a_{1n} \\ a_{21} & a_{22} & \cdots & a_{2n} \\ \cdot & \cdot & \cdots & \cdot \\ a_{m1} & a_{m2} & \cdots & a_{mn} \end{pmatrix}$$

Thus a_{ij} is the element in the ith row and jth column of the $m \times n$ matrix. Capital letters are often used to denote matrices, and sometimes a typical element in brackets (a_{ij}) is used; for example, the 4×3 matrix

$$\begin{pmatrix} b_{11} & b_{12} & b_{13} \\ b_{21} & b_{22} & b_{23} \\ b_{31} & b_{32} & b_{33} \\ b_{41} & b_{42} & b_{43} \end{pmatrix}$$

could be denoted by B or (b_{ij}), $i = 1, 2, 3, 4$; $j = 1, 2, 3$.

An $m \times 1$ matrix, i.e. a matrix consisting of a single column, is called a **column vector,** and contains m elements. For example,

$$\begin{pmatrix} a_1 \\ a_2 \\ a_3 \\ a_4 \\ a_5 \end{pmatrix}$$

is a column vector containing 5 elements.

A $1 \times m$ matrix, i.e. a matrix consisting of a single row, is called a **row vector,** and contains m elements. For example,

$$(x_1, x_2, x_3)$$

is a row vector containing 3 elements.

An $n \times n$ matrix is called a **square matrix** of order n. So, the arrays exhibited in the multiplication table, and in the linear equations representing the four-terminal networks, are all square matrices of orders 3, 2 and 2, respectively.

A 1×1 matrix is called a **scalar;** a scalar, then, consists of a single element and is a square matrix of order 1. Brackets around a scalar (a) are often omitted.

Two matrices are said to be **equal** if and only if the elements of one are equal to the elements of another and are in the same corresponding positions. So if the two matrices (a_{ij}) and (b_{ij}) are equal, then $a_{ij} = b_{ij}$ for all pairs i, j.

5.2. Addition of matrices

Let (a_{ij}) and (b_{ij}) be two matrices, then their **sum** is defined to be the matrix (c_{ij}) where

$$c_{ij} = a_{ij} + b_{ij}.$$

Clearly for two matrices to be **conformable** for addition, i.e. for their sum to exist, then the number of rows of one must equal the number of rows of the other, and likewise for their columns. For example,

$$\begin{pmatrix} -1 & 2 & 4 & -3 \\ 0 & 3 & -2 & 1 \\ 5 & -6 & 3 & -1 \end{pmatrix} + \begin{pmatrix} 0 & 1 & 1 & 2 \\ -3 & 1 & 0 & 4 \\ 7 & -2 & 1 & 3 \end{pmatrix}$$

$$= \begin{pmatrix} -1 & 3 & 5 & -1 \\ -3 & 4 & -2 & 5 \\ 12 & -8 & 4 & 2 \end{pmatrix}.$$

If two matrices (a_{ij}) and (b_{ij}) are conformable for addition then their **difference** $A - B$ is defined to be the matrix (c_{ij}) where

$$c_{ij} = a_{ij} - b_{ij}.$$

The **null matrix** 0 is defined to be any matrix *all* of whose elements are zero. Thus, for any matrix (a_{ij})

$$0 + (a_{ij}) = (a_{ij}).$$

EXERCISES 5a

1. If $A = \begin{pmatrix} 2 & 3 & 4 \\ 1 & 2 & 3 \end{pmatrix}$, $B = \begin{pmatrix} 5 & -3 & 2 \\ 1 & -2 & 0 \end{pmatrix}$,

and $C = \begin{pmatrix} 1 & 3 & 2 \\ -4 & 6 & 5 \end{pmatrix}$,

find (a) $A + B$ (b) $B + C$ (c) $A + (B + C)$ (d) $(A + B) + C$.

2. Prove that addition of matrices (where conformable) is commutative and associative.

3. Vector law of addition (using the word vector in the physical sense).

Two vectors v_1 and v_2 (see Fig. 5.3) may be completely specified by the two matrices (x_1, y_1) and (x_2, y_2). Show that their resultant $R = v_1 + v_2$ is given by

$$R = (x_1, y_1) + (x_2, y_2).$$

Interpret $(x_1, y_1) - (x_2, y_2)$.

Note that we have also the basis for the definition of the sum of two complex numbers.

4. Prove by induction that for any matrix (a_{ij}) and **any positive integral scalar** k that $k(a_{ij}) = (ka_{ij})$.

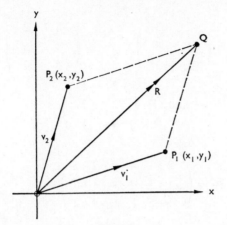

Fig. 5.3.

5.3. Scalar multiplication of matrices

If k is any scalar and (a_{ij}) is any matrix, then the **scalar product** of k and (a_{ij}) is defined to be the matrix (ka_{ij}). For example, λA, where

$$A = \begin{pmatrix} \alpha & \beta \\ \gamma & \delta \\ \varepsilon & \zeta \end{pmatrix}$$

is

$$\begin{pmatrix} \lambda\alpha & \lambda\beta \\ \lambda\gamma & \lambda\delta \\ \lambda\varepsilon & \lambda\zeta \end{pmatrix}.$$

If $(a_{ij}), (b_{ij}), (c_{ij}), \ldots$, are matrices conformable for addition, and $k_1, k_2, k_3, \ldots$, are scalars, then

$$k_1(a_{ij}) + k_2(b_{ij}) + k_3(c_{ij}) + \ldots$$
$$= (k_1 a_{ij}) + (k_2 b_{ij}) + (k_3 c_{ij}) + \ldots$$
$$= (k_1 a_{ij} + k_2 b_{ij} + k_3 c_{ij} + \ldots).$$

For example, if

$$A = \begin{pmatrix} 2 & 3 \\ -1 & 4 \\ 1 & 0 \end{pmatrix}, \qquad B = \begin{pmatrix} -1 & 2 \\ 3 & 1 \\ 5 & 4 \end{pmatrix}$$

$$\text{and } C = \begin{pmatrix} 2 & -1 \\ 2 & 3 \\ -4 & 1 \end{pmatrix},$$

then

$$A - B + 2C = \begin{pmatrix} 2+1+4 & 3-2-2 \\ -1-3+4 & 4-1+6 \\ 1-5-8 & 0-4+2 \end{pmatrix} = \begin{pmatrix} 7 & -1 \\ 0 & 9 \\ -12 & -2 \end{pmatrix}.$$

5.4. Linear transformations

Before starting the theory of multiplication of matrices, we take a brief glimpse at transformations once more—in particular linear transformations. The reader who has not read the section on transformations in Chapter 4, especially questions 8, 9, 10 and 11, Exercise 4d, is advised to do so now. The ensuing discussion refers to Cartesian axes in the plane.

Reflections

The transformation T which maps all points (x, y) to points (x', y') given by

$$x' = x$$
$$y' = -y \qquad \text{(i)}$$

is shown in Fig. 5.4. Thus T reflects all points in the x-axis. Similarly, the transformation which reflects all points in the y-axis is given by

$$x' = -x$$
$$y' = y. \qquad \text{(ii)}$$

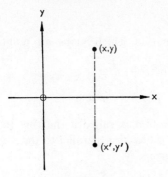

FIG. 5.4.

The transformation which reflects all points in the origin is given by

$$x' = -x$$
$$y' = -y \qquad \text{(iii)}$$

and is shown in Fig. 5.5. Thus if T_1, T_2 and T_3 are the transforma-

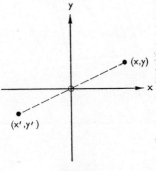

FIG. 5.5.

tions given by the equations (i), (ii) and (iii) respectively, then $T_3 = T_1T_2 = T_2T_1$ (note the commutativity). (See question 8, Exercise 4d in Chapter 4.)

Shearings

The transformation which maps all points (x, y) to points (x', y') given by

$$x' = x + ky$$
$$y' = y, \qquad (iv)$$

where k is a constant is called a shearing transformation, and moves points in a direction parallel to the x-axis. Similarly, the transformation given by

$$x' = x$$
$$y' = y + kx \qquad (v)$$

moves points in a direction parallel to the y-axis. The diagram in Fig. 5.6 shows how a parallelogram has been sheared in a direction

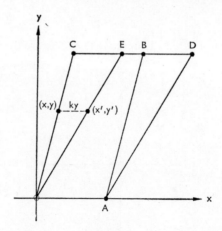

FIG. 5.6.

parallel to the x-axis. If T_4 and T_5 are the transformations given by the equations (iv) and (v) respectively, then $T_4 T_5 = T_5 T_4 = T$, where T is the transformation that shears along the x- and y-axes. Again, note the commutativity.

Rotations

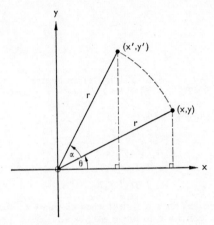

FIG. 5.7.

Suppose now that all points (x, y) are rotated through an angle α (counterclockwise sense taken as positive); then referring to the diagram in Fig. 5.7,

$$x = r\cos\theta \qquad x' = r\cos(\theta + \alpha)$$
$$y = r\sin\theta \qquad y' = r\sin(\theta + \alpha),$$

and therefore upon expansion of $\cos(\theta + \alpha)$ and $\sin(\theta + \alpha)$, we have

$$x' = x\cos\alpha - y\sin\alpha$$
$$y' = x\sin\alpha + y\cos\alpha. \qquad \text{(vi)}$$

If $\alpha = \pi$, $x' = -x$ and $y' = -y$, and we have reflection in the origin, i.e. if T_6 is the transformation given by equations (vi), then when $\alpha = \pi$, $T_6 = T_3$.

EXERCISES 5b

(All questions refer to notation used in above section.)

1. Find the inverses of T_1, T_2, T_3, T_4, T_5 and T_6,
e.g. $T_2(x, y) \to (x', y')$ is given by

$$x' = -x$$
$$y' = y$$

and therefore $T_2^{-1}(x', y') \to (x, y)$ is given by

$$x = -x'$$
$$y = y',$$

i.e.

$$x' = -x$$
$$y' = y.$$

2. Which T_i $(i = 1, \ldots, 6)$ is equal to its own inverse?

3. Prove that (a) $T_1^2 = I$, (b) $T_2^2 = I$, (c) $T_3^2 = I$, where I is the identity transformation.

4. Prove the following: (a) $T_1T_3 = T_3T_1 = T_2$

(b) $T_2T_3 = T_3T_2 = T_1$

(c) $T_1T_4 \neq T_4T_1$

(d) $T_1T_6 \neq T_6T_1$

(e) $T_5T_6 \neq T_6T_5$.

The above expressions are self-evident when diagrams are drawn; however, the object of the exercise is to prove each expression analytically, e.g.

$$T_3T_6(x, y) \to T_3(x', y') \to (x'', y''),$$

where $\left.\begin{array}{l} x' = x\cos\alpha - y\sin\alpha \\ y' = x\sin\alpha + y\cos\alpha \end{array}\right\} T_6(x, y) \to (x', y')$

and

$\left.\begin{array}{l} x'' = -x' \\ y'' = -y' \end{array}\right\} T_3(x', y') \to (x'', y'')$

and therefore,

$\left.\begin{array}{l} x'' = -x\cos\alpha + y\sin\alpha \\ y'' = -x\sin\alpha - y\cos\alpha \end{array}\right\} T_3T_6(x, y) \to (x'', y'').$

Similarly,

$\left.\begin{array}{l} x'' = -x\cos\alpha + y\sin\alpha \\ y'' = -x\sin\alpha - y\cos\alpha \end{array}\right\} T_6T_3(x, y) \to (x'', y'')$

therefore

$$T_3T_6 = T_6T_3.$$

5. Verify the associative law for transformations in the following instances:

(a) $T_1(T_2T_3) = (T_1T_2)T_3$

(b) $T_3(T_4T_6) = (T_3T_4)T_6$

(c) $T_2(T_4T_5) = (T_2T_4)T_5$.

6. Write down the matrices of the coefficients of the equations given by question 4 parts (a), (b), (c).

5.5. Multiplication of matrices

It is a matter of *definition* that any linear transformation can be represented by the linear equations

$$x' = ax + by$$
$$y' = cx + dy,$$

where a, b, c, d are constants (not all zero).

Consider now, two linear transformations T_1 and T_2 given by the following equations (where double suffix notation is used for convenience).

$$\left. \begin{array}{l} x_1'' = a_{11}x_1' + a_{12}x_2' \\ x_2'' = a_{21}x_1' + a_{22}x_2' \end{array} \right\} \quad T_2(x_1', x_2') \rightarrow (x_1'', x_2'')$$

$$\left. \begin{array}{l} x_1' = b_{11}x_1 + b_{12}x_2 \\ x_2' = b_{21}x_1 + b_{22}x_2 \end{array} \right\} \quad T_1(x_1, x_2) \rightarrow (x_1', x_2').$$

We now form the "product" T_2T_1 by solving for x_1'', x_2'' in terms of x_1, x_2,

$$x_1'' = a_{11}(b_{11}x_1 + b_{12}x_2) + a_{12}(b_{21}x_1 + b_{22}x_2)$$
$$x_2'' = a_{21}(b_{11}x_1 + b_{12}x_2) + a_{22}(b_{21}x_1 + b_{22}x_2),$$

i.e.
$$x_1'' = (a_{11}b_{11} + a_{12}b_{21})x_1 + (a_{11}b_{12} + a_{12}b_{22})x_2$$
$$x_2'' = \underbrace{(a_{21}b_{11} + a_{22}b_{21})x_1 + (a_{21}b_{12} + a_{22}b_{22})x_2}$$
$$T_2T_1(x_1, x_2) \rightarrow (x_1'', x_2'')$$

Thus T_2T_1 is a linear transformation given by the linear equations above. The whole analysis may be abbreviated as follows:

$$x_i'' = \sum_{j=1}^{2} a_{ij}x_j', \qquad i = 1, 2.$$

(This means choose a value for i then sum over j, e.g. with $i = 2$,

$$x_2'' = \sum_{j=1}^{2} a_{2j}x_j' = a_{21}x_1' + a_{22}x_2'.)$$

Similarly,

$$x_i' = \sum_{j=1}^{2} b_{ij}x_j, \qquad i = 1, 2.$$

Therefore,

$$x_i'' = \sum_{j=1}^{2} (a_{i1}b_{1j} + a_{i2}b_{2j})x_j, \qquad i = 1, 2$$

or

$$x_i'' = \sum_{j=1}^{2} \sum_{\lambda=1}^{2} a_{i\lambda}b_{\lambda j}x_j, \qquad i = 1, 2,$$

where one first sums over j and then over λ. The matrices of the coefficients of the equations representing T_1, T_2, and T_2T_1 are therefore A, B, and C respectively, where

$$c_{ij} = \sum_{\lambda=1}^{2} a_{i\lambda}b_{\lambda j}.$$

Note that λ denotes the columns of A and the rows of B. For example,

$$c_{12} = \sum_{\lambda=1}^{2} a_{1\lambda}b_{\lambda 2} = a_{11}b_{12} + a_{12}b_{22}.$$

If one writes X'', X' and X for the following matrices,

$$X'' = \begin{pmatrix} x_1'' \\ x_2'' \end{pmatrix}, \qquad X' = \begin{pmatrix} x_1' \\ x_2' \end{pmatrix}, \qquad X = \begin{pmatrix} x_1 \\ x_2 \end{pmatrix},$$

then it seems natural to write the equations for T_1, T_2, and T_2T_1 as follows:

$$X'' = AX', \qquad X' = BX \qquad \text{and} \qquad X'' = ABX.$$

We thus define the **product of two matrices** $A = (a_{ij})$ and $B = (b_{ij})$, and written AB, to be a matrix $C = (c_{ij})$, where

$$c_{ij} = \sum_{\lambda=1}^{n} a_{i\lambda}b_{\lambda j}.$$

For example,

$$\begin{pmatrix} a_{11} & a_{12} & a_{13} \\ a_{21} & a_{22} & a_{23} \end{pmatrix} \times \begin{pmatrix} b_{11} & b_{12} \\ b_{21} & b_{22} \\ b_{31} & b_{32} \end{pmatrix} = \begin{pmatrix} c_{11} & c_{12} \\ c_{21} & c_{22} \end{pmatrix}$$

$$= \begin{pmatrix} a_{11}b_{11} + a_{12}b_{21} + a_{13}b_{31} & a_{11}b_{12} + a_{12}b_{22} + a_{13}b_{32} \\ a_{21}b_{11} + a_{22}b_{21} + a_{23}b_{31} & a_{21}b_{12} + a_{22}b_{22} + a_{23}b_{32} \end{pmatrix},$$

and
$$c_{ij} = \sum_{\lambda=1}^{3} a_{i\lambda}b_{\lambda j},$$

where, for example,

$$c_{21} = \sum_{\lambda=1}^{3} a_{2\lambda}b_{\lambda 1} = a_{21}b_{11} + a_{22}b_{21} + a_{23}b_{31}.$$

Note that we are multiplying the rows of A by the columns of B. The necessary condition for two matrices A and B to be conformable for the product AB (i.e. for AB to exist) is that the number of columns of A must equal the number of rows of B. This follows immediately from the definition of the product, since if $AB = C$, then

$$c_{ij} = \sum_{\lambda=1}^{n} a_{i\lambda}b_{\lambda j},$$

where, as we noted before, λ denotes the columns of A and the rows of B. So, in general, if A is an $m \times n$ matrix then B will be an $n \times p$ matrix, and AB will be an $m \times p$ matrix.

EXAMPLES

1. We confirm that $X'' = AX'$, $X' = BX$ and $X'' = ABX$, are the equations representing T_1, T_2 and T_2T_1 respectively.

Now, $X'' = AX'$ is

$$\begin{pmatrix} x_1'' \\ x_2'' \end{pmatrix} = \begin{pmatrix} a_{11} & a_{12} \\ a_{21} & a_{22} \end{pmatrix} \begin{pmatrix} x_1' \\ x_2' \end{pmatrix}$$

i.e.
$$\begin{pmatrix} x_1'' \\ x_2'' \end{pmatrix} = \begin{pmatrix} a_{11}x_1' + a_{12}x_2' \\ a_{21}x_1' + a_{22}x_2' \end{pmatrix}$$

and since two matrices are equal if and only if elements in corresponding positions are equal, we have

$$x_1'' = a_{11}x_1' + a_{12}x_2'$$
$$x_2'' = a_{21}x_1' + a_{22}x_2'.$$

Similarly for $X' = BX$.

In the case of $X'' = ABX$, we have

$$\begin{pmatrix} x_1'' \\ x_2'' \end{pmatrix} = \begin{pmatrix} a_{11} & a_{12} \\ a_{21} & a_{22} \end{pmatrix} \begin{pmatrix} b_{11} & b_{12} \\ b_{21} & b_{22} \end{pmatrix} \begin{pmatrix} x_1 \\ x_2 \end{pmatrix}$$

and assuming the **associative law** for matrices, to be proved later, we have

$$\begin{pmatrix} x_1'' \\ x_2'' \end{pmatrix} = \begin{pmatrix} a_{11}b_{11} + a_{12}b_{21} & a_{11}b_{12} + a_{12}b_{22} \\ a_{21}b_{11} + a_{22}b_{21} & a_{21}b_{12} + a_{22}b_{22} \end{pmatrix} \begin{pmatrix} x_1 \\ x_2 \end{pmatrix}$$

i.e.

$$\begin{pmatrix} x_1'' \\ x_2'' \end{pmatrix} = \begin{pmatrix} [a_{11}b_{11} + a_{12}b_{21}]x_1 + [a_{11}b_{12} + a_{12}b_{22}]x_2 \\ [a_{21}b_{11} + a_{22}b_{21}]x_1 + [a_{21}b_{12} + a_{22}b_{22}]x_2 \end{pmatrix}$$

$$x_1'' = (a_{11}b_{11} + a_{12}b_{21})x_1 + (a_{11}b_{12} + a_{12}b_{22})x_2$$
$$x_2'' = (a_{21}b_{11} + a_{22}b_{21})x_1 + (a_{21}b_{12} + a_{22}b_{22})x_2.$$

2. If AB exists, then it does not necessarily mean that BA exists. In fact if A is an $m \times n$ matrix and B is an $n \times p$ matrix, then BA will exist only if $m = p$. So, if A and B are given by the following 3×2 and 2×3 matrices,

$$A = \begin{pmatrix} 2 & 1 \\ 3 & 1 \\ -1 & 2 \end{pmatrix}, \qquad B = \begin{pmatrix} 1 & 0 & 3 \\ 2 & -1 & 4 \end{pmatrix},$$

then,

$$AB = \begin{pmatrix} 4 & -1 & 10 \\ 5 & -1 & 13 \\ 3 & -2 & 5 \end{pmatrix}$$

and

$$BA = \begin{pmatrix} -1 & 7 \\ -3 & 9 \end{pmatrix}.$$

3. If A and B are both square matrices of the same order (n say), find expressions for the typical elements in the following matrices: (a) A^2 (b) $(A+B)^2$ (c) $A(AB)$.

(a) Now, $A = (a_{ij}), \qquad B = (b_{ij})$

therefore $A^2 = (a_{ij})^2 = (u_{ij})$ (say),

where $u_{ij} = \sum_{\lambda=1}^{n} a_{i\lambda} a_{\lambda j}.$

(b) $(A+B) = (a_{ij} + b_{ij}) = (c_{ij})$ (say),

therefore $(A+B)^2 = (c_{ij})^2 = (d_{ij})$ (say),

where $d_{ij} = \sum_{\lambda=1}^{n} c_{i\lambda} c_{\lambda j},$

but $c_{ij} = a_{ij} + b_{ij} \Rightarrow c_{i\lambda} = a_{i\lambda} + b_{i\lambda},$

and $c_{\lambda j} = a_{\lambda j} + b_{\lambda j}.$

Therefore $d_{ij} = \sum_{\lambda=1}^{n} (a_{i\lambda} + b_{i\lambda})(a_{\lambda j} + b_{\lambda j}).$

(c) $(AB) = (c_{ij})$ (say),

where $c_{ij} = \sum_{\lambda=1}^{n} a_{i\lambda} b_{\lambda j}.$

Therefore $A(AB) = (a_{ij})(c_{ij}) = (d_{ij})$ (say),

where $d_{ij} = \sum_{\mu=1}^{n} a_{i\mu} c_{\mu j}.$

But, $c_{ij} = \sum_{\lambda=1}^{n} a_{i\lambda} b_{\lambda j} \Rightarrow c_{\mu j} = \sum_{\lambda=1}^{n} a_{\mu\lambda} b_{\lambda j}.$

Therefore $d_{ij} = \sum_{\mu=1}^{n} \left\{ a_{i\mu} \left[\sum_{\lambda=1}^{n} a_{\mu\lambda} b_{\lambda j} \right] \right\},$

where one first sums over μ then over λ.

4. If A and B are both square and of the same order (n, say), then

$$(A+B)^2 = A^2 + AB + BA + B^2.$$

Now, $\qquad\qquad A = (a_{ij}), \qquad B = (b_{ij}),$

therefore $\qquad\quad A^2 = (a_{ij})^2 = (u_{ij}) \qquad$ (say),

where $\qquad\qquad u_{ij} = \sum_{\lambda=1}^{n} a_{i\lambda} a_{\lambda j}.$

Similarly, if $\qquad (v_{ij}) = B^2,$

then $\qquad\qquad v_{ij} = \sum_{\lambda=1}^{n} b_{i\lambda} b_{\lambda j}.$

Also $\qquad\qquad (A+B) = (a_{ij} + b_{ij}),$

therefore $\qquad (A+B)^2 = (a_{ij} + b_{ij})^2 = (w_{ij}) \qquad$ (say),

where $\qquad\qquad w_{ij} = \sum_{\lambda=1}^{n} (a_{i\lambda} + b_{i\lambda})(a_{\lambda j} + b_{\lambda j})$

$$= \sum_{\lambda=1}^{n} a_{i\lambda} a_{\lambda j} + \sum_{\lambda=1}^{n} a_{i\lambda} b_{\lambda j} + \sum_{\lambda=1}^{n} b_{i\lambda} a_{\lambda j} + \sum_{\lambda=1}^{n} b_{i\lambda} b_{\lambda j},$$

i.e. $\qquad\qquad w_{ij} = u_{ij} + x_{ij} + y_{ij} + v_{ij},$

where $\qquad\qquad (x_{ij}) = AB, \qquad$ and $\qquad (y_{ij}) = BA,$

therefore $\qquad \underline{(A+B)^2 = A^2 + AB + BA + B^2.}$

Note that,

$$\sum_{\lambda=1}^{n} b_{i\lambda} a_{\lambda j} = \sum_{\lambda=1}^{n} a_{\lambda j} b_{i\lambda} \neq \sum_{\lambda=1}^{n} a_{i\lambda} b_{\lambda j},$$

i.e. $BA \neq AB$ in general,

and we say that the **operation of multiplication in matrix algebra is non-commutative.**

5. If $AB = 0$, then it does not necessarily follow that $A = 0$ or $B = 0$, e.g.

if $\qquad A = \begin{pmatrix} 0 & k \\ 0 & 0 \end{pmatrix}$ and $\qquad B = \begin{pmatrix} k & 0 \\ 0 & 0 \end{pmatrix},$

then, $\qquad AB = \begin{pmatrix} 0 & 0 \\ 0 & 0 \end{pmatrix} = 0.$

Therefore it is possible to have divisors of zero in a matrix algebra.
See Chapter 6 on rings.

EXERCISES 5c

1. If $A = \begin{pmatrix} 1 & 2 \\ 0 & 1 \end{pmatrix}$, $B = \begin{pmatrix} 3 & 1 \\ 2 & -1 \end{pmatrix}$,

and $\qquad C = \begin{pmatrix} 1 & 0 & 3 \\ -2 & 1 & 0 \end{pmatrix}$,

find (a) AB (b) BA (c) AC (d) BC.

2. If $A = (1 \quad 0 \quad 3 \quad 4)$,

$$B = \begin{pmatrix} -1 \\ 3 \\ 2 \\ -4 \end{pmatrix}, \quad \text{and } C = \begin{pmatrix} 0 & 1 \\ -2 & 3 \\ 2 & -1 \\ 1 & 0 \end{pmatrix},$$

find (a) AB (b) BA (c) AC.

3. If $A = \begin{pmatrix} k & 0 & 0 \\ 0 & 0 & 0 \\ 0 & 0 & 0 \end{pmatrix}$, and $C = \begin{pmatrix} 0 & 0 & 0 \\ 0 & 0 & \lambda \\ 0 & 0 & 0 \end{pmatrix}$,

find matrices B and D (other than the null matrix) such that $AB = BA$ and $CD = DC$. Also find AC and CA.

4. If A and B are both square and of the same order, prove that

$$(A - B)^2 = A^2 - AB - BA + B^2.$$

Illustrate with matrices C and D in question 3.

5. If A, B and C are the matrices given in question 1, find
(a) $A(BC)$ (b) $(AB)C$ (c) $(A+B)C$ (d) $AC+BC$.
Comment on the results.

6. If A is any matrix, and 0 is a null matrix, show that $0 \times A = A \times 0 = 0$.

7. Write down a typical element from each of the following matrices:

(a) AB (b) BA (c) $A(B+C)$ (d) $A^2(B+C)^2$,

where A, B and C are any matrices assumed conformable for each of the operations.

8. Write down the necessary condition for two matrices to commute under the operations of (a) addition, and (b) multiplication. What is the necessary condition for two matrices to commute under both the operations of addition and multiplication? Illustrate geometrically.

Unit matrix

Definition. The unit matrix I_n is a square matrix of order n given by:

$$I_n = (\delta_{ij}), \text{ where } \delta_{ij} = 1$$

if and only if $i = j$, and 0 if $i \neq j$. That is, the **leading diagonal of a unit matrix is occupied by 1's and all the remaining elements are zero.** It follows that if A is any $m \times n$ matrix and I_m and I_n are unit matrices, that

$$I_m A = A I_n = A.$$

To see this, let $I_m = (\delta_{ij})$, where $\delta_{ij} = 1$ if and only if $i = j$, and 0 if $i \neq j$; then

$$I_m A = (\delta_{ij})(a_{ij}) = (u_{ij}) \qquad \text{(say)},$$

where

$$u_{ij} = \sum_{\lambda=1}^{m} \delta_{i\lambda} a_{\lambda j}, \qquad \text{and expanding}$$

$$u_{ij} = \delta_{i1} a_{1j} + \delta_{i2} a_{2j} + \ldots + \delta_{ii} a_{ij} + \ldots + \delta_{im} a_{mj},$$

i.e.

$$u_{ij} = \delta_{ii} a_{ij} = a_{ij}.$$

Thus, $\underline{I_m A = A.}$

Similarly, $A I_n = A.$

For example, if

$$A = \begin{pmatrix} a_{11} & a_{12} & a_{13} \\ a_{21} & a_{22} & a_{23} \end{pmatrix}, \qquad \text{then } I_2 = \begin{pmatrix} 1 & 0 \\ 0 & 1 \end{pmatrix},$$

and

$$I_3 = \begin{pmatrix} 1 & 0 & 0 \\ 0 & 1 & 0 \\ 0 & 0 & 1 \end{pmatrix}$$

If A is a square matrix then the identity matrix I is uniquely determined and we write

$$IA = AI = A.$$

It follows immediately from the definition of the product of two conformable matrices that they do not in general commute. However, the **associative** and **distributive** laws hold as we shall now see.

Associative law

If A is an $m \times n$ matrix, B is an $n \times p$ matrix, and C is a $p \times q$ matrix, then $A(BC) = (AB)C$ is an $m \times q$ matrix.

Proof. **To find $A(BC)$:**

If $\qquad (u_{ij}) = BC,$

then $\qquad u_{ij} = \sum_{\lambda=1}^{p} b_{i\lambda} c_{\lambda j};$

therefore if $\qquad (v_{ij}) = A(BC),$

then $\qquad v_{ij} = \sum_{\mu=1}^{n} a_{i\mu} u_{\mu j}.$

But $\qquad u_{ij} = \sum_{\lambda=1}^{p} b_{i\lambda} c_{\lambda j} \Rightarrow u_{\mu j} = \sum_{\lambda=1}^{p} b_{\mu\lambda} c_{\lambda j},$

and so, $\qquad v_{ij} = \sum_{\mu=1}^{n} a_{i\mu} \left\{ \sum_{\lambda=1}^{p} b_{\mu\lambda} c_{\lambda j} \right\},$

where one first sums over μ then over λ. Thus, expanding,

$$v_{ij} = a_{i1} \sum_{\lambda=1}^{p} b_{1\lambda} c_{\lambda j} + a_{i2} \sum_{\lambda=1}^{p} b_{2\lambda} c_{\lambda j} + \ldots + a_{in} \sum_{\lambda=1}^{p} b_{n\lambda} c_{\lambda j},$$

i.e.

$$\begin{aligned} v_{ij} = \; & a_{i1}(b_{11} c_{1j} + b_{12} c_{2j} + \ldots + b_{1p} c_{pj}) \\ & + a_{i2}(b_{21} c_{1j} + b_{22} c_{2j} + \ldots + b_{2p} c_{pj}) \\ & + \qquad . \qquad . \qquad . \\ & + a_{in}(b_{n1} c_{1j} + b_{n2} c_{2j} + \ldots + b_{np} c_{pj}) \end{aligned}$$

To find $(AB)C$:

If $\qquad\qquad (x_{ij}) = AB,$

then $\qquad\qquad x_{ij} = \sum\limits_{s=1}^{n} a_{is}b_{sj},$

therefore if $\qquad (y_{ij}) = (AB)C,$

then $\qquad\qquad y_{ij} = \sum\limits_{t=1}^{p} x_{it}c_{tj}.$

But, $\qquad\qquad x_{ij} = \sum\limits_{s=1}^{n} a_{is}b_{sj} \Rightarrow x_{it} = \sum\limits_{s=1}^{n} a_{is}b_{st},$

and so, $\qquad\quad y_{ij} = \sum\limits_{t=1}^{p} \left\{ \sum\limits_{s=1}^{n} a_{is}b_{st} \right\} c_{tj},$

where one first sums over t then over s.

Expanding,

$$y_{ij} = \left\{ \sum_{s=1}^{n} a_{is}b_{s1} \right\} c_{1j} + \left\{ \sum_{s=1}^{n} a_{is}b_{s2} \right\} c_{2j} + \ldots + \left\{ \sum_{s=1}^{n} a_{is}b_{sp} \right\} c_{pj}$$

i.e.

$$\begin{aligned}
y_{ij} = &(a_{i1}b_{11} + a_{i2}b_{21} + \ldots + a_{in}b_{n1})c_{1j} \\
&+ (a_{i1}b_{12} + a_{i2}b_{22} + \ldots + a_{in}b_{n2})c_{2j} \\
&+ \qquad\quad . \qquad\quad . \qquad\quad . \\
&+ (a_{i1}b_{1p} + a_{i2}b_{2p} + \ldots + a_{in}b_{np})c_{pj}
\end{aligned}$$

Looking at the two expansions for v_{ij} and y_{ij}, it is clear that $v_{ij} = y_{ij}$ (the rows (columns) in the expansion for v_{ij} equal the columns (rows) in the expansion for y_{ij}). Thus, since $(v_{ij}) = A(BC)$, and $(y_{ij}) = (AB)C$, we have proved that $A(BC) = (AB)C$; so ABC is unambiguous.

Distributive law

If A, B and C are any three matrices conformable for the operations of addition and multiplication, then:

(a) $A(B+C) = AB+AC$

(b) $(A+B)C = AC+BC$.

For example, in case (a), if B is $m \times n$, then C must be $m \times n$, and A will be $q \times m$, for any q; $A(B+C)$ will therefore be $q \times n$.

Proof. Case (a) only is proved here; the proof of (b) is left to the reader.

Now, $\qquad A = (a_{ij}), \qquad B = (b_{ij}), \qquad C = (c_{ij})$

$$\therefore\ B+C = (b_{ij}+c_{ij}),$$

and $\qquad\qquad A(B+C) = (d_{ij}) \qquad \text{(say)},$

where $\qquad\qquad d_{ij} = \sum_{\lambda=1}^{m} a_{i\lambda}(b_{\lambda j}+c_{\lambda j})$

$$= \sum_{\lambda=1}^{m} a_{i\lambda}b_{\lambda j} + \sum_{\lambda=1}^{m} a_{i\lambda}c_{\lambda j},$$

i.e. $\qquad\qquad A(B+C) = AB + AC.$

EXERCISES 5d

1. If $A = \begin{pmatrix} 2 & 0 \\ 1 & 3 \end{pmatrix}, \qquad B = \begin{pmatrix} 1 & 0 & -1 \\ 0 & 2 & -3 \end{pmatrix},$

$C = \begin{pmatrix} 4 & -1 \\ 5 & 2 \\ -2 & 6 \end{pmatrix}, \quad \text{and} \quad D = \begin{pmatrix} 2 & 3 & 1 & 4 \\ 0 & 1 & 1 & 2 \end{pmatrix},$

find (a) ABC (b) BCD (c) $ABCD$ (d) $(A+BC)D$.

2. If $Y = \begin{pmatrix} y_1 \\ y_2 \\ y_3 \end{pmatrix}, \qquad X = \begin{pmatrix} x_1 \\ x_2 \\ x_3 \end{pmatrix},$

$A = \begin{pmatrix} 1 & 0 & 2 \\ 3 & 1 & -1 \\ 4 & 0 & 2 \end{pmatrix}, \quad \text{and} \quad B = \begin{pmatrix} 4 & 0 & 1 \\ 0 & 1 & -2 \\ 3 & 3 & 5 \end{pmatrix},$

write out fully the equations given by:

(a) $Y = AX$ (b) $Y = BX$ (c) $Y = ABX$ (d) $Y = BAX$.

3. Show by induction that the associative law for matrices guarantees the existence of the general product $A_1 A_2 A_3 \ldots A_n$, where the matrices are assumed to be conformable. (*Hint:* see §6.9, Theorem 1 on Groups.)

4. For any square matrix A, A^m is defined to be $AAA \ldots A$ (to m terms), m a positive integer. Prove that $A^m A^n = A^{m+n}$, and $I^n = I$, where n is a positive integer, and I is the identity matrix.

5. Show that for two square matrices A and B of the same order where I is the identity matrix that:

(a) $(A+B)(A-B) = A^2 - AB + BA - B^2$

(b) $(A+I)(A-I) = A^2 - I$

(c) $(A+I)(A^2 - A + I) = A^3 + I$

(d) $(A-I)(A^2 + A + I) = A^3 - I$

(e) $(A+B+I)^2 = A^2 + B^2 + I + AB + BA + 2(A+B)$.

6. Find the 3×3 matrices X which satisfy the following equations, where I and 0 are the unit and zero matrices respectively:

(a) $X^2 - 7X + 12I = 0$ (b) $2X^3 + 3X^2 - 11X - 6I = 0$.

How do the existence of divisors of zero affect your results?

5.6. Transpose of a matrix. Symmetric and skew-symmetric matrices

The **transpose** of a matrix A is defined to be the matrix A' where the columns of A' are the rows of A, and the rows of A' are the columns of A. So, if A is $m \times n$, then A' will be $n \times m$; clearly both products AA' and $A'A$ exist—AA' is square and of order m, and $A'A$ is square and of order n. For example, if

$$A = \begin{pmatrix} a & b & c \\ d & e & f \end{pmatrix}, \quad \text{then } A' = \begin{pmatrix} a & d \\ b & e \\ c & f \end{pmatrix},$$

$$AA' = \begin{pmatrix} a^2 + b^2 + c^2 & ad + be + cf \\ ad + be + cf & d^2 + e^2 + f^2 \end{pmatrix},$$

and

$$A'A = \begin{pmatrix} a^2 + d^2 & ab + de & ac + df \\ ab + de & b^2 + e^2 & bc + ef \\ ac + df & bc + ef & c^2 + f^2 \end{pmatrix}.$$

Clearly the transpose of a transposed matrix is the original matrix, i.e.

$$(A')' = A.$$

We now state and prove an important theorem on products and transposes:

The transpose of a product AB of two conformable matrices is equal to the product (in reverse order) of the transposes, i.e.

$$(AB)' = B'A'.$$

Proof. Let A be $m \times n$ and B be $n \times p$.

Now,

$$A = (a_{ij}),$$

$$A' = (a_{ij})' = (a_{ij}'),$$

where

$$a_{ij}' = a_{ji}.$$

$$B = (b_{ij}),$$

$$B = (b_{ij})' = (b_{ij}'),$$

where

$$b_{ij}' = b_{ji}.$$

If

$$(u_{ij}) = (AB),$$

then

$$u_{ij} = \sum_{\lambda=1}^{n} a_{i\lambda} b_{\lambda j}$$

$$(AB)' = (u_{ij})' = (u_{ij}'),$$

where

$$u_{ij}' = u_{ji},$$

i.e.

$$u_{ij}' = \sum_{\lambda=1}^{n} a_{j\lambda} b_{\lambda i}. \tag{i}$$

Now, let

$$B'A' = (v_{ij}),$$

then

$$v_{ij} = \sum_{\lambda=1}^{n} b_{i\lambda}' a_{\lambda j}',$$

but

$$a_{ij}' = a_{ji},$$

$$\therefore a_{\lambda j}' = a_{j\lambda},$$

also

$$b_{ij}' = b_{ji}$$

$$\therefore b_{i\lambda}' = b_{\lambda i},$$

and so

$$v_{ij} = \sum_{\lambda=1}^{n} b_{\lambda i} a_{j\lambda},$$

i.e.

$$v_{ij} = \sum_{\lambda=1}^{n} a_{j\lambda} b_{\lambda i}. \tag{ii}$$

Hence, from (i) and (ii), $(AB)' = B'A'$.

For example,

if $\qquad A = \begin{pmatrix} a & b \\ c & d \end{pmatrix}$, and $\qquad B = \begin{pmatrix} 1 & 0 & 3 \\ -2 & 2 & 4 \end{pmatrix}$,

then $\qquad AB = \begin{pmatrix} a-2b & 2b & 3a+4b \\ c-2d & 2d & 3c+4d \end{pmatrix}$

and, therefore,

$$(AB)' = \begin{pmatrix} a-2b & c-2d \\ 2b & 2d \\ 3a+4b & 3c+4d \end{pmatrix}.$$

Also, $\qquad A' = \begin{pmatrix} a & c \\ b & d \end{pmatrix}$, and $\qquad B' = \begin{pmatrix} 1 & -2 \\ 0 & 2 \\ 3 & 4 \end{pmatrix}$,

therefore

$$B'A' = \begin{pmatrix} a-2b & c-2d \\ 2b & 2d \\ 3a+4b & 3c+4d \end{pmatrix} = (AB)'.$$

Since we have proved the associative law, we may now consider the product $A_1A_2A_3$ of matrices A_1, A_2 and A_3 (assumed conformable), and the product of their transposes $A_3'A_2'A_1'$:

Since $(A_1A_2A_3)' = A_3'(A_1A_2)'$ by the above theorem, and $(A_1A_2)' = A_2'A_1'$, again by the above theorem, we have therefore $(A_1A_2A_3)' = A_3'A_2'A_1'$.

In general, $(A_1A_2 \ldots A_n)' = A_n' \ldots A_2'A_1'$; this is proved by induction on n, and the proof is left as an exercise to the reader.

Referring to the example given earlier in this section where the matrix A was given by

$$A = \begin{pmatrix} a & b & c \\ d & e & f \end{pmatrix},$$

we note that the elements of the matrix $A'A$ are symmetrically placed about the **leading diagonal** (the leading diagonal of a square matrix M is defined to be the set of elements m_{ii} for all i); to be more precise, we mean that the element in the (i,j)th position is the same as the element in the (j,i)th position, e.g. the element in the first row and third column of $A'A$ is the same as the element in the third row and first column of $A'A$ and is $ac + df$. Similarly, AA' also has this symmetry. Clearly, matrices that have such symmetry can only be square and they remain unchanged by the operation of transposition. We thus have the following definition:

A **symmetric matrix** is any square matrix A such that its transpose A' is equal to itself, i.e. $A' = A$ or $a_{ij}' = a_{ij}$. Other typical examples of symmetric matrices are:

$$\begin{pmatrix} a & 1 \\ 1 & a \end{pmatrix}, \quad \begin{pmatrix} a & h & g \\ h & b & f \\ g & f & c \end{pmatrix}, \quad \begin{pmatrix} 1 & 0 & 0 & 0 \\ 0 & 1 & 0 & 0 \\ 0 & 0 & 1 & 0 \\ 0 & 0 & 0 & 1 \end{pmatrix}.$$

On the other hand, a **skew-symmetric matrix** is defined to be any square matrix A such that $a_{ij} = -a_{ji}$. Since for $i = j$, $a_{ii} = -a_{ii}$ is true only if $a_{ii} = 0$, then the leading diagonal of a skew-symmetric matrix consists entirely of zeros. Typical examples of skew-symmetric matrices are:

$$\begin{pmatrix} 0 & b \\ -b & 0 \end{pmatrix}, \quad \begin{pmatrix} 0 & 1 & 2 \\ -1 & 0 & 3 \\ -2 & -3 & 0 \end{pmatrix}, \quad \begin{pmatrix} 0 & -p & q & -r \\ p & 0 & s & t \\ -q & -s & 0 & -v \\ r & -t & v & 0 \end{pmatrix}.$$

Thus a skew-symmetric matrix A is the negative of its transpose A', i.e. $A = -A'$.

EXERCISES 5e

1. Prove that for *any* matrix A and its transpose A', that the products AA' and $A'A$ exist and are symmetrical.

2. If A and B are both skew-symmetric matrices of order 2, prove that $AB = BA$. If A and B are both **diagonal matrices** (i.e. square matrices whose elements are all zero except those along the leading diagonal), prove that $AB = BA$.

3. Prove for any two matrices A and B that $(A + B)' = A' + B'$. Hence prove by induction on n that

$$(A_1 + A_2 + \ldots + A_n)' = A_1' + A_2' + \ldots + A_n',$$

for matrices $A_1, A_2, \ldots, A_n$.

4. Prove that any square matrix can be expressed as the sum of two matrices, one of which is symmetric and the other skew-symmetric. (*Hint:* let A be any square matrix, then show that $(A + A')$ is symmetric and $(A - A')$ is skew-symmetric.)

5. Since the elements of a matrix A may be complex, we define a **conjugate matrix** $\bar{A}$ to be the matrix A where the elements a_{ij} are replaced by their respective complex conjugates. So $\bar{A} = (\bar{a}_{ij})$, and a typical example of a matrix A and its conjugate $\bar{A}$ is given below:

$$A = \begin{pmatrix} 3+4i & i \\ -1+2i & 2-3i \end{pmatrix}, \qquad \bar{A} = \begin{pmatrix} 3-4i & -i \\ -1-2i & 2+3i \end{pmatrix}$$

where $i = \sqrt{-1}$.

Find the conjugates of the following matrices:

$$\begin{pmatrix} 2-3i & 4+2i & 1-i \\ 3+2i & -5+4i & 3-2i \end{pmatrix}, \qquad \begin{pmatrix} a+ib & a-ib \\ 3+i & 1-i \\ 0 & 2 \end{pmatrix},$$

$$\begin{pmatrix} i & 0 \\ 0 & i \end{pmatrix}, \qquad \begin{pmatrix} a-2i \\ 3a-2bi \\ 1+i \end{pmatrix}, \quad \text{where } a \text{ and } b \text{ are real.}$$

6. Find the products $A\bar{A}$ and $\bar{A}A$, where A is the matrix given in question 5.

7. If the transpose of the conjugate of a given square matrix A is equal to A, i.e. $\bar{A}' = A$, then A is called a **Hermitian matrix**. Thus, $\bar{a}_{ij}' = a_{ij}$, and since $\bar{a}_{ii}' = a_{ii}$ only if a_{ii} is real, it follows that the leading diagonal of a Hermitian matrix consists solely of real numbers. The Hermitian matrix is so named after the French mathematician, Charles Hermite (1822–1901), and is very useful in some branches of physics, especially in quantum mechanics. Some typical Hermitian matrices are:

$$\begin{pmatrix} 2 & 1+i \\ 1-i & 3 \end{pmatrix}, \qquad \begin{pmatrix} 3 & 2-3i & 1+i \\ 2+3i & -2 & 2-i \\ 1-i & 2+i & 1 \end{pmatrix},$$

$$\begin{pmatrix} a & c+id \\ c-id & b \end{pmatrix}, \quad \text{where } a, b, c, d \text{ are all real.}$$

When $A = -\bar{A}'$, then A is called **skew-Hermitian**.

(a) Prove that the operations of finding the transpose and conjugate of a square matrix A are commutative only if A is Hermitian,

i.e.
$$(\bar{A})' = \overline{(A')}.$$

(b) Prove that if A is skew-Hermitian, then the elements in the leading diagonal are either imaginary or zero.

(c) Show that if A is Hermitian, then iA is skew-Hermitian.

(d) Show that any Hermitian matrix A can be written in the form $X + iY$, where X is a real symmetric matrix, and Y is a real skew-symmetric matrix.

5.7. Inverse of a square matrix of order 2

Consider the two equations in two unknowns x_1 and x_2 given below:

$$a_{11}x_1 + a_{12}x_2 = k_1$$

$$a_{21}x_1 + a_{22}x_2 = k_2,$$

where the a's and k's are constants. Writing these equations in matrix form, we have

$$AX = K,$$

where $A = \begin{pmatrix} a_{11} & a_{12} \\ a_{21} & a_{22} \end{pmatrix}$, $\quad X = \begin{pmatrix} x_1 \\ x_2 \end{pmatrix}$, $\quad K = \begin{pmatrix} k_1 \\ k_2 \end{pmatrix}$.

We now wish to solve for X; if we write A^{-1} for the matrix such that

$$A^{-1}A = AA^{-1} = I,$$

where I is the identity matrix, then A^{-1} behaves like an **inverse** (see Chapter 6). Multiplying both sides of our equation by A^{-1} to the left, we have

$$A^{-1}AX = A^{-1}K \Rightarrow IX = A^{-1}K,$$

i.e.
$$X = A^{-1}K.$$

In order to find X we must first know what A^{-1} is in terms of A. Now, A^{-1} was defined to be the matrix such that $A^{-1}A = AA^{-1} = I$, and if we let A^{-1} be given by

$$A^{-1} = \begin{pmatrix} b_{11} & b_{12} \\ b_{21} & b_{22} \end{pmatrix},$$

then we have to find the b's in terms of the a's such that

$$\begin{pmatrix} b_{11} & b_{12} \\ b_{21} & b_{22} \end{pmatrix} \begin{pmatrix} a_{11} & a_{12} \\ a_{21} & a_{22} \end{pmatrix} = \begin{pmatrix} 1 & 0 \\ 0 & 1 \end{pmatrix},$$

i.e. $$\begin{pmatrix} a_{11}b_{11} + a_{21}b_{12} & a_{12}b_{11} + a_{22}b_{12} \\ a_{11}b_{21} + a_{21}b_{22} & a_{12}b_{21} + a_{22}b_{22} \end{pmatrix} = \begin{pmatrix} 1 & 0 \\ 0 & 1 \end{pmatrix}.$$

Since matrices are equal only if corresponding elements are identical, it follows that

$$\left.\begin{array}{r} a_{11}b_{11} + a_{21}b_{12} = 1 \\ a_{12}b_{11} + a_{22}b_{12} = 0 \end{array}\right\} \Rightarrow b_{11} = \frac{a_{22}}{\Delta}, \qquad b_{12} = \frac{-a_{12}}{\Delta},$$

$$\left.\begin{array}{r} a_{11}b_{21} + a_{21}b_{22} = 0 \\ a_{12}b_{21} + a_{22}b_{22} = 1 \end{array}\right\} \Rightarrow b_{21} = \frac{-a_{21}}{\Delta}, \qquad b_{22} = \frac{a_{11}}{\Delta},$$

where $$\Delta = a_{11}a_{22} - a_{21}a_{12}.$$

We also obtain the same expressions for the b's if we solve

$$\begin{pmatrix} a_{11} & a_{12} \\ a_{21} & a_{22} \end{pmatrix} \begin{pmatrix} b_{11} & b_{12} \\ b_{21} & b_{22} \end{pmatrix} = \begin{pmatrix} 1 & 0 \\ 0 & 1 \end{pmatrix}.$$

So, in order that $A^{-1}A = AA^{-1} = I$, we have

$$A^{-1} = \begin{pmatrix} \dfrac{a_{22}}{\Delta} & \dfrac{-a_{12}}{\Delta} \\[2mm] \dfrac{-a_{21}}{\Delta} & \dfrac{a_{11}}{\Delta} \end{pmatrix}$$

i.e. $$A^{-1} = \frac{1}{\Delta} \begin{pmatrix} a_{22} & -a_{12} \\ -a_{21} & a_{11} \end{pmatrix}, \qquad \Delta \neq 0.$$

Δ is called the **determinant of the matrix** A and is often written as

$$\begin{vmatrix} a_{11} & a_{12} \\ a_{21} & a_{22} \end{vmatrix}, \text{ or det } A, \text{ or simply as } |A|;$$

its **value** is $a_{11}a_{22} - a_{12}a_{21}$, and so **a determinant is a scalar.**

Thus, the **inverse matrix** A^{-1} exists only if $|A| \neq 0$ (since division by zero is meaningless). For example, if

$$A = \begin{pmatrix} 1 & -3 \\ 2 & 4 \end{pmatrix}, \quad \text{then } |A| = \begin{vmatrix} 1 & -3 \\ 2 & 4 \end{vmatrix} = 4 - (-6) = 10,$$

and

$$A^{-1} = \frac{1}{10} \begin{pmatrix} 4 & 3 \\ -2 & 1 \end{pmatrix}, \quad \text{i.e. } A^{-1} = \begin{pmatrix} \frac{2}{5} & \frac{3}{10} \\ -\frac{1}{5} & \frac{1}{10} \end{pmatrix}.$$

It is left to the reader to check that $A^{-1}A = AA^{-1} = I$. If, on the other hand,

$$A = \begin{pmatrix} 2 & 1 \\ 6 & 3 \end{pmatrix}, \quad \text{then } |A| = 6 - 6 = 0,$$

and A^{-1} does not exist. When the determinant of a matrix A is zero, we call A a **singular matrix**.

EXERCISES 5f

1. Which of the following matrices have inverses?

(a) $\begin{pmatrix} 0 & 1 \\ 3 & -2 \end{pmatrix}$ (b) $\begin{pmatrix} 2 & 1 \\ 4 & 3 \end{pmatrix}$

(c) $\begin{pmatrix} a & -a \\ a & -a \end{pmatrix}$ (d) $\begin{pmatrix} 3 & -1 \\ 5 & 4 \end{pmatrix}$

Write down the inverses where they exist.

2. Solve the following equations, where solutions exist:

(a) $AX = K$ (b) $BX = C$ (c) $EX = F$,

where

$$A = \begin{pmatrix} 2 & 1 \\ 0 & 3 \end{pmatrix}, \quad K = \begin{pmatrix} 5 \\ 4 \end{pmatrix},$$

$$B = \begin{pmatrix} -3 & 2 \\ 4 & 1 \end{pmatrix}, \quad C = \begin{pmatrix} 1 \\ 2 \end{pmatrix},$$

$$E = \begin{pmatrix} a & b \\ c & d \end{pmatrix}, \quad F = \begin{pmatrix} u \\ v \end{pmatrix},$$

$$X = \begin{pmatrix} x_1 \\ x_2 \end{pmatrix}.$$

3. If A and B are any two non-singular square matrices of order 2, prove that:

    (a) $(A')^{-1} = (A^{-1})'$ (b) $(AB)^{-1} = B^{-1}A^{-1}$.

4. If T_1 and T_2 are linear transformations represented by the following two equations:

$$T_1(x_1, x_2) \to (x_1', x_2'): X' = AX$$

$$T_2(x_1', x_2') \to (x_1'', x_2''): X'' = BX',$$

where, for example, $X' = AX$ is given by

$$\left(\begin{array}{c} x_1' \\ x_2' \end{array} \right) = \left(\begin{array}{cc} a_{11} & a_{12} \\ a_{21} & a_{22} \end{array} \right) \left(\begin{array}{c} x_1 \\ x_2 \end{array} \right), \quad |A| \neq 0,$$

prove that:

    (a) T_2T_1 is given by $X'' = BAX$
    (b) T_1^{-1} is given by $X = A^{-1}X'$, and
        T_2^{-1} is given by $X' = B^{-1}X''$
    (c) $(T_2T_1)^{-1} = T_1^{-1}T_2^{-1}$.

5. With regard to question 4, illustrate the case where T_1 is a rotation transformation and T_2 is a shearing transformation in the direction of the x-axis.

6. If A and B are any two square matrices of order 2, prove that:

    (a) $|AB| = |A||B|$.   (b) If A is singular, then AB is singular.
Write down the converse of (b) and prove that this converse is also true.

5.8. Determinants of order 3

In the last section we met determinants of order 2 in our development of the inverse of a square matrix of order 2. Before we discuss the inverse of a square matrix of order 3, it is necessary to define a **determinant of order 3**:

Definition

The determinant $|A|$ of order 3 of a square matrix A of order 3 where

$$A = \left(\begin{array}{ccc} a_{11} & a_{12} & a_{13} \\ a_{21} & a_{22} & a_{23} \\ a_{31} & a_{32} & a_{33} \end{array} \right),$$

is defined to be the product

$$a_{11}a_{22}a_{33} - a_{11}a_{23}a_{32} - a_{12}a_{21}a_{33} + a_{12}a_{23}a_{31} + a_{13}a_{21}a_{32}$$
$$- a_{13}a_{22}a_{31}.$$

Now, the above product can be written in the form

$$a_{11}(a_{22}a_{33} - a_{23}a_{32}) - a_{12}(a_{21}a_{33} - a_{23}a_{31}) + a_{13}(a_{21}a_{32} - a_{22}a_{31})$$

and it follows from the definition of a determinant of order 2, that the product may be written as

$$a_{11} \begin{vmatrix} a_{22} & a_{23} \\ a_{32} & a_{33} \end{vmatrix} - a_{12} \begin{vmatrix} a_{21} & a_{23} \\ a_{31} & a_{33} \end{vmatrix} + a_{13} \begin{vmatrix} a_{21} & a_{22} \\ a_{31} & a_{32} \end{vmatrix}.$$

These second order determinants are called **minors**; thus, the minor of the element a_{11} is

$$\begin{vmatrix} a_{22} & a_{23} \\ a_{32} & a_{33} \end{vmatrix},$$

the minor of the element a_{12} is

$$\begin{vmatrix} a_{21} & a_{23} \\ a_{31} & a_{33} \end{vmatrix},$$

and the minor of the element a_{13} is

$$\begin{vmatrix} a_{21} & a_{22} \\ a_{31} & a_{32} \end{vmatrix}.$$

If we put the corresponding signs in front of the minors, we obtain what we call **cofactors**; so if we write A_{11}, A_{12} and A_{13} for the cofactors of the elements a_{11}, a_{12} and a_{13} respectively, we have:

$$|A| = a_{11}A_{11} + a_{12}A_{12} + a_{13}A_{13}, \tag{i}$$

where $\quad A_{11} = + \begin{vmatrix} a_{22} & a_{23} \\ a_{32} & a_{33} \end{vmatrix}, \quad A_{12} = - \begin{vmatrix} a_{21} & a_{23} \\ a_{31} & a_{33} \end{vmatrix},$

and $\quad A_{13} = + \begin{vmatrix} a_{21} & a_{22} \\ a_{31} & a_{32} \end{vmatrix}.$

For example, if

$$A = \begin{pmatrix} 1 & 6 & 2 \\ 3 & 1 & 4 \\ 2 & 5 & -1 \end{pmatrix},$$

then,
$$|A| = \begin{vmatrix} 1 & 6 & 2 \\ 3 & 1 & 4 \\ 2 & 5 & -1 \end{vmatrix}$$

$$= 1 \begin{vmatrix} 1 & 4 \\ 5 & -1 \end{vmatrix} - 6 \begin{vmatrix} 3 & 4 \\ 2 & -1 \end{vmatrix} + 2 \begin{vmatrix} 3 & 1 \\ 2 & 5 \end{vmatrix},$$

i.e.
$$|A| = 1(-21) - 6(-11) + 2(13),$$

i.e.
$$\underline{|A| = 71,}$$

and the respective cofactors are $+(-21) = -21$, $-(-11) = +11$, and $+(+13) = +13$.

Referring back to the definition of a third order determinant, it can be seen that the product could have been written as

$$- a_{21}a_{12}a_{33} + a_{21}a_{13}a_{32} + a_{22}a_{11}a_{33} - a_{22}a_{13}a_{31} - a_{23}a_{11}a_{32} + a_{23}a_{12}a_{31},$$

i.e. as

$$- a_{21}(a_{12}a_{33} - a_{13}a_{32}) + a_{22}(a_{11}a_{33} - a_{13}a_{31}) - a_{23}(a_{11}a_{32} - a_{12}a_{31}),$$

or

$$- a_{21} \begin{vmatrix} a_{12} & a_{13} \\ a_{32} & a_{33} \end{vmatrix} + a_{22} \begin{vmatrix} a_{11} & a_{13} \\ a_{31} & a_{33} \end{vmatrix} - a_{23} \begin{vmatrix} a_{11} & a_{12} \\ a_{31} & a_{32} \end{vmatrix}.$$

So, the cofactors of a_{21}, a_{22} and a_{23} are respectively given by

$$A_{21} = - \begin{vmatrix} a_{12} & a_{13} \\ a_{32} & a_{33} \end{vmatrix}, \quad A_{22} = + \begin{vmatrix} a_{11} & a_{13} \\ a_{31} & a_{33} \end{vmatrix}, \quad A_{23} = - \begin{vmatrix} a_{11} & a_{12} \\ a_{31} & a_{32} \end{vmatrix},$$

and we may therefore write

$$\underline{|A| = a_{21}A_{21} + a_{22}A_{22} + a_{23}A_{23}.} \tag{ii}$$

Similarly, if A_{31}, A_{32}, A_{33}, are the cofactors of the elements a_{31}, a_{32}, a_{33}, respectively, then it can be shown, following exactly the same procedure as above, that

$$\underline{|A| = a_{31}A_{31} + a_{32}A_{32} + a_{33}A_{33},} \tag{iii}$$

where

$$A_{31} = + \begin{vmatrix} a_{12} & a_{13} \\ a_{22} & a_{23} \end{vmatrix}, \quad A_{32} = - \begin{vmatrix} a_{11} & a_{13} \\ a_{21} & a_{23} \end{vmatrix}, \quad A_{33} = + \begin{vmatrix} a_{11} & a_{12} \\ a_{21} & a_{22} \end{vmatrix}.$$

Any one of the expressions for $|A|$ in equations (i), (ii), (iii), is called a **row expansion of** $|A|$; so, for example, the expression for $|A|$ given by equation (ii) is obtained by multiplying the elements in the second row of $|A|$ by their respective cofactors.

$|A|$ can also be expanded by columns, and the proof of this is left as an exercise for the reader in Exercises 5g; the column expansions are:

$$|A| = a_{11}A_{11} + a_{21}A_{21} + a_{31}A_{31}, \qquad \text{(iv)}$$

$$|A| = a_{12}A_{12} + a_{22}A_{22} + a_{23}A_{23}, \qquad \text{(v)}$$

$$|A| = a_{13}A_{13} + a_{23}A_{23} + a_{33}A_{33}, \qquad \text{(vi)}$$

where the nine cofactors are as given above in (i), (ii), (iii). A rapid way of writing down any one of the above six expansions amounts to determining rapidly the relevant cofactors, and this may be done as follows: suppose we wish to determine A_{32}, then we delete the third row and second column of $|A|$ and write down the second order determinant from the remaining four elements,

$$\begin{vmatrix} a_{11} & a_{12} & a_{13} \\ a_{21} & a_{22} & a_{23} \\ a_{31} & a_{32} & a_{33} \end{vmatrix}$$

and therefore the numerical value of A_{32} (i.e. the minor of a_{32}) is

$$\begin{vmatrix} a_{11} & a_{13} \\ a_{21} & a_{23} \end{vmatrix}.$$

To determine the sign of A_{32}, or for that matter, any other cofactor, one writes signs (+ or -) in place of the elements in $|A|$ as shown:

$$\begin{vmatrix} + & - & + \\ - & + & - \\ + & - & + \end{vmatrix}.$$

The sign in the third row and second column is $-$, and so

$$A_{32} = - \begin{vmatrix} a_{11} & a_{13} \\ a_{21} & a_{23} \end{vmatrix}.$$

EXAMPLES

1. Evaluate the determinant

$$\begin{vmatrix} 2 & 3 & 0 \\ -4 & 1 & 5 \\ 1 & 2 & -3 \end{vmatrix},$$

by expanding (a) by the second row, and (b) by the third column.

(a) $\Delta = -(-4) \begin{vmatrix} 3 & 0 \\ 2 & -3 \end{vmatrix} + (1) \begin{vmatrix} 2 & 0 \\ 1 & -3 \end{vmatrix} - (5) \begin{vmatrix} 2 & 3 \\ 1 & 2 \end{vmatrix}$

$= 4(-9) + (-6) - 5(1),$

i.e. $\Delta = -47.$

(b) $\Delta = +(0) \begin{vmatrix} -4 & 1 \\ 1 & 2 \end{vmatrix} - (5) \begin{vmatrix} 2 & 3 \\ 1 & 2 \end{vmatrix} + (-3) \begin{vmatrix} 2 & 3 \\ -4 & 1 \end{vmatrix}$

$= 0 - 5(1) - 3(14),$

i.e. $\Delta = -47.$

2. If each of the elements in one row (or column) of a third order determinant Δ are multiplied by some scalar k, then the value of the new determinant Δ' is given by

$$\Delta' = k\Delta.$$

Proof. It follows immediately from any row or column expansion of Δ' that k is a common factor. For instance, if $\Delta = |A|$ in the text, and the first column of Δ has each of its elements multiplied by k, then

$$\Delta' = ka_{11}A_{11} + ka_{21}A_{21} + ka_{31}A_{31},$$

i.e. $\Delta' = k\Delta.$

The result also follows immediately for second order determinants.

3. If any two adjacent rows (or columns) in a third order determinant Δ are interchanged, then the value of the new determinant Δ' is given by

$$\Delta' = -\Delta.$$

Proof. This follows immediately from the definition of a third order determinant. For example, if $\Delta = |A|$ in the text, and the second and third rows of Δ are interchanged,

i.e.
$$\Delta' = \begin{vmatrix} a_{11} & a_{12} & a_{13} \\ a_{31} & a_{32} & a_{33} \\ a_{21} & a_{22} & a_{23} \end{vmatrix},$$

then

$$\Delta' = a_{11}a_{32}a_{23} - a_{11}a_{33}a_{22} - a_{12}a_{31}a_{23} + a_{13}a_{31}a_{22} - a_{13}a_{32}a_{21} = -\Delta.$$

The same holds true for second order determinants.

4. If any two adjacent rows (or columns) are identical in a third order determinant, then the value of that determinant is zero.

Proof. Let the determinant be Δ, then interchanging the two identical rows (or columns) leaves the value of Δ unchanged. But, according to example 3 above,

$$\Delta = -\Delta,$$

which is true only if $\Delta = 0$.

This result is also true for determinants of order 2, and is especially helpful in the quick recognition of singular matrices of orders 2 and 3 (for the latter case, see next section).

EXERCISES 5g

1. Evaluate the determinants,

$$\begin{vmatrix} 1 & 5 & 4 \\ 2 & 3 & 1 \\ -4 & 6 & 2 \end{vmatrix}, \quad \begin{vmatrix} 0 & 1 & 2 \\ 3 & 4 & 5 \\ -1 & -2 & 3 \end{vmatrix},$$

by expanding along (a) the third rows (b) the second columns.

2. Prove that the expressions given in equations (iv), (v), and (vi) in the text are true.

3. Prove that if any two *non-adjacent* rows (or columns) in a third order determinant Δ are interchanged then the value of the new determinant Δ' is given by

$$\Delta' = -\Delta.$$

(*Hint:* consider interchanging the first and third columns, say, then labelling the columns in Δ as 1, 2 and 3, the following *adjacent* interchanges are necessary: $123 \to 213 \to 231 \to 321$.)

4. Prove that if any two *non-adjacent* rows (or columns) in a third order determinant Δ are identical, then $\Delta = 0$. (*Hint:* see question 3 above.)

5. If Δ_1 and Δ_2 are any two determinants of the third order given by

$$\Delta_1 = \begin{vmatrix} a_{11} & a_{12} & a_{13} \\ a_{21} & a_{22} & a_{23} \\ a_{31} & a_{32} & a_{33} \end{vmatrix}, \quad \Delta_2 = \begin{vmatrix} b_{11} & b_{12} & b_{13} \\ b_{21} & b_{22} & b_{23} \\ b_{31} & b_{32} & b_{33} \end{vmatrix},$$

it can be shown that

$$\Delta_1\Delta_2 = \Delta_2\Delta_1 = \begin{vmatrix} c_{11} & c_{12} & c_{13} \\ c_{21} & c_{22} & c_{23} \\ c_{31} & c_{32} & c_{33} \end{vmatrix},$$

where $c_{ij} = \sum_{\lambda=1}^{3} a_{i\lambda}b_{\lambda j}$.

[N.B. Since determinants are scalars, i.e. ordinary numbers—real or complex, it follows that $\Delta_1\Delta_2 = \Delta_2\Delta_1$—i.e. the commutative law holds for multiplication of determinants.]

Prove this theorem in the case for two second order determinants, and illustrate the theorem numerically for two third order determinants.

6. Prove that transposing a determinant of the second or third order (i.e. writing rows for columns and columns for rows) does not alter the value of the determinant.

7. Prove that if each of the elements in any row (or column) of a third order determinant are proportional to each of the elements in any other row (or column) of the determinant, then the value of the determinant is zero. Consider separately the cases where (a) the rows (or columns) are adjacent, and (b) the rows (or columns) are not adjacent.

8. The **adjoint determinant** Δ^* of a third order determinant Δ is defined to be the determinant which is obtained by replacing the elements of Δ by their respective cofactors and then transposing.

Thus if Δ is given by

$$\Delta = \begin{vmatrix} a_{11} & a_{12} & a_{13} \\ a_{21} & a_{22} & a_{23} \\ a_{31} & a_{32} & a_{33} \end{vmatrix},$$

then the adjoint determinant Δ^* is given by

$$\Delta^* = \begin{vmatrix} A_{11} & A_{21} & A_{31} \\ A_{12} & A_{22} & A_{32} \\ A_{13} & A_{23} & A_{33} \end{vmatrix}.$$

Prove that $\Delta\Delta^* = \Delta^3$, i.e. $\Delta^* = \Delta^2$, $\Delta \neq 0$.

(*Hint:* see question 5 on the product of two determinants, and from the expressions for the row expansions of Δ show that the leading diagonal of $\Delta\Delta^*$ consists solely of Δ's. Also show that all the remaining elements in $\Delta\Delta^*$ are each zero.)

5.9. Inverse of a square matrix of order 3

Consider the square matrix A of order 3 given by

$$A = \begin{pmatrix} a_{11} & a_{12} & a_{13} \\ a_{21} & a_{22} & a_{23} \\ a_{31} & a_{32} & a_{33} \end{pmatrix},$$

then the **minor** of any one of the elements is defined to be the minor corresponding to that element in the determinant $|A|$ of the matrix A. Thus the minor of a_{23} is

$$\begin{vmatrix} a_{11} & a_{12} \\ a_{31} & a_{32} \end{vmatrix}.$$

The **cofactor** of any one of the elements in the matrix A is defined to be the cofactor corresponding to that element in the determinant $|A|$. Thus the cofactor of a_{23} is

$$A_{23} = - \begin{vmatrix} a_{11} & a_{12} \\ a_{31} & a_{32} \end{vmatrix}.$$

The **adjoint matrix** (written adj A) of the matrix A is defined to be the matrix which is obtained by replacing the elements of A by their respective cofactors and then transposing. So, adj A is given by

$$\text{adj } A = \begin{pmatrix} A_{11} & A_{21} & A_{31} \\ A_{12} & A_{22} & A_{32} \\ A_{13} & A_{23} & A_{33} \end{pmatrix}.$$

Note the similarity between the above definitions and those given for a determinant.

Consider now, the product adj A . A:

$$\text{adj } A \,.\, A =$$

$$\begin{pmatrix} a_{11}A_{11} + a_{12}A_{12} + a_{13}A_{13} & \begin{matrix} a_{11}A_{21} + a_{12}A_{22} + a_{13}A_{23} \\ a_{11}A_{31} + a_{12}A_{32} + a_{13}A_{33} \end{matrix} \\ a_{21}A_{11} + a_{22}A_{12} + a_{23}A_{13} & \begin{matrix} a_{21}A_{21} + a_{22}A_{22} + a_{23}A_{23} \\ a_{21}A_{31} + a_{22}A_{32} + a_{23}A_{33} \end{matrix} \\ a_{31}A_{11} + a_{32}A_{12} + a_{33}A_{13} & \begin{matrix} a_{31}A_{21} + a_{32}A_{22} + a_{33}A_{23} \\ a_{31}A_{31} + a_{32}A_{32} + a_{33}A_{33} \end{matrix} \end{pmatrix}$$

Each of the terms in the leading diagonal of adj A . A is a row expansion of $|A| = \Delta$ (say). Each of the remaining terms is zero; take for instance the term in the third row and second column of adj A . A,

$$a_{31}A_{21} + a_{32}A_{22} + a_{33}A_{23}$$

$$= -a_{31} \begin{vmatrix} a_{12} & a_{13} \\ a_{32} & a_{33} \end{vmatrix} + a_{32} \begin{vmatrix} a_{11} & a_{13} \\ a_{31} & a_{33} \end{vmatrix} - a_{33} \begin{vmatrix} a_{11} & a_{12} \\ a_{31} & a_{32} \end{vmatrix}$$

$$= \begin{vmatrix} -a_{31} & -a_{32} & -a_{33} \\ a_{11} & a_{12} & a_{13} \\ a_{31} & a_{32} & a_{33} \end{vmatrix} = 0,$$

the latter determinant having the value zero, since each of the elements in the first row is proportional to the corresponding element in the third row (see question 7, Exercise 5g). Thus

$$\text{adj } A \,.\, A = \begin{pmatrix} \Delta & 0 & 0 \\ 0 & \Delta & 0 \\ 0 & 0 & \Delta \end{pmatrix} = \Delta I,$$

where I is the unit matrix.

Similarly, A . adj $A = \Delta I$, and the proof of this is left to the reader; at this stage it would benefit the reader to compare what we have just done above with the solution to question 8, Exercise 5g.

Now in §5.7 we defined an inverse matrix A^{-1} of a matrix A of order 2 as a matrix such that

$$A^{-1}A = AA^{-1} = I.$$

We have the same definition for the **inverse matrix A^{-1} of a matrix A of order 3,** and in order to satisfy this definition we find that

$$A^{-1} = \frac{\text{adj } A}{\Delta}, \qquad \Delta \neq 0;$$

This is shown as follows:

We proved earlier that

$$\text{adj } A \cdot A = \Delta I,$$

i.e. $\qquad \dfrac{\text{adj } A \cdot A}{\Delta} = I,$ since Δ is a scalar.

Multiplying both sides to the right by A^{-1} we obtain,

$$\frac{\text{adj } A \cdot A \cdot A^{-1}}{\Delta} = IA^{-1} = A^{-1},$$

but according to the definition $AA^{-1} = I$,

$$\therefore \quad \frac{\text{adj } A \cdot I}{\Delta} = A^{-1}$$

i.e. $\qquad \dfrac{\text{adj } A}{\Delta} = A^{-1}.$

If $|A| = \Delta = 0$, then we define A to be a **singular matrix** (just as for matrices of order 2), and in this connection we note that the properties of a determinant stated in question 7, Exercise 5g, help us in the rapid recognition of singular matrices.

As numerical examples consider the following:

Let $\qquad A = \begin{pmatrix} 1 & -2 & 3 \\ 0 & 4 & 1 \\ 2 & -3 & 5 \end{pmatrix},$

then $|A| = 1(20+3) - (-2)(0-2) + 3(0-8)$, expanding by the first row,

i.e. $\qquad\qquad\qquad |A| = -5.$

$$\text{adj } A = \begin{pmatrix} 23 & 1 & -14 \\ 2 & -1 & -1 \\ -8 & -1 & 4 \end{pmatrix}.$$

$$A^{-1} = \frac{\text{adj } A}{|A|} = -\frac{1}{5} \begin{pmatrix} 23 & 1 & -14 \\ 2 & -1 & -1 \\ -8 & -1 & 4 \end{pmatrix},$$

i.e.
$$A^{-1} = \begin{pmatrix} -\frac{23}{5} & -\frac{1}{5} & \frac{14}{5} \\ -\frac{2}{5} & \frac{1}{5} & \frac{1}{5} \\ \frac{8}{5} & \frac{1}{5} & -\frac{4}{5} \end{pmatrix}.$$

It is left to the reader to check that $AA^{-1} = A^{-1}A = I$. On the other hand if

$$A = \begin{pmatrix} 3 & 5 & -9 \\ 0 & -2 & 0 \\ -4 & -1 & 12 \end{pmatrix},$$

then A is a singular matrix since each of the elements in the third column are proportional to each of the elements in the first column (proportionality factor $= -3$), and therefore the inverse matrix A^{-1} does not exist.

Having defined the inverse matrix A^{-1} of a non-singular matrix A of order three, we are now in a position to solve three linear equations in three unknowns; let the equations be

$$a_{11}x_1 + a_{12}x_2 + a_{13}x_3 = k_1$$
$$a_{21}x_1 + a_{22}x_2 + a_{23}x_3 = k_2$$
$$a_{31}x_1 + a_{32}x_2 + a_{33}x_3 = k_3,$$

then these equations expressed in matrix notation are

$$AX = K,$$

where $A = (a_{ij})$ $(i, j = 1, 2, 3)$, is the matrix of the coefficients of the set of equations, and X and K are the column vectors given by:

$$X = \begin{pmatrix} x_1 \\ x_2 \\ x_3 \end{pmatrix}, \qquad K = \begin{pmatrix} k_1 \\ k_2 \\ k_3 \end{pmatrix}.$$

Multiplying both sides of our matrix equation by A^{-1} to the left, we obtain,

$$A^{-1}AX = A^{-1}K, \qquad |A| \neq 0,$$

i.e. $$IX = A^{-1}K,$$

or $$\underline{X = A^{-1}K.}$$

Consider the following numerical example:

$$2x + y - z = 3$$
$$x - y + 2z = 1$$
$$3x + 4y + 3z = -2,$$

in matrix notation,

$$\begin{pmatrix} 2 & 1 & -1 \\ 1 & -1 & 2 \\ 3 & 4 & 3 \end{pmatrix} \begin{pmatrix} x \\ y \\ z \end{pmatrix} = \begin{pmatrix} 3 \\ 1 \\ -2 \end{pmatrix}.$$

Here, $\Delta = +2(-11) - 1(-3) + (-1)(7) = -26,$

and $$\text{adj } A = \begin{pmatrix} -11 & -7 & 1 \\ 3 & 9 & -5 \\ 7 & -5 & -3 \end{pmatrix},$$

and therefore $$A^{-1} = -\frac{1}{26} \begin{pmatrix} -11 & -7 & 1 \\ 3 & 9 & -5 \\ 7 & -5 & -3 \end{pmatrix};$$

thus, $$\begin{pmatrix} x \\ y \\ z \end{pmatrix} = -\frac{1}{26} \begin{pmatrix} -11 & -7 & 1 \\ 3 & 9 & -5 \\ 7 & -5 & -3 \end{pmatrix} \begin{pmatrix} 3 \\ 1 \\ -2 \end{pmatrix},$$

i.e. $$\begin{pmatrix} x \\ y \\ z \end{pmatrix} = \begin{pmatrix} \frac{21}{13} \\ -\frac{14}{13} \\ -\frac{11}{13} \end{pmatrix},$$

$$x = \frac{21}{13}, \qquad y = -\frac{14}{13}, \qquad z = -\frac{11}{13}.$$

To conclude this section, we look at some more properties of matrices and their inverses:

(i) *The inverse A^{-1} of a non-singular matrix A is unique*

Assume on the contrary, and let B be another inverse of A, then $BA = AB = I$. Multiplying both sides of $BA = I$ to the right by A^{-1} we have

$$BAA^{-1} = IA^{-1} = A^{-1},$$

but $\qquad\qquad AA^{-1} = I,$

$$\therefore\ BI = A^{-1},$$

i.e. $\qquad\qquad \underline{B = A^{-1}.}$

Similarly, multiplying both sides of $AB = I$ to the left by A^{-1},

$$A^{-1}AB = A^{-1}I = A^{-1},$$

i.e. $\qquad\qquad IB = A^{-1},$

i.e. $\qquad\qquad \underline{B = A^{-1}.}$

Thus, A^{-1} is unique; this result ensures a unique solution to the equation $AX = K$, namely $X = A^{-1}K$.

(ii) *If $AB = 0$, and A is non-singular, then $B = 0$*

It was shown in §5.5 (examples, no. 5) that in general if $AB = 0$, then it does not necessarily follow that $A = 0$ or $B = 0$. However, if A is non-singular, then A^{-1} exists, and therefore multiplying both sides of $AB = 0$ to the left by A^{-1},

$$A^{-1}AB = A^{-1}0 = 0,$$

i.e. $\qquad\qquad IB = 0,$

$$\therefore\ \underline{B = 0.}$$

Similarly if $AB = 0$, and B is non-singular, then $A = 0$.

(iii) *The inverse of the product AB of two non-singular matrices A and B of the same order is equal to the product $B^{-1}A^{-1}$ of their inverses*

Consider the product $(B^{-1}A^{-1})(AB)$:

$$(B^{-1}A^{-1})(AB) = B^{-1}(A^{-1}A)B = B^{-1}IB = B^{-1}B = I.$$

So, by definition of an inverse matrix,

$$\underline{(AB)^{-1} = B^{-1}A^{-1}}.$$

Similarly, for non-singular matrices A, B, C, of the same order,

$$(ABC)^{-1} = [(AB)C]^{-1} = C^{-1}(AB)^{-1} = \underline{C^{-1}B^{-1}A^{-1}},$$

by double application of the theorem.

In general, for non-singular matrices $A_1, A_2, \ldots, A_n$, of the same order,

$$\underline{(A_1A_2\ldots A_n)^{-1} = A_n^{-1}A_{n-1}^{-1}\ldots A_1^{-1}},$$

and it is left to the reader to prove this by induction on n.

(iv) *The operations of transposing and finding the inverse of a non-singular matrix A are commutative, i.e. $(A^{-1})' = (A')^{-1}$*

In §5.6 we proved that for any two matrices A and B conformable for the product, $(AB)' = B'A'$, so for a non-singular matrix A,

$$(AA^{-1})' = (A^{-1})'A',$$

writing $A^{-1} = B$.

Now, $AA^{-1} = I$, therefore $(AA^{-1})' = I' = I$.

Therefore, $I = (A^{-1})'A'$, and by definition of an inverse matrix, the inverse of $A' = (A^{-1})'$,

i.e. $$\underline{(A')^{-1} = (A^{-1})'}.$$

The above four properties are independent of the orders of the matrices involved (except, of course, that the matrices must conform for the product where necessary), and so apply in particular to matrices of orders two and three.

EXERCISES 5h

1. Find the inverses, where they exist, of the following matrices:

(a) $\begin{pmatrix} 1 & 2 & 3 \\ 0 & 3 & 4 \\ -1 & 5 & 2 \end{pmatrix}$
(b) $\begin{pmatrix} 0 & -1 & 3 \\ 4 & 6 & -2 \\ 2 & 1 & -5 \end{pmatrix}$

(c) $\begin{pmatrix} 3 & 6 & 4 \\ 1 & 3 & 2 \\ 1 & 9 & 6 \end{pmatrix}$
(d) $\begin{pmatrix} a & 0 & 0 \\ 0 & b & 0 \\ 0 & 0 & c \end{pmatrix}$

2. Solve the following equations, where solutions exist:

(a) $3x - 4y + 2z = 0$
$4x + y - 3z = 1$
$-x + y - z = 2$

(b) $\alpha + 2\beta - 4\gamma = 1$
$-2\alpha + \beta + 3\gamma = 4$
$-3\alpha - 6\beta + 12\gamma = 24$

(c) $4l - 3m = 3 - 2n$
$m + n + l = 0$
$2l - 4n = 5m - 1$

Check your answers by direct substitution.

3. Transformations T_1, T_2, T_3, T_4 on points in three-dimensional space are given by the linear equations:

$$T_i: A_i X = X', \qquad i = 1, 2, 3, 4,$$

where

$$X = \begin{pmatrix} x \\ y \\ z \end{pmatrix}, \qquad X' = \begin{pmatrix} x' \\ y' \\ z' \end{pmatrix},$$

$$A_1 = \begin{pmatrix} 1 & 0 & 0 \\ 0 & 1 & 0 \\ 0 & 0 & 1 \end{pmatrix}, \qquad A_2 = \begin{pmatrix} 1 & 0 & 0 \\ 0 & 1 & 0 \\ 0 & 0 & -1 \end{pmatrix},$$

$$A_3 = \begin{pmatrix} 1 & 0 & 0 \\ 0 & -1 & 0 \\ 0 & 0 & 1 \end{pmatrix}, \qquad A_4 = \begin{pmatrix} 1 & 0 & 0 \\ 0 & 1 & 0 \\ 0 & 0 & k \end{pmatrix},$$

k some real number.

Prove that: (a) T_1 is the identity transformation,
(b) T_2 reflects points in the x–y plane,
(c) T_3 reflects points in the x–z plane,
(d) T_4 stretches (*not shears*) in the direction of the z-axis.

Draw sketches illustrating these transformations (e.g. transform a unit cube).

4. Write down the inverses A_i^{-1} of the transformation matrices A_i referred to in question 3 and interpret geometrically. Write down the transformation matrices representing the following transformations:

(a) T_2T_3 (b) T_3T_2 (c) T_3T_4 (d) $T_4^{-1}T_3^{-1}$
(e) a stretch in the direction of the x-axis: T_5 (say)
(f) stretching in the directions of both the x-axis and the y-axis: T_6 (say)
(g) T_4T_6 (h) $(T_4T_5)^{-1}$ (j) $T_5^{-1}T_4^{-1}$.

5. Prove that for any non-singular matrix A of order three that,
    (a) $|A^{-1}| = |A|^{-1}$ (b) $(A^{-1})^{-1} = A$ (c) $|\text{adj } A| = |A|^2$.

6. Prove that for any two third order matrices A and B that,
    (a) $|AB| = |A||B|$ (b) if A is singular, then AB is singular.

7. Prove that the inverse of a third order symmetric matrix is symmetric, and that the inverse of a third order Hermitian is Hermitian.

8. The **rank** of any $m \times n$ matrix is defined to be the order of the largest non-vanishing minor of the matrix; e.g. if A and B are the matrices given below, then the rank of A is 3 since $|A| \neq 0$, and the rank of B is 2 since the largest non-vanishing minor is of order 2. The rank of any null matrix is taken to be zero, and the rank of a matrix consisting of a single element is taken to be one.

$$A = \begin{pmatrix} 3 & 2 & 1 \\ -1 & 5 & 4 \\ 4 & -2 & 0 \end{pmatrix}, \quad B = \begin{pmatrix} 3 & 0 & 0 & 1 \\ 0 & 0 & 0 & 2 \\ 0 & 1 & 0 & 4 \end{pmatrix}.$$

Find the ranks of the following matrices:

$$\begin{pmatrix} 2 & 0 & 4 \\ -2 & 1 & 0 \\ 0 & 1 & 5 \end{pmatrix}, \quad \begin{pmatrix} 1 & 3 & 4 \\ 2 & 6 & 8 \\ 0 & 0 & 0 \end{pmatrix}, \quad \begin{pmatrix} 4 & 1 & 0 & 0 \\ -1 & 2 & 3 & -5 \\ 0 & 1 & 0 & 2 \end{pmatrix},$$

$$\begin{pmatrix} 5 & 0 & 1 & 0 & 1 \\ 0 & 2 & 1 & 6 & -2 \\ 1 & 0 & 4 & -3 & 1 \end{pmatrix}, \quad \begin{pmatrix} 3 & 2 & 0 & -2 & 1 \\ 0 & 0 & 1 & 4 & 3 \\ 6 & 4 & 0 & -4 & 2 \\ 0 & 0 & 3 & 12 & 9 \end{pmatrix}.$$

9. Show that for the following three equations to be **consistent** the rank of the matrix of the coefficients must be less than 3:

$$a_{11}x_1 + a_{12}x_2 + a_{13}x_3 = 0$$

$$a_{21}x_1 + a_{22}x_2 + a_{23}x_3 = 0$$

$$a_{31}x_1 + a_{32}x_2 + a_{33}x_3 = 0.$$

(*Hint:* choose any pair of equations and divide each one throughout by x_3, say, and solve for x_1/x_3 and x_2/x_3. Divide the remaining equation throughout by x_3, and substitute the expressions obtained for x_1/x_3 and x_2/x_3 into this equation.)

CHAPTER 6

Algebraic Structure

6.1. It is implicit in all the mathematics that has been presented to the reader at "ordinary level" and, in particular, in the algebra that has so far been developed in this book, that mathematics is built up by logical processes based on axioms. We mean by "logical processes based on axioms" that there is a deductive system in which theorems are shown to be necessary consequences of some previously proved propositions and theorems; these in turn must be proved, and so on. This deductive process would, of course, go on for ever (infinite regression) unless we stopped at some point. Hence, there must be a number of statements called axioms which are accepted as true, and from these we attempt to deduce all other theorems by purely logical argument.

The above scheme of things sounds straightforward enough, but in forming our axioms we run into trouble. The three most important considerations in laying down our structure are (i) our axioms must be **independent,** i.e. no two or more axioms should be equivalent in the sense that one can be deduced from another; (ii) the list of axioms must be **complete** in order that all the theorems in the system (e.g. algebra of sets) may be deduced; (iii) the axioms must be **consistent,** i.e. no two theorems deduced from them must contradict each other. Above all, the axioms should be small in number and simple in nature. It is in the question of completeness and consistency that we run into trouble. A large amount of work has been done in the past thirty years or so in search of consistency and completeness proofs, at least in the algebra of real numbers, with little success. In fact it has been indicated that the existence of such proofs is doubted (within strictly closed systems of concepts).

However, in spite of the "crisis in the foundations" of mathematics, the deductive method seems to be the most natural way of illuminating the essential structure of a subject in mathematics, and we are going to exemplify this point of view when dealing with the elementary theory of groups, rings, fields and the number system.

Before we embark on our study of algebraic structure, one further important point must be made; into any set of axioms must enter certain undefined concepts. For, like axioms themselves, if we are to avoid infinite regressions, we must accept that we "understand" what is meant by a certain undefined concept— intuition helps us in this "understanding". Two examples of undefined concepts, **set,** and **element,** are to be found in the axiom concerning the operation of union on two sets (see Chapter 2) written here again for convenience: "The operation of union on two **sets** A and B, written $A \cup B = C$, is such that the **elements** of C are members of A or B or both A and B." The difficulty in defining set lies in finding only synonyms of set (e.g. collection) for suitable words of description. Likewise for element. We did, however, define operation (see Chapter 2): "An instruction for obtaining sets from given sets", having accepted an intuitive understanding of set!

6.2. Let us consider the situation when we multiply directed numbers by themselves. We recall that

$$(+) \times (+) = (+)$$
$$(+) \times (-) = (-)$$
$$(-) \times (+) = (-)$$
$$(-) \times (-) = (+).$$

Suppose we write x for $(+)$ and y for $(-)$, then for the two elements x and y we have the multiplication table overleaf. To find the product of two elements we locate the point of intersection of the row corresponding to the first element with the column corresponding to the second element. We notice for the

×	x	y
x	x	y
y	y	x

set $\{x, y\}$ that all possible products (e.g. $x \times x$, $x \times y$) are also elements of the set—this property is called **closure**. Also, $xy = yx$—the elements are therefore **commutative** under the operation of multiplication. Multiplication by x leaves each element unchanged, e.g. $x \times x = x$, $x \times y = y$. We call such an element x an **identity element**.

EXERCISES 6a

1. Consider all the possibilities of odd and even numbers being added together, then construct an algebra of two elements, odd and even, with the aid of an addition table and confirm the following properties: (a) closure; (b) commutativity; (c) there is an identity element.

2. Repeat above under the operation of multiplication instead of addition and confirm (a), (b) and (c).

6.3. In an arithmetic multiplication table, we have:

×	1	2	3	4	.
1	1	2	3	4	.
2	2	4	6	8	.
3	3	6	9	12	.
4	4	8	12	16	.
.	.	.	.	.	.

In this case, in addition to the above three properties, we have

$$3 \times 2 \times 4 = (3 \times 2) \times 4 = 3 \times (2 \times 4)$$

and in general,

$$a_1a_2a_3\ldots a_n = a_1(a_2a_3\ldots a_n)$$

$$= a_1a_2(a_3a_4\ldots a_n),$$

etc. for $a_i \in J^+$, $i = 1, 2, \ldots, n$; this property is called **associativity**.

6.4. Let us now consider all the possible rotations of an equilateral triangle in its plane, which bring it into coincidence with itself, about the centroid (Fig. 6.1).

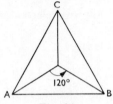

Fig. 6.1.

We can choose the rotations to be in a counter-clockwise sense (being quite arbitrary), and agree to call rotations equal if they differ by an integral number of revolutions (i.e. by $2k\pi$, $k = 0, 1, 2, \ldots, n, \ldots$). Thus a rotation of 120° will carry A to B, B to C, and C to A; let this rotation be written a_1. A rotation of 240° will carry A to C, B to A, and C to B; let this rotation be written a_2. A rotation of 360° produces the same result as a rotation of 0°; let this be written a_0. We now define the addition of two rotations to be the operation of carrying out the first then the second. Exhausting all the possibilities:

$$a_0 + a_0 = a_0$$

$$a_0 + a_1 = a_1 + a_0 = a_1$$

$$a_0 + a_2 = a_2 + a_0 = a_2$$

$$a_1 + a_2 = a_2 + a_1 = a_0$$

$$a_1 + a_1 = a_2$$

$$a_2 + a_2 = a_1$$

and writing these results in the form of an addition table:

+	a_0	a_1	a_2
a_0	a_0	a_1	a_2
a_1	a_1	a_2	a_0
a_2	a_2	a_0	a_1

From the addition table we observe:

(i) The addition of any two elements is itself an element—**closure.**

(ii) Addition is **associative,**

e.g. $a_1 + a_0 + a_2 = a_1 + (a_0 + a_2) = a_1 + a_2 = a_0$

or $a_1 + a_0 + a_2 = (a_1 + a_0) + a_2 = a_1 + a_2 = a_0$.

(iii) There is an **identity element** a_0 such that

$a_0 + a_i = a_i + a_0 = a_i$, where $i = 0, 1, 2$.

(iv) Each element has an **inverse** a^{-1} such that
$a_i^{-1} + a_i = a_i + a_i^{-1} = a_0$ (the identity)
where $i = 0, 1, 2$.
Since
$$a_0 + a_0 = a_0,$$
and $\quad\quad a_1 + a_2 = a_0,$
then $\quad\quad a_0^{-1} = a_0 \quad a_1^{-1} = a_2 \quad a_2^{-1} = a_1$.

(v) Addition is **commutative.**

In the set $\{x, y\}$, $x^{-1} = x$, and $y^{-1} = y$. Although there exists an identity element $1 \in J^+$ under multiplication, there are no inverse elements in J^+,

e.g. if $a = 5$ then $a^{-1} = \dfrac{1}{5}$ in order that

$$a^{-1} \times a = a \times a^{-1} = 1, \text{ but } \frac{1}{5} \notin J^+.$$

EXERCISE 6b

Instead of considering the rotations of an equilateral triangle which bring it into coincidence with itself, consider the rotations of a square in its plane about its centre and construct an addition table for the four elements representing rotations through 0°, 90°, 180° and 270°, respectively. Again treat any two rotations which differ by $2k\pi$ as identical. Confirm the properties found in the algebra of rotations of the equilateral triangle.

6.5. The axioms of addition for the set J are:

(i) For all a, $b \in J$, $(a + b) \in J$ is uniquely determined—**closure**.

(ii) For all a, b, $c \in J$, $(a + b) + c = a + (b + c)$—**associativity**.

(iii) $\exists$ an **identity** $0 \in J$, such that for all $a \in J$,

$$0 + a = a + 0 = a.$$

(iv) $\exists$ an **inverse** $(-a) \in J$ such that for all $a \in J$,

$$(-a) + a = a + (-a) = 0 \qquad \text{(the identity)}.$$

(v) For all a, $b \in J$, $a + b = b + a$—**commutativity**.

6.6. The axioms of multiplication for the set J are:

(i) For all a, $b \in J$, $(ab) \in J$—**closure**.

(ii) For all a, b, $c \in J$, $(ab)c = a(bc)$—**associativity**.

(iii) $\exists$ an **identity** 1 such that for all $a \in J$,

$$1 \times a = a \times 1 = a.$$

(iv) For all a, $b \in J$, $ab = ba$—**commutativity**.

There are no inverse elements in J under multiplication for reasons similar to those given in this connection for J^+.

We will be looking closely into number systems later on in this chapter.

6.7. It was seen in the last chapter that for any 2×2 or 3×3 non-singular matrices, the operation of multiplication is associative although non-commutative. There also exist an identity matrix and inverse matrices. What is true for 2×2 and 3×3 non-singular matrices can be shown to be true for $n \times n$ non-singular matrices, but it is a little beyond the scope of this book. Closure was not discussed, so let us investigate a particular case now:

Let $\quad A = \begin{pmatrix} a_{11} & a_{12} \\ a_{21} & a_{22} \end{pmatrix} \quad$ and $\quad B = \begin{pmatrix} b_{11} & b_{12} \\ b_{21} & b_{22} \end{pmatrix}$

be any two members of the set M of all non-singular 2×2 matrices with integers as elements of the matrices. So we have the following set for the elements:

$$\{\text{all } a \text{ and all } b \in J: (a_{11}a_{22} - a_{12}a_{21}) \neq 0,$$
$$(b_{11}b_{22} - b_{12}b_{21}) \neq 0\}.$$

We saw earlier (§§ 6.5–6) that we have closure under the operation of addition and closure under the operation of multiplication in the set J. Thus, all $(ab) \in J$ (e.g. $[a_{11}b_{12}] \in J$) and all the sums of the products $\in J$ (e.g. $[a_{11}b_{12} + a_{12}b_{22}] \in J$). All the elements of AB are therefore integers. AB is also a 2×2 matrix, but one point still remains: is AB non-singular? For, to say that AB has integers for its elements and that it is 2×2 does not imply that $AB \in M$. From Chapter 5 we know that $|AB| = |A||B|$; therefore since $|A| \neq 0$, and $|B| \neq 0$, $|A||B| = |AB| \neq 0$, and so AB is non-singular.

We have now proved that the above set M is closed under the operation of multiplication, since $AB \in M$ for any $A, B \in M$.

EXERCISES 6c

1. Prove that the 2×2 identity matrix $\in M$.
2. For any matrix $A \in M$, does A^{-1} exist? Is $A^{-1} \in M$? Give reasons.

Summary

Sections 6.1–7 are summed up in the table on page 177. One can see at a glance what properties a particular algebra possesses. Further very important examples will be met later.

A set under a particular operation that has the properties of (i) closure, (ii) associativity, (iii) the existence of identity elements,

Set	Operation	Properties				
		Closure	Associativity	Identity	Inverse	Commutativity
$\{x, y\}$	$\times$	$\checkmark$	$\times$	$\checkmark$	$\checkmark$	$\checkmark$
J^+	$\times$	$\checkmark$	$\checkmark$	$\checkmark$	$\times$	$\checkmark$
Rotations of Δ	$+$	$\checkmark$	$\checkmark$	$\checkmark$	$\checkmark$	$\checkmark$
J	$+$	$\checkmark$	$\checkmark$	$\checkmark$	$\checkmark$	$\checkmark$
J	$\times$	$\checkmark$	$\checkmark$	$\checkmark$	$\times$	$\checkmark$
M	$\times$	$\checkmark$	$\checkmark$	$\checkmark$	$\times$	$\times$

(iv) the existence of inverse elements, is called a **group**. A group which has the property of commutativity is called an **Abelian group,** after the Norwegian mathematician, N. H. Abel (1802–29). Thus, the set of rotations of the equilateral triangle under the binary operation of addition is an Abelian group; J under the binary operation of addition is also an Abelian group. The remaining sets under the corresponding operations are not groups, with the exception of $\{x, y\}$ if one of the elements is "counted twice" to satisfy associativity.

6.8. Formal definition of a group

(i) **Closure:** A group G is a set (finite or infinite) of elements under a binary operation $*$ (say) such that for all a, $b \in G$, $a * b \in G$ is uniquely determined.

(ii) **Associativity:** For all a, b, $c \in G$,

$$a * (b * c) = (a * b) * c.$$

(iii) **Existence of a left identity element:** For all $a \in G$, $\exists$ an $e \in G$ such that $ea = a$.

(iv) **Existence of a left inverse element:** For each $a \in G$, $\exists$ an $a^{-1} \in G$ such that $a^{-1}a = e$.

Should the group be commutative, i.e. for all $a, b \in G, a * b = b * a$, then as mentioned in §6.7 the group is called an Abelian group. A finite group is a group containing a finite number of elements and this number is defined to be the **order of the group.** An infinite group has an infinite number of elements in it.

When there is no possibility of ambiguity, i.e. when only one operation is being considered, the binary operation symbol $*$ is often omitted.

6.9. Basic group theorems

(i) *The operation $*$ over any finite number of elements*

According to axiom (i), ab is uniquely defined, whereas we do not know for the moment what is meant by abc. Does $abc = a(bc)$? (Which means find bc ($= m$ say) and then find am.) Or does $abc = (ab)c$? (Which means find ab ($= n$ say) and then find nc.) There are no other possible interpretations of abc. Now, referring to axiom (ii), we see that $a(bc) = (ab)c$. Thus, as abc could be interpreted as $a(bc)$ or $(ab)c$, we have now deduced the meaning of abc.

Similarly, we can investigate what is meant by $abcd$. We might try $abcd = (abc)d$ or $(ab)(cd)$ or $a(bcd)$. Naturally, the reader can immediately think of other possibilities such as:

$$[(ab)c]d \quad \text{or} \quad [a(bc)]d \quad \text{or} \quad a[(bc)d] \quad \text{or} \quad a[b(cd)]$$

(actually, the possibilities are now exhausted). From above we know that $(ab)c = a(bc)$ and $(bc)d = b(cd)$. Thus it is only necessary to show that $abcd = (abc)d = (ab)(cd) = a(bcd)$ in order to understand completely what is meant by $abcd$:

$$abcd = (abc)d = [a(bc)]d,$$

and so for the three elements a, (bc) and d,

$$[a(bc)]d = a[(bc)d] = a(bcd),$$

i.e. $$abcd = (abc)d = a(bcd).$$

Secondly, $abcd = (abc)d = [(ab)c]d$, and for the three elements (ab), c and d,

$$[(ab)c]d = (ab)(cd).$$

Hence,

$$abcd = (abc)d = (ab)(cd) = a(bcd).$$

Following the above procedure soon defines $abcde$, and using suffixes, in general:

$$a_1a_2a_3 \ldots a_n = a_1(a_2a_3 \ldots a_n)$$
$$= (a_1a_2a_3 \ldots a_k)(a_{k+1}a_{k+2} \ldots a_n).$$

The general case is proved by the principle of induction (see Chapter 3) and the proof is left as an exercise to the reader. As stated in axiom (i), ab is unique, and so $abc = a(bc) = am$, where $m = bc$, is also unique. Likewise $abcd$ is unique, and in general, $a_1a_2a_3 \ldots a_n$ is uniquely determined.

(ii) *Existence of a right inverse element*

As stated in axiom (iv), there exists at least one left inverse element a^{-1} such that for all a, $a^{-1}a = e$, and we now show that there exists at least one right inverse element a^{-1} such that for all a, $aa^{-1} = e$:

$$a^{-1} = ea^{-1} \quad (\exists \ a \text{ left identity element } e)$$
$$= (a^{-1}a)a^{-1} = a^{-1}(aa^{-1}) \quad \text{(associativity)} \qquad \text{(i)}$$

Let w be a left inverse element of a^{-1}, then

$$wa^{-1} = e = w[a^{-1}(aa^{-1})] \quad \text{from equation (i)},$$

i.e. $\quad e = wa^{-1}(aa^{-1}) \quad$ (associativity)

i.e. $\quad \underline{e = e(aa^{-1}) = \underline{aa^{-1}}}.$

(iii) *Existence of a right identity element*

For a right identity element to exist, we must show that $ae = a$ for all $a \in G$:

$$ae = a(a^{-1}a) = (aa^{-1})a \quad \text{(associativity)}$$
$$= ea \quad \text{(theorem 2)}$$

i.e. $\qquad \underline{ae = a.}$

(iv) There are unique elements x and y for x, y ∈ G, such that
$ax = b$ and $ya = b$, for any $a, b \in G$

Now	$ax = b,$
so	$a^{-1}ax = a^{-1}b$
i.e.	$(a^{-1}a)x = a^{-1}b$ (associativity),
i.e.	$ex = a^{-1}b.$
Thus,	$\underline{x = a^{-1}b.}$

Suppose x is not unique, i.e. $ax' = b$ also satisfies the equation,
then $ax' = ax$, therefore

$$x' = ex' = (a^{-1}a)x' = a^{-1}(ax') = a^{-1}(ax) = (a^{-1}a)x = ex,$$

i.e. $\underline{x' = x.}$

Hence, $x = a^{-1}b$ is the unique solution to the equation $ax = b$.
It is left to the reader to show that $y = ba^{-1}$ is the unique solution
of $ya = b$.

(v) The uniqueness of the identity element

Only the existence of a left identity element is stated in axiom
(iii), i.e. there may be several left identity elements in G. However,
theorem 4 shows that every left identity element is the unique
solution of $ya = a$. By theorem 3 we may now drop the description
"left".

(vi) The uniqueness of the inverse element

Similarly, there may be several left inverse elements of a particular element $a \in G$, but theorem 4 shows that every left inverse
element is the unique solution of $ya = e$. By theorem 2, "left"
can be dropped.

In virtue of theorems 5 and 6 we may now draw up an alternative
list of axioms for a group:

(as before) (i) **Closure:** A group G is a set (finite or infinite) of
elements under a binary operation * (say) such
that for all $a, b \in G$, $a * b \in G$ is uniquely determined.

(as before) (ii) **Associativity:** For all a, b, $c \in G$,

$$a * (b * c) = (a * b) * c.$$

   (iii) **Unique identity element:** For all $a \in G$, there is a unique element $e \in G$ such that $ea = ae = a$.

   (iv) **Unique inverse element:** For each $a \in G$, there is a unique element $a^{-1} \in G$ such that for each a

$$a^{-1}a = aa^{-1} = e.$$

It may be argued that axioms (iii) and (iv) in the alternative list are partly redundant, that is one might say that the mere existence of a left identity element (or right—quite arbitrary) is sufficient for axiom (iii) as we have seen that the uniqueness and operation to the left or right of the identity can be deduced. One could argue similarly for the left inverse element of each element. However, the alternative list of axioms is much more convenient than the first list when deciding whether a particular set qualifies itself to be called a group or not.

6.10. Further implications of the group concept

Cancelling. If $ab = ac$, then by theorem 4,

$$b = a^{-1}ac = ec,$$

i.e. $$\underline{b = c.}$$

Similarly, if $ba = ca$, then $b = caa^{-1} = ce$, i.e. $\underline{b = c}$. We can therefore cancel, but a note of warning is necessary: **we can either cancel to the left or cancel to the right but not both for non-Abelian groups.** For example, if $ab = ca$, then $b = a^{-1}ca \neq a^{-1}ac$ for non-Abelian groups. For Abelian groups, of course, order is unimportant:

$$ab = ca \Leftrightarrow ba = ca \Leftrightarrow b = c.$$

Isomorphism. We first met the concept of isomorphism in §2.5 and we now see the implications of this concept in terms of groups. Two groups, G_1 and G_2, are isomorphic if

(i) we can set up a one–one correspondence between the elements $a_1, b_1, c_1, \ldots, \in G_1$, and the elements $a_2, b_2, c_2, \ldots \in G_2$;

(ii) $j_1 \circled{1} k_1 = m_1$ ⎫
                                    ⎬ where $\begin{matrix} j_1 \leftrightarrow j_2 \\ k_1 \leftrightarrow k_2, \\ m_1 \leftrightarrow m_2 \end{matrix}$ and
        $j_2 \circled{2} k_2 = m_2$ ⎭

where G_1 is under the operation $\circled{1}$, and G_2 is under the operation $\circled{2}$.

The identity element in G_1 will correspond to the identity element in G_2. It can be very easily shown that the inverse, j_1^{-1}, of any element $j_1 \in G_1$ corresponds to the inverse, j_2^{-1}, of the element $j_2 \in G_2$, and this is left in the exercises below.

EXAMPLES

1. If $aa = a$, $a \in G$, then prove that $a = e$.

Proof. $ae = a$, but $aa = a$ (given)

$\therefore ae = aa$, and by left cancellation,

$$e = a.$$

2. To prove that $(a^{-1})^{-1} = a$, where $a \in G$.

Proof. Writing $m = a^{-1}$, then $(a^{-1})^{-1} = m^{-1}$ and

$$(a^{-1})(a^{-1})^{-1} = mm^{-1} = e.$$

Multiplying both sides by a to the left of

$$(a^{-1})(a^{-1})^{-1} = e,$$

and we get,

$$a(a^{-1})(a^{-1})^{-1} = ae = a$$
$$\Rightarrow (aa^{-1})(a^{-1})^{-1} = a \qquad \text{(associativity)}$$
$$\Rightarrow e(a^{-1})^{-1} = a$$
$$\Rightarrow (a^{-1})^{-1} = a.$$

3. To prove that in G, $(ab)^{-1} = b^{-1}a^{-1}$ and in general,

$$(a_1 a_2 \dots a_n)^{-1} = a_n^{-1} \dots a_2^{-1} a_1^{-1}.$$

Proof. If the inverse of (ab) is $b^{-1}a^{-1}$, then we have to prove that $(b^{-1}a^{-1})(ab) = e$.

Now, $(b^{-1}a^{-1})(ab) = b^{-1}(a^{-1}a)b$ (associativity)

$$= b^{-1}eb$$

$$= b^{-1}b$$

$$= e.$$

Using the principle of induction (see Chapter 3):

for the case $n = 1$ $(a_1)^{-1} = a_1^{-1}$ which is evidently true;

for the case $n = k$ $(a_1a_2\ldots a_k)^{-1} = a_k^{-1}\ldots a_2^{-1}a_1^{-1}$ which we assume to be true, i.e. we assume the truth of

$$(a_1a_2\ldots a_k)(a_k^{-1}\ldots a_2^{-1}a_1^{-1}) = e;$$

for the case $n = k+1$ $(a_1a_2\ldots a_ka_{k+1})(a_{k+1}^{-1}a_k^{-1}\ldots a_2^{-1}a_1^{-1})$

$$= (a_1a_2\ldots a_k)a_{k+1}a_{k+1}^{-1}(a_k^{-1}\ldots a_2^{-1}a_1^{-1})$$

$$= (a_1a_2\ldots a_k)e(a_k^{-1}\ldots a_2^{-1}a_1^{-1})$$

$$= (a_1a_2\ldots a_k)(a_k^{-1}\ldots a_2^{-1}a_1^{-1})$$

$$= e \quad \text{(by assumption)}.$$

Thus, the truth for the case $n = k$ implies the truth for the case $n = k+1$. Since the formula is true for $n = 1$, we have now proved it in general.

4. To prove that if every element in G is its own inverse, then G is Abelian.

Proof. For $a, b \in G$, $ab \in G$ (closure), and since every element is its own inverse, then for the element (ab), $(ab) = (ab)^{-1}$. From example 3, $(ab)^{-1} = b^{-1}a^{-1} = ba$, since $b^{-1} = b$ and $a^{-1} = a$.
Therefore $(ab)^{-1} = \mathbf{ab} = \mathbf{ba}$.

5. Show that the set $\{0, 1, 2\}$ under the operation of addition (mod 3) is a group isomorphic to the group of congruence rotations of the equilateral triangle discussed in §6.4. The operation table for the group $\{0, 1, 2\}$ is shown below:

+	0	1	2
0	0	1	2
1	1	2	0
2	2	0	1

All the conditions for two groups to be isomorphic are clearly satisfied if one compares the above operation table with that for the group of rotations of the triangle shown here again for quick reference:

+	a_0	a_1	a_2
a_0	a_0	a_1	a_2
a_1	a_1	a_2	a_0
a_2	a_2	a_0	a_1

EXERCISES 6d

1. Which of the following systems are groups?
   (i) All odd integers under addition
   (ii) All odd integers under multiplication
   (iii) All even integers under addition
   (iv) All even integers under multiplication
   (v) $m \times n$ matrices with integral elements under the operation of addition
   (vi) Non-singular matrices under multiplication with rational numbers as elements.

2. Show that in an operation table for a finite group every element occurs once and only once in each row and each column. (*Hint:* notice carefully how an element $c = a * b$ is located in an operation table (§6.2) then use theorem 4 in §6.9.)

3. Using the result found in question 2, show that there is only one possible operation table for a group of order 3.

4. Again, using the above result, write down all the possible operation tables for groups of order 4, and deduce that all groups of order 4 are Abelian.

5. If a finite group of order n has as its elements $a, a * a, a * a * a, \ldots, a * a * \ldots * a$ (n terms), show that at least one of the elements is the identity element.

6. Show that, in a group under $\times$, the equation $ax = b$ has the unique solution $x = a^{-1}b$, and the equation $ya = b$ has the unique solution $y = ba^{-1}$. If the group is Abelian, show that each of the equations have the unique solution $x = \dfrac{b}{a}$ $\left(\text{or } y = \dfrac{b}{a}\right)$.

7. Show that a group G is Abelian if $b^{-1}a^{-1}ba = e$ for $a, b \in G$.

8. Is a Boolean Algebra a group or not? Give the reasons for your answer.

9. If the set $S = \{0, 1, 2, 3, 4\}$ is under the operation of addition (mod 5), show that S is a group.

10. (a) Prove that if two groups G_1 and G_2 are isomorphic under the correspondence $a_1 \leftrightarrow b_1$, $a_2 \leftrightarrow b_2$, etc., where $a_1, a_2, \ldots \in G_1$, and $b_1, b_2, \ldots \in G_2$, then the inverses also correspond, i.e. $a_1^{-1} \leftrightarrow b_1^{-1}$, $a_2^{-1} \leftrightarrow b_2^{-1}$, etc.

(b) Prove that the cube roots of unity under the operation of multiplication is a group isomorphic to the group of rotations of an equilateral triangle.

6.11. Subgroups

Definition. A subset H of a group G such that all the elements of H satisfy the four group axioms is called a subgroup.

Let us look at this definition closely. Firstly, for all a, $b \in H$, $a * b \in H$ must be uniquely determined. Secondly, there must be a unique identity element in H. As there is a unique identity element in G and because $H \subseteq G$, then the unique identity element in H must in fact be the unique identity element in G. Thirdly, each element in H must have a unique inverse element also in H. There is no need to state explicitly that the associative property must hold in H; for, since it holds in G and $H \subseteq G$, then in particular it will hold in H.

Thus, necessary and sufficient conditions for the subset H of the group G to be a subgroup are:

(i) For all a, $b \in H$, $a * b \in H$ must be uniquely determined.

(ii) The unique identity element in H must be the unique identity element in G.

(iii) Each element in H must have a unique inverse element in H. In particular, G is considered a subgroup of itself, and the unique set which consists of the identity e alone is regarded as a subgroup of every group, including itself. A **proper subgroup** is a subgroup which is neither G nor e alone.

Consider now, the group of four elements defined in the following table:

*	a_0	a_1	a_2	a_3
a_0	a_0	a_1	a_2	a_3
a_1	a_1	a_0	a_3	a_2
a_2	a_2	a_3	a_0	a_1
a_3	a_3	a_2	a_1	a_0

From the table we soon see that the group is Abelian. Furthermore, in higher mathematics especially, one often meets groups whose elements combine as in the above table; such groups are called **Klein four-groups** after the German mathematician, Felix Klein (1849–1925). A Klein four-group has three subgroups of order 2:

$$a_0, a_1; \qquad a_0, a_2; \qquad \text{and} \qquad a_0, a_3.$$

Each subgroup contains the identity element a_0, and one other element. It is easily seen from the table for the entries a_0, a_1; a_0, a_2; a_0, a_3, respectively, that each subgroup satisfies the conditions above for a subset to be a subgroup.

Exercises 6e

1. Can you find any subgroups of order 3 in a Klein four-group? If not, why not?

2. Consider the transformations T_1, T_2, T_3 and T_4 which transform any point (x, y) in the plane as follows:

$$T_1(x, y) \rightarrow (x, y)$$
$$T_2(x, y) \rightarrow (x, -y)$$
$$T_3(x, y) \rightarrow (-x, y)$$
$$T_4(x, y) \rightarrow (-x, -y).$$

Thus, T_1 is the identity transformation, T_2 a reflection in the x-axis, T_3 a reflection in the y-axis, and T_4 a reflection in the origin. Using the usual definition for combining transformations (see Chapter 4), confirm that the set $\{T_1, T_2, T_3, T_4\}$ is a Klein four-group and write down its subgroups.

3. What groups in §§ 6.4, 6.5 and 6.7 have subgroups?

4. Explain how the alternative list of axioms for a group is much more convenient than the original list when deciding on the necessary and sufficient conditions for a subset H of a group G to be a subgroup.

5. Prove that the congruence rotations of a rhombus form a group. (There are four rotations to consider: One of them is a 180° rotation about one of the diagonals, another one is a 180° rotation about the remaining diagonal and the other two rotations are 180° about the centroid of the rhombus and the identity rotation.)

6. Show that the group of rotations of a rhombus is isomorphic with the Klein four-group. How many subgroups of order 2 are there? Write them down.

7. Prove that every group of order 4 is isomorphic to either Klein's four-group or to the rotation group of a square. Write down the subgroups of the rotation group of a square.

8. If H_1 and H_2 are subgroups of G, then prove that $H_1 \cap H_2$ is also a subgroup of G.

6.12. Cyclic groups

If we consider any element a which is a member of the finite group G under the group operation $*$, we may write

$$a * a = a^2,$$

on the strict understanding that a^2 is just an abbreviated way of writing $a * a$. Likewise we may write the following combinations of a with itself in this abbreviated form:

$$a * a * a = a^3,$$

and, in general,

$$a * a * \ldots * a \ (n \text{ terms}) = a^n, \ n \in J^+.$$

It therefore follows immediately that

$$a^m * a^n = a^{m+n}, \ m, \ n \in J^+.$$

Now, $a \in G$, and therefore $a * a = a^2 \in G$ (closure) and so $a * (a * a) = a * a^2 = a^3 \in G$ (closure) and so on, until in general $a^n \in G$. Thus, since a^m, $a^n \in G$, we have $a^m * a^n = a^{m+n} \in G$. So all the combinations of a are elements of G, and therefore all their inverses will be members of G. It seems natural to write the inverse of a^n as a^{-n}, and so,

$$\text{for } a^n, \ a^{-n} \in G, \ a^{-n} * a^n = a^n * a^{-n} = e,$$

where e is the identity element in G.

Now, $a^n * a^0 = a^{n+0} = a^n$ is true if we define $\underline{a^0 = e}$, i.e.

$$\underline{a^m * a^n = a^{m+n}, \; m, \, n \in J_0^+,}$$

on the understanding that $a^0 = e$.

Thus, $a^{-n} * a^n = a^n * a^{-n} = e = a^0$, for $n \in J_0^+$, and therefore we have proved that,

$$\underline{a^m * a^n = a^{m+n}, \; m, \, n \in J.}$$

If the group G is of the order $g < n$, then the number of elements in G ($=g$) is less than the number of "powers" of a—the latter elements being members of G. So in the sequence of "powers" of a: $a^0, a^1, a^2, a^3, \ldots, a^n$, not all the "powers" will be distinct; let u be the first value for the "power" of a such that

$$a^u = a^v, \qquad u > v \geqslant 0,$$

where a^v occurs earlier in the sequence. "Multiplying" both sides to the right by a^{-v},

$$a^u * a^{-v} = a^v * a^{-v} = a^0 = e,$$

i.e. $$a^{u-v} = e,$$

or $$\underline{a^p = e,}$$

where $p = u - v$ is a positive integer, since $u > v$.

We have therefore proved that at least one of the "powers" of a is the identity element, and the smallest "power" for this to be true is p. So for any positive integer k, $a^{kp} = e^k = e$, and for any positive integer $q \leqslant p$,

$$a^{kp} * a^q = \underline{a^{kp+q} = a^q.}$$

Therefore the sequence of "powers" of a repeats itself in "cycles"— each cycle containing p elements.

Lastly, we note that $a^{p-q} * a^q = a^{p-q+q} = a^p = e$, so by definition of an inverse, the inverse of a^q is a^{p-q},

i.e. $$\underline{a^{-q} = a^{p-q},}$$

this means that since $p - q \geqslant 0$, a^{p-q} is a member of the sequence of "powers" of a and therefore a^{-q} is a member of this sequence. We therefore have the following theorem:

If a is any element $(\neq e)$ of the group G, then the sequence $a^0, a^1, a^2, \ldots, a^{p-1}, (a^p = a^0 = e)$, is a subgroup H of G.

The theorem follows immediately from the above development:

(i) *Closure*

$$a^m * a^n = a^{m+n} \in H, \; a^m, \; a^n \in H \text{ for } m, \; n \in J.$$

(ii) *Identity*

$$a^0 = a^p = e \in H, \; p \in J^+.$$

(iii) *Inverses*

$$a^{-q} = a^{p-q} \in H, \; p \geqslant q, \; p, \; q \in J^+.$$

We also have two definitions:

The group H is called a **cyclic group of order p** generated by a (the latter sometimes called a **generator**).

The **order of the element $a \in H$** is defined to be the positive integer p.

In short then, we may say that a group is cyclic if it is generated by one of its elements. For example, the congruence group of the equilateral triangle (i.e. rotations into itself) in §6.4 is a cyclic group of order 3:

$*$	a_0	a_1	a_2
a_0	a_0	a_1	a_2
a_1	a_1	a_2	a_0
a_2	a_2	a_0	a_1

Here a_0 is the identity element; consider a_1 say, then $a_1{}^0 = a_0$ by definition, $a_1{}^1 = a_1$, $a_1{}^2 = a_2$ $(a_1{}^3 = a_0)$. Therefore the group is generated by the element a_1 whose order is 3; this group could, however, be generated by the element a_2. Note on the other hand that the Klein four-group is not cyclic.

Although a cyclic group is generated by one of its elements, there is nothing stated in the definition of a cyclic group that implies that such a group can be generated by *every one* of its elements (excluding the identity element). For example, consider the cyclic group C of order 4 whose elements are combined according to the operation table below:

*	a_0	a_1	a_2	a_3
a_0	a_0	a_1	a_2	a_3
a_1	a_1	a_2	a_3	a_0
a_2	a_2	a_3	a_0	a_1
a_3	a_3	a_0	a_1	a_2

a_0 is the identity element; a_1 is a generator since, $a_1^0 = a_0$ (by definition), $a_1^1 = a_1$, $a_1^2 = a_2$, $a_1^3 = a_3$ ($a_1^4 = a_0$). Similarly, a_3 is a generator, but a_2 is not, since $a_2^2 = a_0$ and therefore $a_3^3 = a_0$.

EXAMPLES

1. Although the Klein four-group is not cyclic, each of its three subgroups is cyclic:

*	a_0	a_1	a_2	a_3
a_0	a_0	a_1	a_2	a_3
a_1	a_1	a_0	a_3	a_2
a_2	a_2	a_3	a_0	a_1
a_3	a_3	a_2	a_1	a_0

Klein's four-group. a_0 is the identity element.

Subgroups

*	a_0	a_1
a_0	a_0	a_1
a_1	a_1	a_0

*	a_0	a_2
a_0	a_0	a_2
a_2	a_2	a_0

*	a_0	a_3
a_0	a_0	a_3
a_3	a_3	a_0

$a_1{}^0 = a_0$ (by definition), $a_1{}^1 = a_1$ $(a_1{}^2 = a_0)$

$a_2{}^0 = a_0$ (by definition), $a_2{}^1 = a_2$ $(a_2{}^2 = a_0)$

$a_3{}^0 = a_0$ (by definition), $a_3{}^1 = a_3$ $(a_3{}^2 = a_0)$.

2. The cube roots $1, \omega, \omega^2$ of unity, under the operation of multiplication form a cyclic group.

Since $\qquad 1^{\frac{1}{3}} = e^{2k\pi i/3}, \qquad k = 0, 1, 2$ (where e is the exponential base)

then $\qquad 1 = e^0, \ \omega = e^{2\pi i/3}, \qquad \omega^2 = e^{4\pi i/3},$

and $\qquad \omega^3 = e^{2\pi i} = e^0 = 1;$

also, $\qquad \omega^4 = \omega \times \omega^3 = \omega \times 1 = \omega.$

*	1	ω	ω^2
1	1	ω	ω^2
ω	ω	ω^2	1
ω^2	ω^2	1	ω

Group table for cube roots of 1.

3. Any cyclic group is Abelian.

Consider any two elements, a^m and a^n, of the group, where a is a generator, then $a^m * a^n = a^{m+n} = a^{n+m} = a^n * a^m$, since addition of integers is commutative.

4. The set of integers $\{0, 1, 2, 3\}$ under the operation of addition (mod 4) form a cyclic group isomorphic with the rotation group of a square.

The addition table (mod 4) of the set of integers $\{0, 1, 2, 3\}$ and the operation table for the rotation group of a square are given below:

*	0	1	2	3
0	0	1	2	3
1	1	2	3	0
2	2	3	0	1
3	3	0	1	2

$\{0, 1, 2, 3\}$ under addition (mod 4).
0 is the identity element.

*	a_0	a_1	a_2	a_3
a_0	a_0	a_1	a_2	a_3
a_1	a_1	a_2	a_3	a_0
a_2	a_2	a_3	a_0	a_1
a_3	a_3	a_0	a_1	a_2

Rotation group of a square.
a_0 is the identity element.

Note that the isomorphism is evident since there is a one–one correspondence between the numbers of the set $\{0, 1, 2, 3\}$ and the suffices of a, and for example where

$$a_1 \leftrightarrow 1, \qquad a_2 \leftrightarrow 2, \qquad a_3 \leftrightarrow 3,$$

we have

$$1 + 2 \ (\text{mod } 4) = 3$$

and

$$a_1 * a_2 = a_3,$$

i.e.

$$1 + 2 \ (\text{mod } 4) \leftrightarrow a_1 * a_2.$$

The rotation group of the square is cyclic; a_1 and a_3 are the generators. Thus, since the two groups are isomorphic, the group $\{0, 1, 2, 3\}$ under addition (mod 4) must be cyclic.

EXERCISES 6f

1. Show that two cyclic groups of the same order are isomorphic. Consider in particular cyclic groups of orders 2, 3 and 4.

2. With reference to the group $\{0, 1, 2, 3\}$ under addition (mod 4), write down the inverse of each element. Also write down the generators. Note that since this is an "additive group", i.e. a group under the operation of addition, we do not refer to "powers" a^n of any element a, but of "multiples" na. So, by definition $0a = 0$, $1a = a$, $2a = a+a$, and so on until in general, $na = a+a+ \ldots +a$ (n terms).

3. Give an example of an infinite cyclic group, i.e. a cyclic group of infinite order. Show that an infinite cyclic group has an infinite number of cyclic subgroups each of which are isomorphic to the given group. Is the set J under the operation of addition a cyclic group?

4. Construct an operation table for the congruence rotations of a regular pentagon; these rotations (five of them essentially) are made by rotating the pentagon in its plane about its centroid through integral multiples of 72° successively. Show that the set of rotations form a cyclic group of order 5 isomorphic to the group of the fifth roots of unity under the operation of multiplication.

5. Show that every group of prime order is cyclic. Illustrate in the cases of cyclic groups of orders 2, 3, 5 and 7 (in the latter case, the seventh roots of unity under the operation of multiplication will help). Further, show that a cyclic group of prime order has no proper subgroups.

6. Show that a group of prime order is generated by every one of its elements (except the identity element). Illustrate in the case of the group of rotations of a pentagon.

7. Prove that the nth roots of unity given by $1^{1/n} = e^{2k\pi i/n}$, $k = 0, 1, 2, \ldots$, $(n-1)$, for all positive integral n, under the operation of multiplication form a cyclic group of order n. Further, prove that the congruence rotations of an n-sided regular polygon form a cyclic group of order n which is therefore isomorphic to the above group of nth roots.

8. Prove that the set J_0^+ of all positive integers including zero under the operation of addition (mod 4) is a cyclic group of order 4. (*Hint:* show that the group addition table is identical to the table for the group in question 2 by noting that any member of J_0^+ is congruent (mod 4) to either 0, 1, 2, 3 or 4; e.g. $8 \equiv 0$ (mod 4), $17 \equiv 1$ (mod 4), etc.)

9. Prove that the set J_0^+ under the operation of addition (mod n) is a cyclic group of order n, whereas J_0^+ under the operation of multiplication (mod n) is not even a group.

RINGS

6.13. Definition of a ring

So far in this chapter we have studied the properties of a set whose elements are combined according to only *one* operation. If we are to understand better the structure of elementary algebra, not to mention more abstract structures such as those found in the study of matrices, polynomials and quaternions, then we must investigate the properties of a set whose elements are combined according to *two* operations. For example, the set J of all integers under the operation of addition forms an "additive" Abelian group, whereas J under the operation of multiplication is not a group since there are no inverses; however, J under $\times$ is closed, associative, commutative, and there exists an identity $1 \in J$. Also, the **distributive law** which *connects the two operations* $+$ *and* $\times$ holds in J:

For any a, b, $c \in J$,

$$a(b + c) = ab + ac$$

and

$$(b + c)a = ba + ca.$$

Since J is commutative under $\times$,

$$a(b + c) = (b + c)a.$$

Note that J under $+$ has an identity element 0, called a **zero;** J under $\times$ has an identity element 1, called a **unity.**

Consider on the other hand the set $V = \{x : x = 2n,\ n \in J\}$, i.e. V is the set of all positive and negative even integers including zero (0); V under $+$ is an additive Abelian group. V under $\times$ is not a group since there is no unity (1), and there are no inverses; however, V under $\times$ is closed, associative, and commutative. Further, the distributive rule holds in V.

Finally, let us look at the set M of all square matrices of order n whose elements are real numbers; M under $+$ is an additive Abelian group, whilst under $\times$, it is not a group since there exist singular matrices in M. Still, M under $\times$ is closed and associative and there exists a unity—namely, the identity matrix. The distributive rule holds in M.

The above observations are conveniently tabulated below:

		Under ×					Under + and ×
	Set	Closed	Associative	Unity	Inverses	Commutative	Distributive
All are additive Abelian groups	J	√	√	√	×	√	√
	V	√	√	×	×	√	√
	M	√	√	√	×	×	√

Note that the sets J, V and M under both the operations of addition and multiplication have something in common—they are all additive Abelian groups, and under × they are all closed and associative. Further, the distributive rule which connects + and × holds in each case. J, V and M under + and × are called **rings;** we have the following definition:

A **ring** is a set S whose elements are combined according to (i) an operation called "addition" and denoted by +, and (ii) an operation called "multiplication" and denoted by ×, such that S has the following properties: (a) It is an additive Abelian group, (b) it is closed and associative under ×, and (c) the distributive rule connects the two operations + and × so that for any a, b, $c \in S$,

$$a(b+c) = ab+ac,$$

and
$$(b+c)a = ba+ca.$$

In general, then, a ring may or may not have a unity—if it has, then we refer to the ring as a **ring with unity.** If the elements of the ring are commutative under ×, then we call the ring a **commutative ring.**

EXERCISES 6g

1. Examine whether the following sets form rings:
    (i) the set J^+ of all positive integers,
    (ii) the set R of all rational numbers,
    (iii) the set R^* of all real numbers,
    (iv) the set C of all complex numbers,
    (v) the set J under $+ \pmod 4$ and under $\times \pmod 4$.

2. Which of the rings in question 1 have a unity? Which rings are commutative?

3. Is it possible for a ring R to have the following property: $\exists\ a, b \in R$ such that $ab = 0 \not\Rightarrow a = 0$ or $b = 0$?

Illustrate your answer with reference to one of the rings in question 1 above. (See property (iii) in §6.14.)

6.14. Properties of rings. Subrings

Consider the ring R, then for all a, b, $c \in R$ we have:

(i) $0 \times a = a \times 0 = 0$

Proof. $0 \times a = (0 + 0) \times a = 0 \times a + 0 \times a$ (distributive rule). Therefore $0 \times a = 0$ (0 by definition being a unique additive identity).

Similarly $a \times 0 = 0$.

(ii) $a = 0 \Rightarrow ab = 0$

Proof. Whether b is zero or not, the proof follows immediately from property (i). Similarly if $b = 0$, then $ab = 0$.

(iii) **Existence of divisors of zero**

It does not necessarily follow that if $ab = 0$, then either $a = 0$ or $b = 0$. For example, the ring M of square matrices of §6.13 contains many pairs of matrices A and B such that $AB = 0 \not\Rightarrow A = 0$, or $B = 0$ (where 0 is the null matrix), e.g. with third order matrices,

$$\begin{pmatrix} 0 & \lambda & 0 \\ 0 & 0 & 0 \\ 0 & 0 & 0 \end{pmatrix} \begin{pmatrix} 0 & 0 & \varphi \\ 0 & 0 & 0 \\ k & 0 & 0 \end{pmatrix} = \begin{pmatrix} 0 & 0 & 0 \\ 0 & 0 & 0 \\ 0 & 0 & 0 \end{pmatrix},$$

where λ, φ and k are non-zero numbers. (Also see Chapter 2 on Boolean algebra, and Chapter 5 on product of matrices.) If $ab = 0$, and neither $a = 0$ nor $b = 0$, then a is called a **left divisor of zero**, and b is called a **right divisor of zero**.

The above three properties are the most important; however, there are several more and these are left as exercises (6h).

A set H which is a subset of a ring R, is itself a ring—called a **subring of R**—if H satisfies the list of axioms in the definition of a ring. *Necessary and sufficient* conditions for H to be a subring of the ring R can be drawn up, just as conditions for a subset of a group to be a subgroup were drawn up in § 6.11 on groups. Thus H is a subring of the ring R if:

(a) for all a, $b \in H$, $a + b \in H$, and $ab \in H$;

(b) $0 \in H$;

(c) for all $a \in H$, $-a \in H$.

These are necessary and sufficient conditions for H to be a subring of R; there is no need to state the associative law under $+$, and under $\times$, since this law holds in R and will therefore hold in particular in H. Likewise, since the distributive rule holds in R, then it will hold in H. For example, J is a commutative ring with unity, and the set V of all positive and negative integers including 0, is a commutative subring (without unity) of J.

Exercises 6h

1. Prove that for all $a, b, c \in R$:

   (i) $-(a+b) = -a-b$

   (ii) $a(-b) = -ab$

   (iii) $-c(a+b) = -ca-cb$

   (iv) $-c(a-b) = -ca+cb$

   (v) $(-a)(-b) = ab$.

2. Prove that if $a^{-1}, b^{-1} \in R$, then the additive inverse of $(a+b) = -(a+b)$, and $(ab)^{-1} = b^{-1}a^{-1}$.

3. If a ring has a unity, prove that this unity is unique.

4. If R is a commutative ring, prove that the cancellation law for multiplication holds, i.e. for $a, b, c \in R$ and c is not a divisor of zero, then $ac = bc \Rightarrow a = b$. (*Hint:* consider $ac - bc$.)

5. If $a, b \in R$, then $a + x = b$ has the unique solution $x = b - a$.

6. A set S consists of ordered pairs of real numbers (x_1, y_1), (x_2, y_2), ..., and the ordered pairs are operated on as follows:

$$(x_1, y_1) + (x_2, y_2) = (x_1 + x_2, y_1 + y_2)$$
$$(x_1, y_1)(x_2, y_2) = (x_1 x_2, y_1 y_2).$$

Prove that S is a commutative ring with unity and with divisors of zero. Write down the unity, and give two examples of divisors of zero.

7. Prove that under the operations of $+$ and $\times$ the set R^* of all real numbers is a ring, and under the same operations the set C of all complex numbers is a ring. Hence show that R^* is a subring of C.

8. Show that a Boolean algebra B is a commutative ring with divisors of zero. (See Chapter 2 on Boolean algebra.)

FIELDS

6.15 Definition and properties of a field

A **field** F is a commutative ring with unity, each of whose non-zero elements have a unique inverse with respect to multiplication. So, a field is both an additive Abelian group and (excluding 0) a multiplicative Abelian group, and the distributive rule which connects the two operations denoted by $+$ and $\times$ holds; it is a useful refresher to state the axioms of a field in detail:

For all $a, b, c \in F$

(i) *Closure* (a) $a + b \in F$ and is uniquely determined.

(b) $a \times b \in F$ and is uniquely determined.

(ii) *Associativity* (a) $a + (b + c) = (a + b) + c$.

(b) $a \times (b \times c) = (a \times b) \times c$.

(iii) *Identities* (a) $\exists$ a unique $0 \in F$ such that $0 + a = a + 0 = a$.

(b) $\exists$ a unique $1 \in F$ such that $1 \times a = a \times 1 = a$.

(iv) *Inverses* (a) $\exists$ a unique $(-a) \in F$ such that
$(-a) + a = a + (-a) = 0$.

(b) $\exists$ a unique $b^{-1} \in F$, $b \neq 0$, such that
$b^{-1} \times b = b \times b^{-1} = 1$.

(v) *Commutativity* (a) $a + b = b + a$.

(b) $a \times b = b \times a$.

(vi) *Distributivity* $a \times (b + c) = (a \times b) + (a \times c)$.

In view of (v) we may, of course, write (vi) as follows:

$$a(b + c) = (b + c)a = ab + ac = ba + ca,$$

using the familiar juxtaposition of symbols in place of $\times$.

The set R^* of all real numbers for example is a field, and likewise the set C of all complex numbers is a field. Necessary and sufficient conditions for a subset H of F to be a field, i.e. for H to be a **subfield**

of F, are derived in an exactly analogous fashion to that of finding conditions for a subset of a ring to be a subring and this is left as an exercise below.

It is an immediate consequence of the definition of a field F that there can be **no divisors of zero in F**; this is so because every *non-zero* element a in F has a unique inverse a^{-1}, so that if $ab = 0$ then $a^{-1}ab = 0$, i.e. $1b = 0$ or $b = 0$.

EXERCISES 6i

1. Which of the following systems are fields?

    (i) The set of integers J under $+$ and $\times$.

    (ii) The set of rationals R under $+$ and $\times$.

    (iii) The set of real numbers R^* under $+$ and $\times$.

    (iv) The set of complex numbers C under $+$ and $\times$.

    (v) The set V of numbers of the form $a + b\sqrt{2}$, where a and b are integers, under $+$ and $\times$.

    (vi) The set W of numbers of the form $a + b\sqrt{2}$, where a and b are rationals, under $+$ and $\times$.

    (vii) The set J of integers under $+$ (mod 4) and under $\times$ (excluding 0) (mod 4).

    (viii) The set J of integers under $+$ (mod 5) and under $\times$ (excluding 0) (mod 5).

2. Write down necessary and sufficient conditions for a subset of a field to be a subfield.

Show that R^* is a subfield of C. Further, show that R is a subfield of R^*, and R is a subfield of W. (Referring to the sets in question 1 above.)

3. Prove that the equations $a + x = b$ and $cx = d$ have unique solutions in a field. Illustrate by finding the solutions of the equations $3 + x = 4$ and $3x = 2$ in the field given in question 1 (viii) above.

4. Prove that in a field F, where $a, b, c \in F$, that

$$ac = bc \Rightarrow a = b \; (c \neq 0).$$

Solve the equation $x^3 - 7x^2 + 12x = 0$, where

    (a) the solutions are in the field of rationals, and

    (b) the solutions are in the field of integers (mod 3).

5. Prove that necessary and sufficient conditions for a subset H of a field F to be a subfield are that for all $a, b \in H$, $a - b \in H$ and $ab^{-1} \in H$ ($b \neq 0$).

6. Prove that in any field, the additive group can never be isomorphic to the multiplicative group. (*Hint:* try setting up a one–one correspondence between all the elements in the two groups—paying special attention to the identities.) Illustrate your answer by referring to the two groups in the field of integers (mod 5).

Answers

EXERCISES 1a

1. (a) I will read a book and it is summer.
   (b) I will read a book and/or it is summer.
   (c) I will not read a book and/or it is summer.
   (d) I will read a book and/or it is not summer.
   (e) It is not true that I will read a book and it is summer.
   (f) I will read a book or it is summer.
   (g) As in (f).

EXERCISES 1b

4.

p	q	$p \Rightarrow q$
1	1	1
0	1	1
0	0	1

p	q	$p \Leftrightarrow q$
1	1	1
0	0	1

5. (a) not an implication.
   (b) an implication.
   (c) an implication.
   (d) not an implication.
   (e) not an implication.
   (f) an implication.

6. (a) an equivalence.
   (b) not an equivalence.
   (c) an equivalence.
   (d) an equivalence.
   (e) not an equivalence.
   (f) an equivalence.

EXERCISES 1c

1. (a) true.   (b) false.   (c) true.   (d) true.
2. (a) true.   (b) true.   (c) true.
3. false.
4. true.
7. false (2 is an even prime).

201

EXERCISES 2a

20. Subset 1. $A \cap B \cap C \cap D$
Subset 2. $A' \cap B \cap C \cap D$
Subset 3. $A \cap B' \cap C \cap D$
Subset 4. $A \cap B \cap C' \cap D$
Subset 5. $A \cap B \cap C \cap D'$
Subset 6. $A' \cap B' \cap C \cap D$
Subset 7. $A' \cap B \cap C' \cap D$
Subset 8. $A' \cap B \cap C \cap D'$
Subset 9. $A \cap B' \cap C' \cap D$
Subset 10. $A \cap B' \cap C \cap D'$
Subset 11. $A \cap B \cap C' \cap D'$
Subset 12. $A' \cap B' \cap C' \cap D$
Subset 13. $A' \cap B' \cap C \cap D'$
Subset 14. $A' \cap B \cap C' \cap D'$
Subset 15. $A \cap B' \cap C' \cap D'$
Subset 16. $A' \cap B' \cap C' \cap D'$

EXERCISES 2b

1. (a) $p \wedge [(\bar{p} \wedge q) \vee (p \wedge \bar{q})] \wedge q = c$, i.e. open circuit.

(b) $p \wedge [(q \wedge r) \vee (\bar{q} \wedge r)] \wedge [(\bar{r} \wedge p) \vee (q \wedge \bar{p})]$
$\qquad = (p \wedge r) \wedge [\{(\bar{r} \wedge p) \vee q\} \wedge (\bar{p} \vee \bar{r})].$

(c) $(p \wedge q \wedge r) \vee [p \wedge (\bar{q} \vee \bar{r})] = p.$

(d) $(p \wedge q) \vee r \vee p \vee (q \wedge \bar{r}) = p \vee r \vee q.$

8. Not a Boolean algebra, for although $b = 0$ (the identity under $+$) and $c = 1$ (the identity under $\times$), there is no complement a' (so that $a + a' = 1$ and $a \times a' = 0$) and no complement c'.

EXERCISES 2c

1. 99. **2.** 23. **3.** 33. **4.** Inconsistent information (since number of English males would now be 5 instead of 6). **5.** 15.

6. (a) $n(A) + n(B) + n(C) + n(D)$.

(b) $n(A) + n(B) + n(C) + n(D) - n(A \cap B) - n(C \cap D)$.

(c) $n(A) + n(B) + n(C) + n(D) - n(A \cap B) - n(A \cap C) - n(B \cap C)$
$\qquad\qquad\qquad\qquad\qquad + n(A \cap B \cap C).$

(d) $n(A) + n(B) + n(C) + n(D) - n(A \cap B) - n(B \cap C)$.

EXERCISES 3b

3. $r = 0$. **5.** $2(n-1)!$ **6.** (i) $2(n-2)!$ (ii) $(n-3)(n-2)!$ **7.** 15,120; 3,780.

9. $(x+1)2^n - 1$. **10.** (i) $^{365}P_n$ (ii) 365^n. **11.** 252. **12.** (i) ^qP_m (ii) $24pqrs$ ($m = 4$).

EXERCISES 3d

1. $\frac{5}{18}$. **2.** $\frac{2}{9}$. **3.** (i) $\frac{2}{5}$ (ii) $\frac{2}{5}$ (iii) $\frac{3}{5}$ (iv) $\frac{1}{5}$ (v) $\frac{4}{5}$. **5.** $\frac{1}{2!} - \frac{1}{3!} + \ldots - \frac{1}{52!}$.
8. 0·4096.

EXERCISES 4b

1. $R = \{(5,7), (5,9), (6,7), (6,9), (7,9)\}$.

2. $R = \{(1,5), (1,6), (1,7), (1,8), (1,9), (2,6), (2,8), (3,6), (3,9), (4,8)\}$.

6. Both are equivalence relations.

7. Not possible, since although $xRy \Rightarrow yRx$ (symmetry) and $(xRy) \wedge (yRx)$ $\Rightarrow xRx$ (transitivity), i.e. $xRx \Rightarrow$ reflexivity is true only if there is a y such that xRy, i.e. not true for all x.

EXERCISES 4c

3.
Equivalence classes	Canonical forms
$\{\ldots, -4, 0, 4, 8, \ldots\}$	0
$\{\ldots, -3, 1, 5, 9, \ldots\}$	1
$\{\ldots, -2, 2, 6, 10, \ldots\}$	2
$\{\ldots, 1, 3, 7, 11, \ldots\}$	3

5. Equivalence classes are:
(i) 9 students taking 3 subjects.
(ii) 14 students taking English and French but not Maths.
(iii) 16 students taking Maths. and French but not English.
(iv) 12 students taking Maths. and English but not French.
(v) 20 students taking English only.
(vi) 5 students taking French only.
(vii) 23 students taking Maths. only.

EXERCISES 4d

1. (a) range given by $2 \leqslant f(x) \leqslant 27$.

(b) 3, 6, $u^2 + 2u + 6$.

(c) $-5 \leqslant u \leqslant 3$.

2. (a) domain $= R^*$, range $= R_0^{*+}$.

(b) 22, 3, $4\frac{1}{2}$, 30.

3. $\{(1,\alpha), (2,\alpha)\}, \{(1,\beta), (2,\beta)\}, \{(1,\gamma), (2,\gamma)\}, \{(1,\alpha), (2,\beta)\}$,
$\{(1,\alpha), (2,\gamma)\}, \{(1,\beta), (2,\alpha)\}, \{(1,\beta), (2,\gamma)\}, \{1,\gamma), (2,\alpha)\}$,
$\{(1,\gamma), (2,\beta)\}$.

4. (a) domain $= R^*$, range $= 1$.

(b) domain $= J$, range $= 1$ if x is zero or even, or -1 if x is odd.

5. (a) $x = \sin y$, i.e. $y = \sin^{-1} x$.

(b) no inverse.

(c) $x = \dfrac{1}{y}$, i.e. $y = \dfrac{1}{x}$ (no change).

(d) no inverse.

(e) no inverse.

(f) no inverse.

(g) $f^{-1} = \{(2,1), (5,2), (9,3)\}$.

7. $27x^3 + 108x^2 + 138x + 58$, $3x^3 - 6x + 10$.

EXERCISES 5a

1. (a) $\begin{pmatrix} 7 & 0 & 6 \\ 2 & 0 & 3 \end{pmatrix}$ (b) $\begin{pmatrix} 6 & 0 & 4 \\ -3 & 4 & 5 \end{pmatrix}$

(c) $\begin{pmatrix} 8 & 3 & 8 \\ -2 & 6 & 8 \end{pmatrix}$ (d) $\begin{pmatrix} 8 & 3 & 8 \\ -2 & 6 & 8 \end{pmatrix}$.

EXERCISES 5b

2. $T_1 = T_1^{-1}$, $T_2 = T_2^{-1}$, $T_3 = T_3^{-1}$.

6. (a) $\begin{pmatrix} -1 & 0 \\ 0 & 1 \end{pmatrix}$ (b) $\begin{pmatrix} 1 & 0 \\ 0 & -1 \end{pmatrix}$

(c) $\begin{pmatrix} 1 & k \\ 0 & -1 \end{pmatrix}$, writing transformations in the form:
$$x' = ax + by$$
$$y' = cx + dy$$

EXERCISES 5c

1. (a) $\begin{pmatrix} 7 & -1 \\ 2 & -1 \end{pmatrix}$ (b) $\begin{pmatrix} 3 & 7 \\ 2 & 3 \end{pmatrix}$

(c) $\begin{pmatrix} -3 & 2 & 3 \\ -2 & 1 & 0 \end{pmatrix}$ (d) $\begin{pmatrix} 1 & 1 & 9 \\ 4 & -1 & 6 \end{pmatrix}$

2. (a) (-11) (b) $\begin{pmatrix} -1 & 0 & -3 & -4 \\ 3 & 0 & 9 & 12 \\ 2 & 0 & 6 & 8 \\ -4 & 0 & -12 & -16 \end{pmatrix}$

(c) $(10 - 2)$.

3. $B = \begin{pmatrix} 0 & 0 & 0 \\ 0 & u & v \\ 0 & w & x \end{pmatrix}$, $D = \begin{pmatrix} p & q & 0 \\ 0 & 0 & 0 \\ r & s & 0 \end{pmatrix}$,

where u, v, w, x, p, q, r and s are not all zero; $AC = CA = 0$ (the null matrix). Thus A, B, C and D are all divisors of zero.

5. (a) $\begin{pmatrix} 9 & -1 & 21 \\ 4 & -1 & 6 \end{pmatrix}$ (b) $\begin{pmatrix} 9 & -1 & 21 \\ 4 & -1 & 6 \end{pmatrix}$

(c) $\begin{pmatrix} -2 & 3 & 12 \\ 2 & 0 & 6 \end{pmatrix}$ (d) $\begin{pmatrix} -2 & 3 & 12 \\ 2 & 0 & 6 \end{pmatrix}$

(a), (b) verify the associative law, and (c), (d) verify the distributive law.

7. (a) $\sum\limits_{\lambda=1}^{n} a_{i\lambda}b_{\lambda j}$, where A is $m \times n$, and B is $n \times p$.

(b) $\sum\limits_{\lambda=1}^{t} b_{ii}a_{ij}$, where B is $s \times t$, and A is $t \times u$.

(c) $\sum\limits_{\lambda=1}^{n} a_{i\lambda}(b_{\lambda j}+c_{\lambda j})$, where A is $m \times n$, and both B and C are $n \times p$.

(d) $\sum\limits_{\mu=1}^{n} \left[\left\{ \sum\limits_{\lambda=1}^{n} a_{i\lambda}(b_{\lambda\mu}+c_{\lambda\mu}) \right\} \left\{ \sum\limits_{\lambda=1}^{n} a_{\mu\lambda}(b_{\lambda j}+c_{\lambda j}) \right\} \right]$,

where A, B and C are all square matrices of order n, and one first sums over μ then over λ.

EXERCISES 5d

1. (a) $\begin{pmatrix} 12 & -14 \\ 54 & -49 \end{pmatrix}$ (b) $\begin{pmatrix} 12 & 11 & -1 & 10 \\ 32 & 34 & 2 & 36 \end{pmatrix}$

(c) $\begin{pmatrix} 24 & 22 & -2 & 20 \\ 108 & 113 & 5 & 118 \end{pmatrix}$ (d) $\begin{pmatrix} 16 & 17 & 1 & 18 \\ 34 & 40 & 6 & 46 \end{pmatrix}$.

2. (a) $y_1 = x_1 + 2x_3$ (b) $y_1 = 4x_1 + x_3$
    $y_2 = 3x_1 + x_2 - x_3$ $y_2 = x_2 - 2x_3$
    $y_3 = 4x_1 + 2x_3$ $y_3 = 3x_1 + 3x_2 + 5x_3$
(c) $y_1 = 10x_1 + 6x_2 + 11x_3$ (d) $y_1 = 8x_1 + 10x_3$
    $y_2 = 9x_1 - 2x_2 - 4x_3$ $y_2 = -5x_1 + x_2 - 5x_3$
    $y_3 = 22x_1 + 6x_2 + 14x_3$ $y_3 = 32x_1 + 3x_2 + 13x_3$

6. (a) $(X-3I)(X-4I) = 0$, i.e. $X = 3I = \begin{pmatrix} 3 & 0 & 0 \\ 0 & 3 & 0 \\ 0 & 0 & 3 \end{pmatrix}$,

and $X = 4I = \begin{pmatrix} 4 & 0 & 0 \\ 0 & 4 & 0 \\ 0 & 0 & 4 \end{pmatrix}$

(b) $(2X+I)(X+3I)(X-2I) = 0$, i.e. $X = -\frac{1}{2}I = \begin{pmatrix} -\frac{1}{2} & 0 & 0 \\ 0 & -\frac{1}{2} & 0 \\ 0 & 0 & -\frac{1}{2} \end{pmatrix}$,

$$X = -3I = \begin{pmatrix} -3 & 0 & 0 \\ 0 & -3 & 0 \\ 0 & 0 & -3 \end{pmatrix},$$

and $X = 2I = \begin{pmatrix} 2 & 0 & 0 \\ 0 & 2 & 0 \\ 0 & 0 & 2 \end{pmatrix}$.

The matrices X in (a) and (b) do not represent all the possible 3×3 matrices that satisfy the equations because there exist several divisors of zero; e.g. in case (a) above,

$$X = \begin{pmatrix} 3 & 0 & 0 \\ 0 & 4 & 0 \\ 0 & 0 & 4 \end{pmatrix} \text{ also satisfies the equation where}$$

$$(X-3I) = \begin{pmatrix} 0 & 0 & 0 \\ 0 & 1 & 0 \\ 0 & 0 & 1 \end{pmatrix}, \text{ and } (X-4I) = \begin{pmatrix} -1 & 0 & 0 \\ 0 & 0 & 0 \\ 0 & 0 & 0 \end{pmatrix}$$

are two divisors of zero.

EXERCISES 5e

5. $\begin{pmatrix} 2+3i & 4-2i & 1+i \\ 3-2i & -5-4i & 3+2i \end{pmatrix}$, $\begin{pmatrix} a-ib & a+ib \\ 3-i & 1-i \\ 0 & 2 \end{pmatrix}$,

$\begin{pmatrix} -i & 0 \\ 0 & -i \end{pmatrix}$, $\begin{pmatrix} a+2i \\ 3a+2bi \\ 1+i \end{pmatrix}$.

6. $A\bar{A} = \begin{pmatrix} 27-i & 1-i \\ -3+9i & 15+i \end{pmatrix}$, $\bar{A}A = \begin{pmatrix} 27+i & 1+i \\ -3-9i & 15-i \end{pmatrix}$.

EXERCISES 5f

1. (a) $\begin{pmatrix} \frac{2}{3} & 1 \\ 3 & 0 \end{pmatrix}$ (b) $\begin{pmatrix} \frac{3}{2} & -\frac{1}{2} \\ -2 & 1 \end{pmatrix}$ (c) no inverse.

(d) $\begin{pmatrix} \frac{4}{17} & \frac{1}{17} \\ -\frac{5}{17} & \frac{3}{17} \end{pmatrix}$.

2. (a) $x_1 = \frac{11}{6}$, $x_2 = \frac{4}{3}$. (b) $x_1 = \frac{3}{11}$, $x_2 = \frac{10}{11}$.

(c) if $ad - bc = \Delta \neq 0$, $x_1 = \frac{1}{\Delta}(du - bv)$, $x_2 = \frac{1}{\Delta}(av - cu)$.

EXERCISES 5g
1. 46, -18.

EXERCISES 5h

1. (a) $\begin{pmatrix} \frac{14}{13} & -\frac{11}{13} & \frac{1}{13} \\ \frac{4}{13} & -\frac{5}{13} & \frac{4}{13} \\ -\frac{3}{13} & \frac{7}{13} & -\frac{3}{13} \end{pmatrix}$ (b) $\begin{pmatrix} \frac{7}{10} & \frac{1}{20} & \frac{2}{5} \\ -\frac{2}{5} & \frac{3}{20} & -\frac{3}{10} \\ \frac{1}{5} & \frac{1}{20} & -\frac{1}{10} \end{pmatrix}$

(c) no inverse. (d) $\begin{pmatrix} \frac{1}{a} & 0 & 0 \\ 0 & \frac{1}{b} & 0 \\ 0 & 0 & \frac{1}{c} \end{pmatrix}$.

2. (a) $x = -\frac{3}{2}$, $y = -\frac{33}{12}$, $z = -\frac{39}{12}$.
(b) no solution. (c) $l = -\frac{2}{7}$, $m = -\frac{5}{7}$, $n = 1$.

4. $A_1^{-1} = \begin{pmatrix} 1 & 0 & 0 \\ 0 & 1 & 0 \\ 0 & 0 & 1 \end{pmatrix}$, $A_2^{-1} = \begin{pmatrix} 1 & 0 & 0 \\ 0 & 1 & 0 \\ 0 & 0 & -1 \end{pmatrix}$,

$A_3^{-1} = \begin{pmatrix} 1 & 0 & 0 \\ 0 & -1 & 0 \\ 0 & 0 & 1 \end{pmatrix}$, $A_4^{-1} = \begin{pmatrix} 1 & 0 & 0 \\ 0 & 1 & 0 \\ 0 & 0 & \frac{1}{k} \end{pmatrix}$.

(a) $\begin{pmatrix} 1 & 0 & 0 \\ 0 & -1 & 0 \\ 0 & 0 & -1 \end{pmatrix}$ (b) $\begin{pmatrix} 1 & 0 & 0 \\ 0 & -1 & 0 \\ 0 & 0 & -1 \end{pmatrix}$

(c) $\begin{pmatrix} 1 & 0 & 0 \\ 0 & -1 & 0 \\ 0 & 0 & k \end{pmatrix}$ (d) $\begin{pmatrix} 1 & 0 & 0 \\ 0 & -1 & 0 \\ 0 & 0 & \frac{1}{k} \end{pmatrix}$

(e) $\begin{pmatrix} \lambda & 0 & 0 \\ 0 & 1 & 0 \\ 0 & 0 & 1 \end{pmatrix}$, λ some real number.

(f) $\begin{pmatrix} \lambda & 0 & 0 \\ 0 & \mu & 0 \\ 0 & 0 & 1 \end{pmatrix}$, λ and μ real numbers.

(g)
$$\begin{pmatrix} \lambda & 0 & 0 \\ 0 & \mu & 0 \\ 0 & 0 & k \end{pmatrix}, \lambda, \mu \text{ and } k \text{ real numbers.}$$

(h)
$$\begin{pmatrix} \frac{1}{\lambda} & 0 & 0 \\ 0 & 1 & 0 \\ 0 & 0 & \frac{1}{k} \end{pmatrix}$$

(j)
$$\begin{pmatrix} \frac{1}{\lambda} & 0 & 0 \\ 0 & 1 & 0 \\ 0 & 0 & \frac{1}{k} \end{pmatrix}.$$

8. 3, 1, 3, 3, 2.

EXERCISES 6d

1. (i) not a group (not closed)
   (ii) not a group, even if 0 is included (no inverses)
   (iii) a group, if 0 is included
   (iv) not a group, even if 0 is included (no inverses)
   (v) a group
   (vi) a group.

8. A group under union, not a group under intersection (no inverses).

EXERCISES 6e

6. 3; $\{a_0, a_1\}$, $\{a_0, a_2\}$, $\{a_0, a_3\}$, where a_0 is the identity.

7. One proper subgroup: $\{a_0, a_2\}$, where a_0 is the identity, and a_2 is a rotation of 180° about the centroid.

EXERCISES 6f

3. The set $J_0{}^+$ under addition is an infinite cyclic group; it has only one generator, namely 1.

In general for any infinite cyclic group, the "powers" (or "multiples" as the case may be) of any one of the elements can never exceed the order of the group; thus no member of the sequence of "powers" of an element will be identical to a member occurring earlier in the sequence, and so there will be only one generator. Clearly, there are an infinite number of cyclic subgroups in an infinite cyclic group, and each subgroup contains the sole generator of the parent group.

J under addition is not a cyclic group, since none of its elements is a generator.

EXERCISES 6g

1. (i) not a ring (no zero)
  (ii) a commutative ring with unity
  (iii) a commutative ring with unity
  (iv) a commutative ring with unity
  (v) not a ring (not closed under $\times$).

2. 1 (ii), (iii), (iv).

3. Yes, possible (see divisors of zero).

EXERCISES 6h

6. Unity is $(1,1)$. Divisors of zero: $(0, \lambda)$ and $(\mu, 0)$, where λ and μ are any real numbers.

EXERCISES 6i

1. (i) not a field (no multiplicative inverses)
  (ii) a field
  (iii) a field
  (iv) a field
  (v) not a field (no multiplicative inverses)
  (vi) a field
  (vii) not a field [or even a ring since J is not closed under $\times$ (mod 4)]
  (viii) a field.

3. $3 + x = 4 \Rightarrow x = 1; 3x = 2 \Rightarrow x = 4.$

4. (a) $x = 0, 3, 4.$ (b) $x = 0$ (twice), 1.

Bibliography

ADLER, I., **The New Mathematics**, Dobson, London, 1959.

ALEXANDROFF, P. S., **Introduction to the Theory of Groups**, Blackie, London and Glasgow, 1959.

ALLEN, R. G. D., **Basic Mathematics**, Macmillan, London, 1962.

ARCHBOLD, J. W., **Algebra**, Pitman, London, 1961.

BENNER, C. P., NEWHOUSE, A., RADER, C. B. and YATES, R. L., **Topics in Modern Algebra**, Harper, New York, 1962.

BIRKHOFF, G. and MACLANE, S., **A Survey of Modern Algebra**, Macmillan, New York, 1953.

BRIGGS, W. and BRYAN, G. H. (rev. WALKER, G.), **The Tutorial Algebra**, Vol. II, University Tutorial Press, London, 1960.

COURANT, R. and ROBBINS, H., **What is Mathematics?**, Oxford University Press, New York, 1961.

DANTZIG, T., **Number, The Language of Science**, Allen & Unwin, London, 1962.

FANG, J., **Abstract Algebra**, Schaum's, New York, 1963.

FLETCHER, T. J. (Ed.), **Some Lessons in Mathematics**, Cambridge University Press, London, 1964.

HOHN, F. E., **Applied Boolean Algebra**, Macmillan, New York, 1960.

KEMENEY, J. G., MIRKIL, H., SNELL, J. L. and THOMPSON, G. L., **Finite Mathematical Structures**, Prentice-Hall, New Jersey, 1964.

MAXWELL, E. A., **Algebraic Structure and Matrices**, Cambridge University Press, London, 1965.

SINGH, J., **Mathematical Ideas**, Oldbourne Science Library, London, 1962.

Index